Law, Femicide, and Countercolonial-Feminist Praxis

This book unearths the buried legacies of modern legal thought, exposing femicide's entanglements with colonialism, Black Atlantic slavery, and their enduring afterlives, while forging countercolonial pathways to justice.

In the wake of Marielle Franco's assassination – a Black feminist city councilor murdered in Rio de Janeiro in 2018 – and amid the global resurgence of far-right authoritarianism, the entanglements of femicide, White supremacy, misogyny, and colonial juridico-political architectures have come into stark focus. Challenging dominant frameworks for understanding gender-based violence, this book draws on the insights of Black, Indigenous, queer, and feminist thinkers, engaging both written and oral traditions. Through transdisciplinary methodology grounded in deep listening to grassroots activists across the territory now known as Brazil, here acknowledged as theory-makers, it exposes femicide as an enduring *colonial racial-patriarchal order* and lays bare the limitations of liberal legal frameworks. By questioning the colonial foundations of legal order, the book cultivates and seeds terrains to imagine and enact transformative justice and generative forms of redress – engaging with *choreographies of survival* that gesture toward a *politics of vitality*.

This book will appeal to academics, researchers, activists, and students with interests across a range of disciplines, including critical legal studies; critical Black studies; Indigenous and Amerindian studies; gender and feminist studies; critical criminology; legal anthropology; social movements; Brazilian studies; and anticolonial, decolonial, and postcolonial studies.

Juliana Streva is a transdisciplinary legal scholar born and raised in Brazil, currently working as a Fung Global Fellow at Princeton University, USA.

Law, Femicide, and Countercolonial-Feminist Praxis

Choreographies of Survival and the Limits of Justice

Juliana Streva

Routledge
Taylor & Francis Group
a GlassHouse Book

First published 2026
by Routledge
4 Park Square, Milton Park, Abingdon, Oxon OX14 4RN

and by Routledge
605 Third Avenue, New York, NY 10158

Routledge is an imprint of the Taylor & Francis Group, an informa business

A GlassHouse book

British Library Cataloguing-in-Publication Data
A catalogue record for this book is available from the British Library

Library of Congress Cataloging-in-Publication Data
Names: Streva, Juliana Moreira author
Title: Law, femicide, and countercolonial-feminist praxis : choreographies of survival / Juliana Streva.
Description: Abingdon, Oxon [UK] ; New York, NY : Routledge, 2026. | Includes bibliographical references and index.
Identifiers: LCCN 2025008491 (print) | LCCN 2025008492 (ebook) | ISBN 9781032755908 hardback | ISBN 9781032755915 paperback | ISBN 9781003474692 ebook
Subjects: LCSH: Sex crimes—Law and legislation—History | Sex discrimination—Law and legislation—History | Women—Crimes against—Law and legislation—History | Feminist jurisprudence | Colonies | Knowledge, Theory of | Women—Crimes against—Law and legislation—Brazil
Classification: LCC K5194 .S77 2026 (print) | LCC K5194 (ebook) | DDC 345/.0252—dc23/eng/20250306
LC record available at https://lccn.loc.gov/2025008491
LC ebook record available at https://lccn.loc.gov/2025008492

ISBN: 978-1-032-75590-8 (hbk)
ISBN: 978-1-032-75591-5 (pbk)
ISBN: 978-1-003-47469-2 (ebk)

DOI: 10.4324/9781003474692

Typeset in Sabon
by Apex CoVantage, LLC

Contents

Acknowledgments *vii*

Part –1 Legal Under/Grounds and the Front Door of Violence 1

Minus One 1
Choreographies of Survival 5
From the Unspeakable to Speakable 8
Language of Rights 12
Incommensurability: Mathematics of Violence 15
Surface: The Front Door of Violence 18
Grammar of the Ground: Geologies 19

Part 0 Subject-Positions: Bodies and Territories 28

Zero Degree 28
The Human Script: Colonial Fractures, Separability 30
Colonial "Justice" 32
Blame-Shifting: Dress Code and Legal Normativity 33
Sexual Violence and Colonial Epistemology 37
Beyond Legal Victimhood 40
Slavery1 and Slavery2 42
Labor: Racial and Gendered Ontologies of Difference 45
Colonial Family 52
Inheritance 52

Part 1 Colonial Racial-Patriarchal Order: Nation-State and Democracy 65

Re-membering 65
Nation, Nationalism 66

Politics of Silencing/Speakability 71
Monologue 72
Myth 1: Harmony 75
Myth 2: Independence 79
Colonial Pact: The Constitutional Law 81
Representative Democracy 84
First Wave 87

Part 2 Seeding a Politics of Vitality: Countercolonial-Feminist Praxis and the Limits of Justice 94

Marielle Franco 94
Legal Ethnography Otherwise: Deep Listening 98
Seeding: Politics of Vitality 107
Radical Legal Praxis and the Limits of Justice 112
Beyond Representation 136

After-words/After-worlds 161

Appendix 1 167
Appendix 2 169
Index 177

Acknowledgments

There is no better place to begin this tender work of thanks than by turning to the activists who welcomed me into their lives, carving precious time from their relentless days to share their life journeys, their visions of law and politics, and their struggles. This book would not have been possible without the experience of listening to and learning with you. To Ana Karen de Oliveira, Ana Paula Ferreira de Lima, Andreza da Silveira Jorge, Charlene da Silva Borges, Edna da Silva Pinho de Oliveira, Elvira Eliza França, Florismar Ferreira da Silva, Gabriele Roza, Joana Montanha Galvão, Joyce Alves Gomes, Laina Crisóstomo Queiroz, Larissa Guedes Menezes, Lívia Ferreira da Silva, Luzarina Varela da Silva, Kathleen Cristine Feitosa, Kátia Brasil, Manuelita Carolina Machado, Mayara Andrade da Cruz, Márcia dos Santos Moreira, Maria Alice da Silva Paulino, Marklize dos Santos Siqueira, Michelle Barbosa Andrews, Morgana Neves Moltalvão, Nayara Lorena da Silva Goés, Natália Damazio Ferreira, Natalia Kleinsorgen Bernardo Borges, Nelise Antonia Aragão Fagundes (Baiana), Noélia Pires da Silva, Noelle Coelho Resende, Perpétua Pereira Cerqueira (Suni Kokama), Roberta de Pádua, Sandra Benites, Sandra Muñoz, and Shirley da Luz Villela: I am profoundly grateful for your trust and generosity. This project was made possible by my PhD scholarship from the *Human Rights Under Pressure* program at Freie Universität Berlin, funded by Deutsche Forschungsgemeinschaf (DFG), and further developed through my fellowships and postdoctoral positions at the Maria Sibylla Merian Centre Conviviality-Inequality in Latin America (Mecila), the *Beyond Social Cohesion: Global Repertoires of Living Together* research consortium (RePLITO) funded by Berlin University Alliance, and my current role as a Fung Global Fellow at Princeton University. While the constraints of time and the transdisciplinary scope of this project presented their institutional challenges, the financial support I received was indispensable, as such support always is, to the making of my and any academic endeavor. This book carries the imprint of the wisdom, generosity, and unwavering support of those who, in both direct and subtle ways, have guided and encouraged me along this journey.

My deep thanks to my doctoral supervisors, Helmut Aust and Avner de-Shalit, for their attentive readings and support to my unconventional legal project. I am also grateful to my students and colleagues at the Department of Law and the Institute for Latin American Studies (LAI) at Freie Universität Berlin, as well as my colleagues at the Institute for International and Regional Studies (PIIRS) at Princeton University for cultivating intellectual spaces of exchange and reflection. My appreciation extends to the Routledge team and editors for believing in this work and helping bring it to fruition.

To my family and dearest friends, I am endlessly grateful for your support and love. Special thanks to my dear friends Iracema Dulley, Marie Petersmann, Pegah Byroum-Wand, and Ana Luiza Braga, who generously read previous versions of this work and shared their thoughtful insights. Emily Babson, thank you for your flexibility, enthusiasm, and the care you brought to your developmental editing contributions to this project. I also wish to acknowledge the often-invisible reproductive work that underpins the creation of books and worlds. From the workers who clean university halls to administrative staff who keep everything running smoothly: your labor sustains the everyday life of the university and made this work possible. Last, but never least, this work exists because of the Black, Indigenous, queer, and feminist activists, artists, and scholars whose worldviews and practices of world-making otherwise have been a profound source of inspiration and companionship. This book stands as a small part of a larger continuum, nurtured by many hands, steps, gestures, and choreographies of liberation. To all who have touched this work in speakable and unspeakable ways, words will not be enough to thank you. This is, and always will be, for you.

Part −1

Legal Under/Grounds and the Front Door of Violence

Minus One

The ground beneath us holds layered depths, a dense assemblage of living and nonliving matter formed in and of the Earth, that inherited the weight of memory and history. Far from a static or inert foundation, the Earth is a breathing, dynamic terrain: a landscape in constant motion. At times, the geological under/ground feels solid, cemented, seemingly unchangeable; at others, it erodes, fractures, and trembles, opening fissures beneath our feet. Yet these collapses are more than mere reactions and ruptures; they are openings for worlding otherwise. In the wake of exhaustion, dry and depleted soils are moistened again, inviting seeds to germinate and cultivating lifeways. In this spiral of collapse and regeneration, the under/ground becomes both an archive of what has been and a fertile terrain for insurgent possibilities of undoing and unsettling the foundations of colonial geological order.

Engaging transdisciplinary onto-epistemologies, this book challenges traditional legal frameworks by exploring how femicide is shaped, enforced, and continually remade through the enduring entanglements of law and colonialism – a dynamic I describe as the *colonial racial-patriarchal order*. In doing so, it confronts the promises of liberal emancipation and safety, promises often realized through individualistic measures of incarceration and punishment. This project seeks to reframe the way legal scholarship addresses gender-based violence by contesting the entrenched genealogies and geologies of modern law, liberal democracy, and the postcolonial nation-state. By shifting attention from singular, tragic cases to the everyday practices of survival, refusal, and generative redress, this work is not only informed but inspired by countercolonial-feminist practices and epistemologies.

I adopt the term "countercolonial" (*contracolonial*) inspired by its invocation by Black, quilombola, Amerindian, and land activists and intellectuals in Brazil (cf. Bispo dos Santos 2015; Núñez 2023). Closely aligned with anticolonial ontologies and epistemologies (Césaire 1950; Fanon 1961; Cusicanqui 2010), a countercolonial framework not only recognizes the enduring legacies of colonial violence but also foregrounds the persistent resistance and

DOI: 10.4324/9781003474692-1

struggles for liberation that actively contest these structures to this day. Unlike decolonial or postcolonial schools of thought, terms often developed and circulated within academic circles, the notion of countercolonial does not emerge from scholarly theory. Rather, it emerges from historically grounded knowledge, articulated through grassroots activists.

It is important to acknowledge the foundational contribution of quilombola activist, poet, and intellectual Antônio Bispo dos Santos to the conceptualization and popularization of the term *countercolonial* in Brazil, as well as its adoption in the present work. For Bispo dos Santos, *countercolonial* designates a mode of resistance rooted in the continuous, embodied refusal of those historically subjected to colonial domination—those who, as he insists, were *never truly colonized* (Bispo dos Santos et al. 2020; Bispo dos Santos 2024). This book draws deeply from his grounded theorization and honors his lifelong commitment to Black and quilombola struggles. At the same time, it respectfully diverges from the assertion that colonization could be fully escaped or that something could be kept external to it. The perspective advanced here understands colonization as a pervasive and enduring formation, unfolding through intertwined processes of invasion, occupation, accumulation, dehumanization, and extraction. Its reach is structural and saturating, leaving no life, body, or territory untouched; implicating not only those subjugated by its violence but also those complicit in or benefiting from its operations. Yet, in alignment with Bispo dos Santos, this work embraces the notion of the *countercolonial* as a vital framework for foregrounding ontological and epistemic practices of refusal and alternative worldmaking enacted from within, against, and beyond the colonial order. It is in this spirit that the term *countercolonial* is engaged here, not as a static concept, but as a living, situated, and relational praxis of resistance and transformation.

I do not seek to extract or transplant scientific knowledge from the so-called global North to the global South, nor to reduce the complexity of situated ontologies and epistemologies into singular and totalizing narrative. Instead, I propose here to listen to resonances and nurtures confluences, weaving dialogues that moves across borders, practices, and disciplines. By decentering and displacing canonical scholarship on legal thought and political theory from within, this work engages with Black Radical Traditions as it traverses the colonial borders of Brazil, the Caribbean, and the United States, while also fostering dialogues between Amerindian and Indigenous epistemologies from Brazil and Canada.[1] Acknowledging the colonial and White genealogies underlying of scientific "production" of

1 In this book, "White," "Black," and "Indigenous" are capitalized to emphasize their use as sociopolitical constructs, rather than as mere chromatic descriptors. These terms were forged within the classificatory logic of colonialism, which sought to hierarchize human life through racialized categories. The term "Indigenous" is employed with a critical awareness of its colonial origins, rooted in the European misnomer "Indian," itself a product of the mistaken belief that the Americas were part of India. While the term "Amerindian" has been introduced in some Latin American traditions as a localized alternative, I have chosen to use both "Indigenous" and "Amerindian" in acknowledgment of the ways many communities across the territories now known as Brazil have reclaimed and mobilized this term in naming themselves and their collective struggles.

knowledge, this work understands both academic written traditions and nonacademic oral traditions as forms of knowledge and theory-making.[2] Attuned to the distinct linguistic, economic, and sociopolitical conditions in which these onto-epistemologies take form, this book embraces both the tensions and the transformative possibilities that emerge through grounded and transdisciplinary coalitions.

It is in this grounds that the book poses the following questions: Are we not witnessing a global resurgence of authoritarianism through a hypermasculine reaction against anticolonial, antiracist, queer, and feminists' struggles to confront and transform the neocolonial architectures of violence and inequality? How, then, might we draw on ancestral and enduring choreographies of survival to reimagine what law and justice could look and sound like? And how might these practices, rooted in collective memory and ancestral struggle, guide us toward deeper approaches to redress and repair, beyond the limits of liberal and colonial legal frameworks?

•

Susana Chávez Castillo, a Mexican human rights activist and poet, was 36 when her life was violently interrupted on her way to visit friends in 2011. I have chosen not to recount the details of the murder scene here, following the caution of scholars from critical Black studies like Saidiya Hartman, who warns of "the ease with which such scenes [of violence] are reiterated, the casualness with which they are circulated" (1997, 1). Repeated portrayals of violence can dull our sensitivity to the horror of racial- and gender-based brutality. Instead of sparking outrage or fostering meaningful reflection, they can "inure us to pain by virtue of their familiarity" (Hartman 1997). Rather than risk this numbing effect, this work aims to engage more deeply with the structural conditions that sustain violence.

Yet, an official statement demands attention here. The attorney general of Chihuahua swiftly dismissed any connection between Susana Castillo's murder and her activism. He suggested that she had encountered three strangers with whom she might have gone "to have fun," attributing her death to alleged drug and alcohol use that supposedly led these men to "lose control" (Martínez 2011; Nájar 2011; Milenio 2011). Instead of rigorously addressing the brutality and systemic nature of the crime, this statement subtly implicates Castillo as complicit in her own murder, further normalizing and obscuring the deeper structures of violence that led to her death. Susana Chávez Castillo's life was not only brutally cut short – *brought to the ground* – but also institutionally dehumanized.

2 Instead of reinforcing the colonial binary hierarchization of the written over the oral form, I address them in relation: the speaker and the writer, the act of listening and the act of reading. Therefore, speaking-writing refers to a relational movement that is possible only when listening-reading is its counterpart (see Part 2; cf. Gonzalez 1983; Martins 1997; Smith 1999; Kilomba 2015; Wekker 2016; Streva and Dulley 2023).

The internationally known political slogan *ni una menos* (not one [woman] less) draws its inspiration from Castillo's poetry. Her 1995 poem, *Ni una mujer menos, ni una muerta más* (Not one woman less, not one more dead), distills an urgent demand for women's right to live. The activist was a member of the movement *Nuestras hijas de regreso a casa* (Our daughters back home), founded by relatives of disappeared girls and women in Ciudad Juárez.[3] Today, *ni una menos* has become a rallying cry for women's transnational struggle for survival, embodying a collective demand for a politics that resists femicide.

The minus one here signifies the systemic denial of life within a structure in which life and death are no longer natural occurrences but have become fundamental instruments of political and legal normativity and control. Brazilian philosopher Denise Ferreira da Silva (2018) conceptualizes "–1" as a symbol of *dysselection*,[4] negation, and subjugation, a framework that reveals the pervasive scenes of violence within this order. This concept enables us to read such scenes not as isolated events but as expressions of a broader ecosystem, one that governs who is nurtured with life and who is cast into erasure.

In conversations with Black feminist activists in Brazil, I often heard the verb *tombar* used to describe the violent loss of comrades and loved ones. In Portuguese, *tombar* signifies the act of falling or being brought down – a term that can refer to both the felling of a tree and the death of a person. In both cases, what falls returns to the Earth, merging with it once more. This concept of returning to the ground evokes a cyclical understanding of existence, where death does not mark an end but a transformation. It becomes soil, root, and memory, nurturing the ground from which new forms of life and resistance can emerge.

Interestingly, in Brazilian legislation (Decree-Law n. 25/1937), the term *tombar* assumes a profoundly different meaning. Instead of evoking loss or collapse, the legal concept of *tombamento* refers to the act of granting public protection to entities recognized as cultural heritage, whether material or immaterial. This designation is based on the cultural, historical, or artistic value attributed to them, and aims to safeguard these assets as collective memories for future generations.

This dual resonance of *tombar* bridges seemingly opposing ideas: one of profound loss and another of preservation and recognition, underscoring the layered meanings embedded in language and its entanglement with memory, resistance, and the possibilities of transformation. This interplay between

3 The border town of Juárez exemplifies the recurring and systematic practices of disappearance and femicide that have come to define a broader context of violence against women in Mexico. A landmark case that brought international attention to this crisis is *González et al. v. Mexico*, commonly referred to as the *Campo Algodonero* (Cotton Field) case. For further details, see Appendix 2.

4 The concept of "dysselection" is coined by Sylvia Wynter in her analysis of the processes of racialization inherent in colonial slavery. For a more detailed discussion, see Part 0.

loss and the generative potential of memory forms a central thread engaged throughout the chapters of this book.

•

I remember being around 13 when rumors began circulating about a man prowling our neighborhood in Volta Redonda, a municipality in the state of Rio de Janeiro where I grew up. The stories shared a haunting consistency: he lurked near the river's edge, naked but for a cape, concealed in the trees, waiting to assault women. The bus stop stood along that very margin of the river. Many in the neighborhood caught the early bus to reach school or work downtown, but as I entered a double-shift technical high school, I often returned home in the evening, usually disembarking as the sole passenger at my stop. Each time, I would brace myself, mentally rehearsing the sprint home. After a full day, I'd draw on whatever strength I had left, force my tired body into motion, and race as fast as I could toward home.

With the advent of mobile phones, it became routine for my female friends and I to check in with each other upon returning home safely – an unspoken precaution that our cisgender male friends never seemed to need. This choreography wasn't about an isolated urban legend confined to a particular neighborhood, city, or region; it was a collective response to an ever-present, almost inevitable specter of violence. These stories, remembered and shared, connect personal experiences to collective memory, bridging the empirical with the theoretical, and the intimate with the political.

In revisiting these scenes of everyday violence, this book proposes a radical shift in how legal scholars engage with femicide, raising critical questions about theorizing violence in ways that refuse its reinscription and normalization. While socio-legal scholarship often converges on definitions of femicide and gender-based violence, the colonial and legal underlying forces that shape these phenomena and what they reveal about our world remain largely elusive.

Choreographies of Survival

The notion of survival is framed through its etymological roots in the late Latin *supervivere*, meaning to live "beyond" and to persist. Survival, then, is not merely the painful act of enduring under systemic violence, as usually conceived; it is an assertion of livability that transcends and defies these structures – an insistence on living beyond and despite them. It embodies what U.S. Black feminist poet Audre Lorde (1977) describes as the fierce tenacity of those "never meant to survive" and what Brazilian Black writer Conceição Evaristo (2015) calls the determination of those who "refused to die" (*combinamos de não morrer*).

The experience of surviving apocalypse is neither a recent phenomenon nor confined to dystopian imaginations. For centuries, the Euro-modern world has been built on structures of colonial violence, perpetuating cycles of death, genocide, feminicide, and ecocide. Black, Indigenous, and queer activists remind us that, since the onset of modernity, apocalypse – often dismissed as distant or exceptional – has been an enduring, lived reality for communities placed outside the bounds of colonial normativity (Mombaça 2018; Ferreira da Silva 2019; Krenak 2019, 2022; Malunguinho 2020; IndigenousAction 2020). This reality is not one of ruin alone but a continual resurgence, a site where life insists on itself, where new forms of relationality, knowledge, and resistance emerge from within the very fractures of a collapsing world. In this sense, survival is more than resistance or reaction to violence; it involves cultivating strategies, knowledge, tactics, and practices that enable life to thrive even within the colonial and neocolonial structures of today. These practices shape what I term a "politics of vitality" (further developed in Part 2), signaling an insistence on life that goes beyond mere endurance.

To deepen these concepts of survival tactics and strategies, I turn to U.S. writer Ursula Le Guin's *The Carrier Bag Theory of Fiction* (1989). Le Guin reimagines technology not as a narrative of conquest, war, or destruction but through the simple, nurturing image of a carrier bag. This seemingly humble tool for gathering, moving, and sharing emerges as a technology of life-sustenance and interdependence. By departing from violent, masculinized narratives of dominance, Le Guin offers a feminist perspective that privileges nurturing and caring over destruction. In this spirit, I bring together tactics, strategies, and technologies as onto-epistemological tools – tools that open, gather, carry forward, and activate a deeper politics of vitality.

The concept of "choreographies," as invoked in the subtitle of this book, *Choreographies of Survival*, offers an experimental and improvised reframing of legal ethnography. Traditionally rooted in the etymology of *ethno* (people) and *graphia* (writing), ethnography's practice of observation is reimagined here as a form of deep listening and engaged writing that moves alongside, and learns with, the ongoing "movements" (*choreo*) of survival. This shift – from *ethno* (people) to *choreo* (movements) – reorients writing itself, inviting us to rethink the interplay between movement and writing, while broadening the very notion of "choreography" beyond its traditional theorizations within dance and performance studies.

In *Exhausted Dance*, André Lepecki, Brazilian writer and curator working on performance studies, traces the emergence of "choreography" to 1589, when a precursor to the word appeared in the title of Thoinot Arbeau's *Orchesographie*, a Jesuit manual that codified and disciplined movement – literally, the writing (*graphia*) of dance (*orchesis*). This codification, Lepecki argues, coincided with the unfolding and consolidation of Western (colonial) modernity. From the Renaissance onward, dance became implicated in a kinetic mode of being-in-the-world, ordered and disciplined through a grammar of control and capture (Lepecki 2006, 6–7).

In contrast to this history framework of *orchesographie*, which sought to discipline and contain bodies within prescribed orders, this book seeks a stark different understanding of *choreo-graphy*. Here, writing is no longer conceived as a tool for dictating movement but is instead shaped and vibrated by movement itself – a practice that joins and composes with the everyday struggles for liberation. This methodological, theoretical, and political reorientation embraces choreography as a generative, undisciplined practice. Saidiya Hartman's invocation of choreography in *Wayward Lives, Beautiful Experiments* (2019) as bodies in motion, as elaboration of the possible, as flight, as movement for freedom resonates deeply here. Similarly, Fahima Ife's concept of "anachoreography" in *Maroon Choreographies* frames movement as "born in wildness, in fugitivity, in refusal" (2021, xi). The 35th São Paulo Bienal, *Coreografias do Impossível* (Choreographies of the Impossible), curated by Diane Lima, Grada Kilomba, Hélio Menezes, and Manuel Borja-Villel, explores the multifaceted meanings of choreography as a poetic and political practice. The booklet of the exhibition frames choreography as repetitions that inscribe space; as the articulation of movement, time, and space; and bodily inscription in space and time through both rehearsed and improvised motion (2024, 20).

Within this framework, choreography is understood as an active, embodied practice of writing, one that learns with oral traditions, embodied knowledge, and world-making strategies. It refuses the rigid confines of colonial orders. Choreography becomes a dynamic, living mode of inquiry, grounded in the soil of collective resistance and creativity.

Ultimately, *choreographies of survival* return to a question posed by Denise Ferreira da Silva's (2014, 68), which lingers across the social, ethical, political, and juridical spheres:

> Where is that place where what shouldn't happen to anyone happens every day?

•

In the following sections of this introduction, I define key concepts and movements that form the foundation of this book's inquiry. A central concept is Diana Russell's framing of *femicide*, which I examine alongside the debates and reformulations advanced by Marcela Lagarde and Rita Segato. These frameworks enable us to explore how language has the power to transform the unspeakable into the speakable, shaping not only the discourse of rights in contemporary politics but also the distinct boundaries between legal language and the vernacular of lived experience. I then turn to critique the dominant framework of the *mathematics of violence* – a framework rooted in the quantification and statistical representations of violence, often rendering it abstract and impersonal. I argue that this approach fails to account for lives and experiences that are inherently incommensurable and unquantifiable, and I call for a contestation and sabotage of these dominant structures of knowledge production. In contrast to the widely used metaphor of the "iceberg" to understand femicide and gender-based violence, I offer the imagery of the *front door*. This metaphor invites us to consider not only the architecture of what is hidden behind it but also the very ground upon which this structure stands. It challenges us to think about the visible and invisible forces that shape the foundations of violence and justice. Finally, I situate the geological grammar – excavation, soil, ground, territory – that permeates this book, speaking to both the material, earthy aspects of violence and its deeper, ecopolitical significations. These terms allow for a layered understanding of the terrain we must walk through as we excavate the historical and structural underpinnings of colonial violence.

From the Unspeakable to Speakable

Gender-based violence has long been shaped by a politics of silencing (further developed as *politics of silencing/speakability* in Part 1), a silence that becomes, as the U.S. feminist poet and activist Adrienne Rich (1995) described, not only unspoken but also *unspeakable*. In her poetic work, Rich evokes the profound erasures that render certain narratives and voices inaccessible:

> Whatever is unnamed, undepicted in images, whatever is omitted from biography, censored in collections of letters, whatever is misnamed as something else, made difficult-to-come-by, whatever is buried in the memory by the collapse of meaning under an inadequate or lying language – this will become, not merely unspoken, but *unspeakable*.
>
> (1995, 278)

Prior to the 1970s, violence against women often went unnamed, relegated to the realm of private matters or justified as a defense of (male) "honor."[5] When this violence was discussed, it was treated as an embarrassing secret, whispered among close friends who would quickly change the subject if it arose in public (Morrison 2006).

This absence of language capable of fully conveying these experiences played a crucial role in maintaining silence around gendered violence. This linguistic void has, however, also catalyzed a critical shift in the discourse on violence, underscoring the need for terminology that not only brings such context of violence into public awareness but also drives transformation, rendering it *speakable* (McMillan 2007).

Historically, the term "homicide" has been regarded as a neutral legal term for the ultimate act of violence: to kill someone. Yet its etymological roots reveal something else. The Latin term *homin* translates to "man," embedding within the word a presumption of male universality. Feminist scholars and activists have responded to this embedded bias by advocating for alternative terms, such as "murder," to more accurately reflect the various embodiments of violence (Campbell 1992; Vásquez 2009).

5 Further elaborated in the section *Language of Rights* (Part 1) and Appendix 2.

It was not until 1976 that the term "femicide" gained public prominence, when South African feminist writer and activist Diana Russell introduced it during the International Tribunal on Crimes against Women held in Brussels. As one of the Tribunal's organizers, Russell invoked this concept to name and condemn the misogynistic murders of women and girls committed by men. She credits the initial use of the term to Carol Orlock in 1974, who was compiling an anthology on femicide that remained unpublished. In her address, Russell powerfully stated (Russell and Radford 1992, xiv):

> The names of those who I have read out [17 women who had been murdered in the San Francisco Bay] to you today will soon be obliterated. No demonstrations have accompanied them to the grave, no protests rocked the city, no leaflets were passed out, and no committees were formed. But today we have remembered them. And tomorrow we must act to stop femicide!

Diana Russell emphasized the urgent need for a specific term to confront the misogynistic murder of women, with the goal of facilitating movement-building and advocacy against it. We cannot fight what we cannot name. Femicide, while not a new form of violence, is a term crafted to render not necessarily visible but primarily *speakable* the most extreme manifestation of violence against women. It confronts the normalization of systematic killings, making a call to action that exposes the historical and persistent ethical indifference to violence against women.

Russell continued to refine and expand the concept in the 1990s, particularly in the anthology *Femicide: The Politics of Woman Killing*, a collaborative work with Jill Radford. In its introduction, Russell and co-author Jane Caputi frame femicide not as an aberration but as a gendered, politically motivated crime, set within the broader context of social transformations, including instances when women "entered traditional male territory" (Russell 1992, 13). Femicide, therefore, is read as a manifestation of male backlash against feminism and gender equality, rooted in the structure of male supremacy. They describe our current era as one of "gynocide" (Russell 1992, 19), one in which women are both living and dying under conditions of targeted violence.

Russell and Radford's approach is primarily gender-focused, but it also acknowledges their various forms of entanglement. Their concept of femicide sometimes extends beyond direct murder to include indirect forms of death-making arising from misogynistic norms and social practices. They also expand the definition to include other dimensions of violence, coining terms like "racist femicide," "homophobic femicide," and "lesbicide" to address the unique vulnerabilities faced by women of different racial, sexual, and social identities (Radford 1992, 7).

Russell and Caputi also underscore how responses from the police, media, and broader public to crimes against "women of color," impoverished women, lesbians, sex workers, and women with substance dependencies have been "abysmal – generally apathy laced with pejorative stereotyping and victim blaming" (Russell and Caputi 1992, 15). This reinforces the understanding that femicide is not a random, unexpected event; it occupies the far end of a continuum of violence against women, fueled by systemic biases and grounds of indifference.

Today, femicide is recognized as a transnational and global issue, although its academic and policy influence has been most significant in criminology and feminist studies in Latin America, the United States, and Australia, and only more recently developed in Europe. The term has achieved particular resonance and urgency in Latin America, recognized as one of the most dangerous regions in the world for women. This continent alone contains more than half of the 25 countries globally with the highest rates of femicide.

Building upon Diana Russell's foundational work, the Mexican feminist anthropologist Marcela Lagarde introduced the Spanish term *feminicidio* in 1992. For Lagarde (2008), physical murder is the terminal point on a spectrum of violence, which she describes as encompassing verbal threats, emotional manipulations, psychological abuse, and physical assault, all of which may culminate in feminicide. Feminicidio, as Lagarde defines it, is the targeted killing of women due to their gender, situated within a political context marked by systemic silence, omission, negligence, or even complicity from state authorities. This type of violence, she argues, is preventable, thus making the state accountable for failing to implement the necessary protections, preventive measures, and mechanisms of accountability and reparation (Lagarde 2007; Lagarde and Roberts 2010).

Lagarde's terminology resonates deeply with the language of law and the framework of international human rights. Her dual roles as an anthropologist and as a politician – serving in the Mexican Federal Congress from 2003 to 2006 – positioned her to influence legislative change. During her tenure, Lagarde was instrumental in passing the Feminicide Law in the Federal Penal Code and the General Law on Women's Access to a Life Free of Violence, and in establishing the Special Feminicide Commission to investigate the systemic killings of women in Ciudad Juárez (Lagarde 2007; cf. Appendix 2).

However, Russell (2011) expressed reservations about Lagarde's conceptualization of feminicidio, identifying several areas of concern. First, Russell contends that Lagarde's focus on impunity as a defining element of feminicidio implies that the crime only applies when the state fails to prosecute or punish perpetrators. In cases where the state effectively intervenes, the crime would ostensibly no longer be categorized as feminicidio. For Russell, impunity, while often associated with femicide, should not be a defining criterion, as it risks limiting the term's applicability on a global scale. Second, Russell objects to the term "feminicidio" due to its linguistic proximity to "femininity," which could inadvertently reinforce stereotypical gender roles. Last, she warns that the distinction between feminicidio and femicide risks creating unnecessary divisions within a movement that ought to be unified in combating the misogynistic killings of women across Latin America and beyond.

The paper *Femi-geno-cidio como crimen en el fuero internacional de los Derechos Humanos*, later published as a chapter of her book *La guerra contra las mujeres*, Brazilian-based Argentine feminist anthropologist and writer Rita Segato (2010) introduces the term *femo-geno-cídio* to describe crimes systematically and impersonally targeting women for destruction based solely on gender. Segato explores the intersection of law and narrative, suggesting that prescribing a specific legal understanding could fortify a collective pursuit of justice. In examining resistance within legal discourse, the author emphasizes how patriarchal foundations shape societal hierarchies and thereby complicating transformative legal efforts.

Segato addresses the nuanced terminology surrounding violence against women in Latin America, focusing on the terms "feminicidio" and "femicide" and their distinct implications. She highlights the divergence emphasized in the edited volume *No olvidamos ni aceptamos: Femicidio en Centroamérica 2000–2006*, in which Lagarde's concept of feminicidio is associated with the notion of impunity. Nevertheless, Segato (2010) notes the increasing adoption of the term "feminicidio" within Latin American media circles and daily discussions, reflecting a grassroots push for both legal recognition and collective acknowledgment. She argues that patriarchy's perpetuation and the state's role in preserving men's capacity for violence with impunity are central concerns, underscoring the confusion in criminal investigations and the lack of specificity in addressing gender based violence. To combat these issues, Segato advocates for an approach that acknowledges the spectrum of violence against women while resisting the privatization of gender-related crimes.

The debates surrounding femicide, feminicidio, and femi-geno-cídio highlight the intricate intersections of language, social movements, and advocacy in capturing the systemic dimensions of gender-based violence. These terms open pathways for examining how language can serve as both a tool of resistance and a catalyst for change, galvanizing public awareness while also challenging and holding accountable the structures that sustain such violence. Rather than treating these terms as divergent and divides, I propose to engage with their distinct insights as part of a shared critical landscape. Here, I adopt femicide for its expansive scope, which not only encompasses but also reaches beyond questions of state responsibility and criminal impunity, allowing for a fuller exploration of the social, historical, and structural underpinnings of gender-based violence.

Language of Rights

In speaking about language, it is important to distinguish between the "language of rights" and "legal language." The language of rights refers to a broad, politically charged vernacular, often employed by activists and social movements advocating for transformative change. It emphasizes the instrumental role of law as a tool for individuals and communities. The grammar of rights offers a juridico-political lexicon through which a range of issues – such as the right to mobility, housing, education, healthcare, food sovereignty, land, and bodily autonomy – can be vocalized. Law is a discursive field; thus, the struggle for rights involves not only shaping and enforcing laws but also the public assertion and dissemination of legal terms in daily interactions. This dual struggle underscores the battle to claim legal language not only in courts but also in everyday life (Segato 2016).

In contrast, legal language refers to the technical vocabulary embedded in legislation and judicial decisions. This jargon is predominantly confined to legally trained professionals – lawyers, judges, scholars, and practitioners. Within this context, law operates as the medium through which states and institutions acknowledge and legitimize distinct boundaries and interests. The struggle for rights thus becomes a struggle for inscription within the legal framework.

The discourse of human rights is somehow located between both languages and has been regarded as the universal language of "humanity." Later in this book (Part 0), I examine how the category of the "Human," as defined by Western humanism, was shaped by the historical conditions of colonial slavery. The discourse of human rights emerged from the universal embedded in international law. Initially, international law focused on regulating interstate relations, particularly in the context of war and peace. Although the human rights system, designed to protect individuals from state-sanctioned violence, played a significant role in these relations, it remained notably limited, particularly in its failure to address forms of violence within the private sphere, including widespread violations committed against women.

Following the Second World War, human rights discourse assumed a central role in shaping the international legal agenda. A paradigm shift expanded the definition of violence beyond the traditional framework of interstate wars to include interpersonal violations. Feminist activists strategically leveraged human rights discourse to advance the claim that "women's rights are human rights" (Sellers 2009), using this discourse as a tool for transnational advocacy.

International conferences have played a crucial role in shaping global debates on violence against women. The First World Conference on Women, held in Mexico City in 1975, produced the World Plan of Action and inaugurated the United Nations Decade for Women (1975–1985). This conference signaled a critical juncture in advancing social demands and solidifying government commitments to achieving gender equality (ECLAC 2006). The momentum generated in Mexico City was sustained through subsequent conferences, including the International Conference on Women in Copenhagen (1980) and the Third World Conference on Women in Nairobi (1985). These global conferences, far from being top-down initiatives, reflected the widespread activism of women across the world, laying a foundational framework for the landmark international conferences on women's rights in the 1990s.

At a time when many countries were enduring military dictatorships, women emerged as powerful symbols of resistance, advocating for justice. The First World Conference, along with the regional Economic Commission for Latin America and the Caribbean (ECLAC) conferences, created unprecedented opportunities for women to participate in decision-making at all levels. This wave of activism culminated in significant events such as the Human Rights Conference in Vienna (1993), the International Conference on Population and Development in Cairo (1994), and the Fourth World Conference on Women in Beijing (1995). A key precursor to the Beijing conference was the pre-conference held in Mar del Plata in 1994, where women from 16 Latin American and Caribbean countries gathered. These gatherings fostered groundbreaking collective deliberation and collaboration, further solidifying the transnational movement for women's rights.[6]

These events highlight just one dimension of the broader efforts by women activists, who have been central in transforming approaches to gender-based violence within both national and international legal frameworks. Through decades of persistent political organizing, they have steadily pushed violence against women to the forefront of the international human rights agenda, leading to the recognition of "domestic violence" as a critical public and political issue.

The recognition of gender-based violence as a human rights violation marks a departure from classical liberal theory's rigid dichotomy between the private and public spheres, and between the domestic and political (Bunch 1990; Charlesworth, Chinkin, and Wright 1991; Chinkin 1999). This shift broadens the conceptual foundations of human rights theory, extending its scope to

6 In 1994, in Mar del Plata, Argentina, the nations of Latin America and the Caribbean adopted the *Regional Programme of Action for Women of Latin America and the Caribbean, 1995–2001*, in preparation for the Fourth World Conference on Women, held in Beijing in 1995. This program provided an updated assessment of the status of women in the region, proposed public policies aimed at reducing gender inequalities, and addressed emerging issues that had not been included in the earlier *Regional Plan of Action for the Integration of Women into Latin American Economic and Social Development*, adopted in Havana. The *Regional Programme of Action* emphasized the critical role of women in "advancing democratization processes" across the region and underscored the need for a cultural transformation to dismantle patriarchal systems and dominant gender norms. These systems perpetuated subordination, devaluation, and discrimination against women in multiple spheres of life (cf. ECLAC 2022, 5).

include violations occurring within the private sphere, even when perpetrated by individuals and reinforced by sociocultural norms and stereotypes.

Despite the Inter-American Court's reluctance to adopt terms such as "femicide" or "feminicide," several Latin American countries have, in recent years, incorporated the concept of feminicide into their national legal frameworks, criminalizing it as a distinct offense. In Brazil, the Feminicide Law No. 13.104/2015 arose from a report on violence against women produced by the Joint Parliamentary Committee of Inquiry between 2012 and 2013. In its final version, however, the Brazilian National Congress substituted the term "gender" with "female sex," a change that reflects a reductionist and conservative stance on the scope of gender-based violence and the subjects it affects.

The criminalization of femicide in Brazil, in theory, has two main objectives. First, it seeks to transform the discourse on violence against women, historically framed by patriarchal constructs such as "crime of passion" or "legitimate defense of male honor" – justifications often couched in narratives of "strong emotions," "love," or "jealousy." Previously, these explanations were considered as mitigating factors in cases of intentional murder of women, but they now constitute a distinct legal category. Second, the law aims to spotlight the extent and particular context of gender-based violence. By designating femicide as a specific offense, this legislation enables more precise data collection – such as jurisprudence and statistics – that are perceived as crucial for developing targeted public policies to combat this pervasive issue.

The distinction between what is *in jure* (according to law) and what is *de facto* (in reality) underscores the disjunction between legal frameworks and lived experiences. In practice, many women engaged in anti-violence grassroots mobilizations have emphasized a pervasive lack of accessible information about legal definitions and tools, particularly concerning gender-based violence. This gap in legal awareness often impedes their ability to determine whether their experiences can even be recognized or addressed within formal legal classifications of violence. In response to this challenge, grassroots women activists have committed significant effort to consciousness-raising and knowledge-sharing initiatives, organizing collective workshops and group meetings. These spaces become critical sites where women collaboratively unpack the complexities of violence, reflect on their experiences, and build the capacity to navigate and challenge legal systems. As recounted by numerous activists across Brazil, this process of collective engagement has been transformative, enabling many to recognize, articulate, and confront the violence they have endured.

Despite this, mainstream legal frameworks largely continue to marginalize the role of grassroots movements in shaping both national and international law, erasing their contributions from legal history. Dominated by functionalist perspectives, these frameworks typically depend on reductive, top-down approaches to decision-making and lawmaking (Rajagopal 2003). As a result, legal scholarship often focuses on the linear progression of rights, comparative laws, case analysis, doctrine, and jurisprudence. Such approaches often produce dehistoricized, decontextualized normative analyses, distorting social movement claims by reducing them to mere demands for inclusion, rather than addressing the deeper structural conditions that sustain gender-based violence.

Incommensurability: Mathematics of Violence

In the beginning of 2019, the third year of the research that culminated in this book, I began systematically documenting femicides that took place in the months following Brazil's election. This endeavor was spurred by a perceived link between shifts in democratic representation, the proliferation of ultra-masculinity, cisheteronormative, and racist political rhetoric and policies, and the rising incidence of gender-based violence. Given the scarcity of monthly official reports on violence, which are made available only on an annual basis, I took on this mapping effort to furnish a more substantive, detailed analysis of the landscape of violence during this period.

My decision to do so was also influenced by prevailing Western scientific methodologies, which frequently prioritize numerical data even when critical, qualitative insights are sought. Scientific research, academic studies, and institutional reports on violence are often grounded in statistics, rendering violence in the form of tables and numbers, what Canadian scholar on Black feminist thought and Black geographies Katherine McKittrick (2014, 16) calls "breathless, archival numeric evidence" and what U.S. scholar in gender and women's studies Eric A. Stanley (2021, 5) describes as a "wicked archive of murders." These frameworks risk stripping human narratives into cold forensic numbers, reinforcing the calculative logic that can desensitize us to the lived realities they aim to represent.

Drawing from national and local news sources, I tallied instances of femicide, including both consumed and attempted murders, targeting heterosexual, lesbian, bisexual, pansexual, cisgender, transgender, and travesti[7] women. For 52 consecutive days, I immersed myself in Brazilian digital media reports

7 "Travesti" is a term used in Brazil to describe subjects assigned male at birth who challenge gender norms by adopting female names, pronouns, clothing, cosmetics, and other performative markers of femininity. Unlike transgender women, travestis do not consider themselves as women, but rather as travesti. This identity therefore embodies a distinct and complex refusal of binary gender categorizations. Scholars have interpreted travesti as a form of refusal against "an imposed dominant expectation of womanhood that centers on people who are cisgender, heteronormative, able-bodied, elitist, and white" (Santana 2019, 123); and as a form of identification that disrupts "both normative expectations of femininity and trans politics structured around assimilation and respectability" (Rizki 2019, 149). For further discussion, see Part 0, section *Blame-Shifting: Dress Code and Legal Normativity.*

of such cases, each one of them bringing me closer to intimate and often devastating accounts from the families and loved ones of the person who was murdered – those who *tombaram*.

This process exposed me to disturbing images and unsettling stories, each of which contributed to what I came to understand as a "horror mapping." Over time, this mapping evolved into a detailed ten-page document, cataloging key information for each case: the relationship between "perpetrator" and "victim"; any third-party interventions; how authorities and media classified the crime; identified motives – often tied to jealousy or the unacceptance of a breakup; crime location; and identifying markers for each victimized woman, including race or ethnicity, gender identity, sexual orientation, and pregnancy status.

During this time, Brazilian media began reporting on a surge in femicide, often calling it a "pandemic" of violence against women. This spike, beginning in late 2018 during presidential campaigns and coinciding with national elections, signaled an alarming trend (Oliva 2019; Vilela 2019; Senado 2019). In São Paulo, the largest city in Brazil and Latin America, the murder rate against women rose by 220 percent in the first half of 2019. This same period saw a decline in intentional murders of men (Acayaba and Arcoverde 2019; Adorno 2019a, 2019b).

Against this backdrop, the Brazilian Forum of Public Security, in collaboration with the Center for Violence Studies at the University of São Paulo and the newspaper *O Globo*, launched the *Monitor da Violência* (Violence Monitor). This project disclosed previously unreleased data from the Brazilian Ministry of Women (renamed the Ministry of Women, Family, and Human Rights), showing nearly a 60 percent increase in calls to the Center for Assistance to Women in Situations of Violence, or "Service 180," between January and February of 2019 (BRASIL 2018; Velasco, Caesar, and Reis 2019). The dramatic rise in femicide underscores the entangled material and symbolic connections among representative democracy, masculinity, law, and violence. This examination reveals a powerful interplay between specific acts and broader structural dynamics – local and global, particular and universal – and between empirical phenomena and theoretical frameworks.

While it was suggested that I open this book with this map of femicide, I have chosen instead to omit it deliberately, for both conceptual and personal reasons. Compiling this mathematics of violence came at a high emotional cost. Engaging daily with reports of brutal violence left me bearing an overwhelming sense of despair about the world as we know it. By the 52nd day, the strain became unbearable, manifesting itself physically and signaling the need to pause the project. I share this intimate, embodied experience because no table, chart, or infographic can elicit the visceral impact that each of these narratives had on me. Engaging with hundreds of accounts of terror, brutality, and lives abruptly cut short revealed an emotional depth that resists numeric representation. They are incommensurable. As such, this table is visually absent – a refusal to distill these stories into mere statistics. They are uncountable.

This mathematics of violence has come under critical scrutiny, particularly in Black scholarship that examines the archives of slavery and its reverberations (B. Nascimento 1974; Hartman 2008; Ferreira da Silva 2009; McKittrick 2014). Katherine McKittrick contends that such a mathematics reinforces a view of Black life as mere objecthood, rendering it knowable only through data, while masking the fuller, untold dimensions of Black livability (2014, 17). This ostensibly neutral "science" is, as she writes, "trusted as innocuously objective, thus providing an alibi for racism" (McKittrick 2014, 23). In response to this dehumanizing reduction of Black existence to numbers, Brazilian Black historian and poet Beatriz Nascimento insists, "we are the lived history of Black people, not numbers" (1974, 97; my translation).[8]

In the novel *2666*, Chilean author Roberto Bolaño (2004) dedicates the chapter "The Part About the Crimes" to narrating violence against women in Santa Teresa, a fictionalized version of Juarez, Mexico. Stretching over nearly three hundred pages, the chapter confronts the reader with over one hundred cases of femicide between 1993 and 1997. Rather than summing up the number of victims, Bolaño's narrative dwells on each case, constructing a hauntingly forensic account that mirrors the tone of legal and mediatic reports I encountered during my own research. Bolaño's narrative resists the structure of conventional detective fiction; each account begins anew, violence accumulating without resolution, foreclosing any semblance of closure or comprehension, producing a sense of desperation that has no easy solution. They were incommensurable and uncountable.

The reliance on metrics raises critical questions for scholars committed to examining and challenging the architectures of violence. How can we engage with numerical inventories without succumbing to the dehumanizing and numbing forces of scientific objectification? In this work, I confront the dominant statistical frameworks applied to gender-based violence, extending McKittrick's concept of "the racial economy of the archive" (2014, 22) to what I call the mathematics of violence, a system that is both racialized and gendered. This perspective demands a "betrayal" of official archives and a radical critique of the colonial drive to catalog and quantify, a drive that persists in today's quantitative, empirically oriented research.

This work seeks to break through the restrictive and impersonal boundaries of data, insisting on the necessity of reinhabiting lives that statistical representation often flattens. Here, each story claims its own weight, resisting reduction into mere numbers, while numbers themselves may be

8 From the original: "Somos a história viva do preto, não números."

invoked – but only when they convey a nuanced understanding rather than a numbing effect. By prioritizing the lived experiences behind metrics, this approach foregrounds the depth of life that data alone cannot capture, confronting the limitations of quantification in excavating the profound layers of systemic violence.

Surface: The Front Door of Violence

In discussions of gender-based violence, the metaphor of the "tip of the iceberg" is frequently used to convey both visible forms of harm and the hidden layers that underpin them. Human rights reports, for instance, often illustrate violence as an iceberg: acts like murder, sexual assault, and physical violence hover above the surface, while submerged layers – coercive control, emotional abuse, isolation, threats, manipulation, shaming, economic exploitation, restrictions on freedom – extend deep beneath.

While this imagery captures the stratified nature of violence, I propose a rethinking of it. The image of a lone, submerged island fails to grasp the ways in which gendered violence is entangled within social and spatial terrains and relations – a complex ecology of harm that unfolds across boundaries, refusing simplification. Rather than an isolated mass beneath the surface, gendered violence is woven into the fabric of everyday life, blurring the lines between private and public, domestic and political, body and land, silence and voice.

Instead, I propose the imagery of the "front door" of violence. This term is not meant to reduce femicide or any form of gender-based violence to the confines of the home or imply restriction within four walls. Rather, the front door serves as a threshold, a boundary that marks the liminal space between what is visible and invisible, and, mostly important, what is heard and silenced. It is an entry point, opening onto the layered, intersecting dimensions of violence that traverse physical and symbolic spaces alike, revealing how this violence permeates the everyday while remaining, in many ways, hidden in plain sight.

The notion of the front door recalls Austrian-Czech novelist and writer Franz Kafka's parable *Before the Law* (1915), in which a person stands at the threshold, held back by a gatekeeper, spending his life waiting outside the "door of the law," unable to gain entry. Although Kafka's character is identified as a man, this image of the door resonates across legal and philosophical thought as a symbol of the opacity and inaccessibility of legal systems. Kafka's door, an emblem of justice withheld, lays bare the chasm between the promises of law and its enactments.

The connection between architectural boundaries and juridical limits also appears in the work of anthropologists Jean and John Comaroff (2006), who note how law has historically been described as the walls of governance and nationhood, an image invoked by thinkers like Thomas Hobbes and Hannah

Arendt. Yet beyond its role as a threshold, a door can signify departure and closure, isolation and escape. Caribbean-Canadian poet and writer Dionne Brand speaks of "the door of no return" as both a physical and metaphorical marker of the violent rupture of the transatlantic slave trade and its enduring legacies. For Brand, this door embodies the "creation place of Blacks in the New World Diaspora" and the "end of traceable beginnings" (2001, 15).

Similarly, the front door of violence can be understood as a site of rupture and reinvention – a space where refusal, escape, disruption, and transformation become possible. This door is not simply a threshold but an invitation to confront the architectures of violence that remain concealed within social and legal orders. Through this door, the grounding forces that uphold systems of violence can be disrupted and unsettled, making space for world-making otherwise.

Grammar of the Ground: Geologies

The gesture of passing through the *front door* invites us to engage with the layered architectures and geologies of femicide. What lies below this threshold is not only the structure of a house but also the very ground upon which it stands – the soil, sediment, and histories it contains. The ecological grammar and materiality of the ground have long been vital to Black, Indigenous, and anticolonial movements, where geography and geology emerge as sites of resistance, memory, and possibility. This vocabulary is likewise significant to this work. Under colonial and settler-colonial regimes, forms of genocide and femicide are not solely assaults on human bodies but also simultaneous acts of ecocide, as attacks on the Earth's capacity to sustain life and nurture connection.

This book draws inspiration from a lineage of Latin American and Caribbean countercolonial ontologies and epistemologies: Frantz Fanon's conceptualization on "zone of being and zone of nonbeing" (1952) and the condition of the "wretched of the earth" (1961); Sylvia Wynter's elaboration on the plantation as a site of forced transplantation onto "stranger" soil and Black resistance (1970s); Beatriz Nascimento's articulation of the *quilombo* (maroon) as both material territory and a living symbol of Black liberation (1989, 1992); Édouard Glissant's evocation of fertile, muddy soil as a space of opacity (1990); Katherine McKittrick's exploration of "demonic grounds" and Black geographies (2006); Leanne Betasamosake Simpson's concept of land as pedagogy (2014); Geni Núñez's call to reforest imaginaries (2021); Antonio Bispo dos Santos's reflections on belonging to the land and replanting words (2023a, 2023b); Kathryn Yusoff's critique of extractive "White Geology," geological lens through which to examine the foundations of colonialism and capitalism (2018, 2024). Together, these thinkers inform this book and provide tools to excavate the layered grounds of dispossession and resistance. Earth entails more than a site of violence, embodying a living terrain of insurgency, where the seeds of alternative futures might take root.

Drawing from the image of the ground, this book unfolds like a rhizome, burrowing into the subterranean layers of modern law and the violent geologies it sustains, particularly those shaped by what I term *Racial and Gendering ontologies of difference*. These layers expose a colonial world-making project rooted in extraction, dispossession, and invasion, while also bearing witness to enduring acts of resistance, refusal, and reinvention. Within these vital and contested terrains, this book traces ancestral and contemporary seeds of radical transformation that challenge and reach beyond the imposed territories of law.

In this context, "beyond" holds a layered significance. It conveys both a stance "in front of" the law – what I later in this introduction refer to as the front door of violence – and a dynamic movement that disrupts and reconfigures legal ordering. This beyond gestures toward a reimagining of legal reasoning and modern conceptions of justice, stepping into terrains where *choreographies of survival* are rehearsed. Here, the beyond is not merely a confrontation with existing frameworks; it is an act of cultivating spaces for emergent possibilities, where justice is refigured to exceed the confines of colonial legal geologies.

Beyond, in its dual sense of both confronting and surpassing, embodies a spiral temporality that interlaces past, present, and future. This temporal framework disrupts Western narratives of linear progress, fostering a rereading of space and time that opens possibilities for radical transformation (Streva, Case, and Petersmann 2024).

While grounded in the material conditions and geologies of Brazil, this work resists reduction to a case study or confinement within the boundaries of area studies, a limitation often imposed by Eurocentric academic frameworks. Theoretical inquiry is always, by necessity, located in specific soils and histories, and this book embraces the place from which it speaks. At the same time, it seeks to unsettle and challenge the political economy of knowledge that elevates the global North as the primary producer of theory while relegating the global South to the role of raw data supplier (Smith 1999; Cusicanqui 2010; Macharia 2016; Streva and Dulley 2023).

Drawing from Brazil's colonial geologies and the grounded *choreographies of survival* enacted within its borders, this work hopes to reveal how local struggles illuminate transnational patterns of dispossession and resistance. The legal terrains of violence mapped here are not exceptional to Brazil; rather, they are deeply entangled with globalized regimes of racialized and gendered subjugation. Attuned to these interconnections, this work listens closely to grassroots movements led by women in Brazil who resist racist- and gender-based violence. Through oral histories, embodied knowledge, and strategies of livability, these movements challenge dominant frameworks and propose radical reorientations for theorizing and living otherwise.

Law, here, is understood not merely as a mechanism for responding to violence but as a terrain where the architectures of violence have been historically constructed, embedded, and sustained. To engage with femicide through this perspective is to excavate the legal geologies of colonial racial-patriarchal order, tracing their sedimented histories from the first circle of colonialism in Brazil to their contemporary manifestations. Thus, moving beyond reductive, surface-level framings that treat femicide as merely a criminal category, a tragic anomaly, or a matter of impunity, this work interrogates the contradictions embedded within the very geologies of law.

The *choreographies of survival* are approached as enactments of countercolonial-feminist praxis – embodied modes of theorizing and acting on their own terms. This book embraces a broader conception of "theory," one that transcends the confines of intellectual academic pursuits. Instead, theory emerges from lived, situated movements, encompassing the dynamics of kinetics, context, politics, positionality, and relationality. It is a process deeply rooted in life itself. As Betasamosake Simpson observes, "It is intimate and personal, with individuals themselves holding the responsibilities for finding and generating meaning within their own lives" (2014, 7).

Through intimate conversations with women activists across Rio de Janeiro, Salvador, and Manaus, this book approaches these exchanges not as "detached data" but as relational and embodied practices of listening to, learning with, and speaking *nearby*.[9] These encounters reflect theory as something lived, shared, and redefined in the mutual recognition of struggle, rooted in the collective movement toward justice beyond colonial and patriarchal scripts. Thus, this inquiry is not merely an excavation of the past but a practice of learning with and listening to the living, enduring struggles of those who have borne the brunt of these systems (further elaboration on listening in Part 3).

•

Part 0, *Subject-Positions: Bodies and Territories*, excavates the buried histories of colonial fractures and the hierarchical constructions of Racial and Gendered ontologies of difference, particularly the fabrication of "White conquest-driven masculinity." Through the metaphorical front door of violence, this section uncovers the submerged historiographies that permeate and shape modern law and ontological subject-positions. Anchored in the diasporic and dialectical histories of Brazil, it reframes liberal grammars of identity, protection, justice, labor, and family. By excavating the structural role of law in normalizing gender-based violence, it reveals the enduring colonial architectures embedded within these frameworks. This part interrogates

9 For more about the concept and practice of "speaking nearby," see Trinh (1992).

the unspoken underpinnings of modern legal systems, exposing the intersections of colonial violence with legal norms and societal structures.

Part 1, *Colonial Racial-Patriarchal Order: Nation-State and Democracy*, expands the focus from the micro to the macro, analyzing how the colonial construction of the nuclear family facilitated the political formation of the nation-state. This section traces the entanglement of private and public spheres, showing how the colonial dismemberment of the "Human" gave rise to the citizen as a political figure. By examining Brazil's nation-building process, the analysis uncovers the mechanisms of silencing and speakability, as well as the infantilization of women, particularly Black and Indigenous peoples. It critiques national mythologies, such as those of harmony, *mestiçagem*, and independence, revealing their role in perpetuating the colonial pact. This part also examines constitutional frameworks through the lens of the social contract, exposing the persistence of systemic violence in liberal democratic ideals. Ultimately, it investigates how national narratives of unity mask the material and ontological fragmentation produced by colonial racial-patriarchal order.

Part 2, *Seeding a Politics of Vitality: Countercolonial-Feminist Praxis and the Limits of Justice*, marks a narrative shift, centering on the murder of Marielle Franco as a lens to examine choreographies of survival and grassroots feminist praxis. This section engages with theorizations and practices enacted by women in grassroots movements, employing a cross-disciplinary methodology of *deep listening* within a multimodal legal ethnography. It introduces the concept of a "politics of vitality," rooted in Black, Indigenous, queer, and feminist struggles that resist, challenge, and reimagine the law. By exploring political ecologies of the seed (*semente*), this part connects radical legal praxis with the possibilities of decolonial, transformative, and reparative justice and redressive pathways. The concluding sections grapple with the challenges of democratic representation, engaging anticolonial theories and practices of lawmaking and unmaking. Together, these chapters offer a vision of justice that moves beyond colonial and liberal frameworks, imagining new possibilities for collective survival and liberation.

Bibliography

35 Bienal de São Paulo. 2024. *Aqui, numa coreografia de retornos, dançar é inscrever no tempo*. Curated by Diane Lima, Grada Kilomba, Hélio Menezes, and Manuel Borja-Villel. São Paulo: Ministério da Cultura, Fundação Bienal de São Paulo e Itaú.

Acayaba, Cíntia, and Léo Arcoverde. 2019. "Casos de feminicídio aumentam 44% no 1° semestre de 2019 em SP." *O Globo*, July 8.

Adorno, Luís. 2019a. "Governo Doria muda metodologia e homicídio contra mulher salta de 71 a 227." *UOL*, March 9.

Adorno, Luís. 2019b. "SP divulgou dados menores sobre violência contra a mulher por 8 anos." *UOL*, May 9, sec. Segurança Pública.

Bispo dos Santos, Antônio Nego. 2015. *Colonização, Quilombos: Modos e Significados*. Brasília: Universidade de Brasília, Coordenação CNPq.
Bispo dos Santos, Antônio Nego. 2023a. *A Terra Dá, a Terra Quer*. São Paulo: Ubu Editora.
Bispo dos Santos, Antônio Nego. 2023b. "Estamos no começo do replantio das palavras": uma conversa com Antônio Bispo dos Santos (Nego Bispo). Interview by Edgar Rodrigues Barbosa Neto, Natalino Neves da Silva, and Walter Francisco Figueiredo Lowande. *PerCursos, Florianópolis* 24 (eo601): 1–26.
Bispo dos Santos, Antônio Nego. 2024. "Nego Bispo – Trajetórias." *Itaú Cultural*. https://www.youtube.com/watch?v=Tqt9BnrolFg.
Bispo dos Santos, Antônio Nego, Natacha Simei Leal, Greice Martins, Henrique Junio Felipe, and SuzEvany Lima da Silva. 2020. "Das Confluências, Cosmologias e Contra-Colonizações. Uma Conversa com Nego Bispo." *Revista Entrerios, Programa de Pós-Graduação em Antropologia* 2 (1): 73–84.
Bolaño, Roberto. 2004. *2666*. Translated by Natasha Wimmer. London: Picador.
Brand, Dionne. 2001. *A Map to the Door of no Return*. Toronto: Vintage Canada.
BRASIL. 2018. "Relatório Geral 2018. Ligue 180 – Central de Atendimento à Mulher." Report published by the Brazilian Ministry of Women, Family and Human Rights. https://www.gov.br/mdh/pt-br/centrais-de-conteudo/ligue-180/relatorio-ligue-180-2018.pdf.
Bunch, Charlotte. 1990. "Women's Rights as Human Rights: Toward a Re-Vision of Human Rights." *Human Rights Quarterly* 12 (4): 486–498.
Campbell, Jacquelyn. 1992. "'If I Can't Have You, No One Can': Power and Control in Homicide of Female Partners." In *Femicide. The Politics of Woman Killing*, edited by Diana Russell and Jill Radford. New York, Toronto, and Oxford: Twayne Publishers, Maxwell Macmillan International.
Césaire, Aimé. 1950. *Discourse on Colonialism*. Translated by Joan Pinkham. New York: Monthly Review Press.
Charlesworth, Hilary, Christine Chinkin, and Shelley Wright. 1991. "Feminist Approaches to International Law." *The American Journal of International Law* 85 (4): 613–645.
Chinkin, Christine. 1999. "A Critique of the Public/Private Dimension." *EJIL* 10 (2): 387–395.
Comaroff, John L., and Jean Comaroff. 2006. "Law and Disorder in the Postcolony. An Introduction." In *Law and Disorder in the Postcolony*, 1–56. Chicago and London: The University of Chicago Press.
Cusicanqui, Silvia Rivera. 2010. "Ch'ixinakax Utxiwa: A Reflection on the Practices and Discourses of Decolonization." In *Ch'ixinakax Utxiwa. On Practices and Discourses of Decolonization*, translated by Molly Geidel, 46–70. Cambridge: Polity Press.
ECLAC (Economic Commission for Latin America and the Caribbean). 2006. "Regional Programme of Action for the Women of Latin America and the Caribbean and Other Regional Consensuses." LC/G.2239/Rev.1. Santiago: United Nations. https://repositorio.cepal.org/server/api/core/bitstreams/307267f1-f432-4e15-8dff-d2e41b5889d2/content.
ECLAC (Economic Commission for Latin America and the Caribbean). 2022. "45 Years of the Regional Gender Agenda." LC/MDM-E.2022/4. Santiago: United Nations.
Evaristo, Conceição. 2015. "A Gente Combinamos de Não Morrer." In *Olhos d'Água*. Rio de Janeiro: Pallas.
Fanon, Frantz. 1952. *Black Skin, White Masks*. Translated by Richard Philcox. New York: Grove Press.

Fanon, Frantz. 1961. *The Wretched of the Earth*. Translated by Richard Philcox. New York: Grove Press.
Ferreira da Silva, Denise. 2009. "No-Bodies: Law, Raciality and Violence." *Griffith Law Review* 18 (2): 212–236.
Ferreira da Silva, Denise. 2014. "Ninguém: Direito, Racialidade e Violência." *Revista Meritum, Belo Horizonte* 9 (1): 67–117.
Ferreira da Silva, Denise. 2018. "Hacking the Subject: Black Feminism and Refusal Beyond the Limits of Critique." *philoSOPHIA* 8 (1): 19–41.
Ferreira da Silva, Denise. 2019. "An End to 'This' World." *Text Zur Kunst*. Interviewed by Susanne Leeb and Kerstin Stakemeier. April, Section Debates.
Glissant, Édouard. 1990. *Poetics of Relation*. Ann Arbor: The University of Michigan Press.
Gonzalez, Lélia. 1983. "Racismo e Sexismo na Cultura Brasileira." In *Por um Feminismo Afro-Latino-Americano*, edited by Flavia Rios and Márcia Lima, 75–93. Rio de Janeiro: Zahar.
Hartman, Saidiya. 1997. *Scenes of Subjection: Terror, Slavery, and Self-Making in Nineteenth-Century America*. 2nd ed. New York and London: Oxford University Press.
Hartman, Saidiya. 2008. "Venus in Two Acts." *Small Axe (SX26). A Caribbean Journal of Criticism* 12 (2): 1–14.
Hartman, Saidiya. 2019. Wayward Lives, Beautiful Experiments. Intimate Histories of Social Upheaval. New York and London: W.W. Norton & Company.
Ife, Fahima. 2021. *Maroon Choreography*. Durham and London: Duke University Press.
IndigenousAction (AI). 2020. "Rethinking the Apocalypse: An Indigenous Anti-Futurist Manifesto." https://www.indigenousaction.org/rethinking-the-apocalypse-an-indigenous-anti-futurist-manifesto/.
Kafka, Franz. 1915. *Before the Law*. New York: Schocken Books.
Kilomba, Grada. 2015. "Decolonising Knowledge." In *The Struggle Is Not Over Yet. An Archive in Relation*, 191–208. Berlin: Archive Books.
Krenak, Ailton. 2019. *Ideias Para Adiar o Fim Do Mundo*. São Paulo: Companhia das Letras.
Krenak, Ailton. 2022. Earth's Fever. A Short History of Extractivism. Interview by Eric Macedo and Camila de Caux. A Perfect Storm. https://aperfectstorm.net/earths-fever/.
Lagarde, Marcela. 2007. "El Derecho Humano de Las Mujeres a Una Vida Libre de Violencia: La Ley General de Acceso de Las Mujeres a Una Vida Libre de Violencia." *Revista Mexicana de Ciencias Políticas y Sociales* XLIX (200): 143–165.
Lagarde, Marcela. 2008. "Antropología, Feminismo y Política: Violência Feminicida y Derechos Humanos de las Mujeres." In *Retos Teóricos y Nuevas Práticas*, edited by Margaret Bullen and Carmen Diez Mintegui. Donostia, Spain: Ankulegi.
Lagarde, Marcela, and Charlie Roberts. 2010. "Preface: Feminist Keys for Understanding Feminicide: Theoretical, Political, and Legal Construction." In *Terrorizing Women: Feminicide in the Americas*. Durham: Duke University Press.
Le Guin, Ursula K. 1989. "The Carrier Bag Theory of Fiction [1986]." In *Dancing at the Edge of the World: Thoughts on Words, Women, Places*. New York: Groves Press.
Lepecki, André. 2006. *Exhausting Dance. Performance and the Politics of Movement*. New York and London: Routledge.
Lorde, Audre. 1977. "The Transformation of Silence into Language and Action." In *I Am Your Sister: Collected and Unpublished Writings of Audre Lorde*. Oxford and New York: Oxford University Press.

Macharia, Keguro. 2016. "On Being Area-Studied." *GLQ: A Journal of Lesbian and Gay Studies. Duke University Press* 22 (2): 185–189.

Malunguinho, Erica. 2020. Conversa com Erica Malunguinho. Encontro com Estudantes, Professorxs e Pesquisadorxs. Interview by Juliana Streva. Video-Zoom.

Martínez, Juan Manuel. 2011. "La Activista Susana Chávez es Asesinada en Ciudad Juárez, Chihuahua." *Expasión*, November 1. https://expansion.mx/nacional/2011/01/11/la-activista-susana-chavez-es-asesinada-en-ciudad-juarez-chihuahua.

Martins, Leda Maria. 1997. *Afrografias da Memória*. 2 ed. rev. São Paulo and Belo Horizonte: Perspectiva and Mazza Edições.

McKittrick, Katherine. 2006. *Demonic Grounds. Black Women and the Cartographies of Struggle*. Minneapolis and London: University of Minnesota Press.

McKittrick, Katherine. 2014. "Mathematics Black Life." *The Black Scholar* 2 (44): 16–28.

McMillan, Lesley. 2007. *Feminists Organising Against Gendered Violence*. New York: Palgrave MacMillan.

Milenio. 2011. "Niega Fiscal de Chihuahua que Homicidio de Susana Chávez Fuera por su Activismo." *Milenio*, December 1. https://archive.ph/20120630184705/http://www.milenio.com/node/619686#selection-459.0-459.79.

Mombaça, Jota. 2018. "The Time Has Come, in Which the Lights of this Epoch Were Lit Everywhere." Translated by Jess Oliveira. *L'Internationale Online. Originally from Buala, 09/2020*. https://www.internationaleonline.org/opinions/131_the_time_has_come_in_which_the_lights_of_this_epoch_were_lit_everywhere/.

Morrison, Adele M. 2006. "Changing the Domestic Violence (Dis)Course: Moving from White Victim to Multi-Cultural Survivor." *University of California, Davis* 39: 1061–1120.

Nájar, Alberto. 2011. "A Susana Chávez 'La Mataron por ser Mujer'." *BBC Mundo*, December 1. https://www.bbc.com/mundo/noticias/2011/01/110112_mexico_juarez_susana_chavez_an.

Nascimento, Beatriz. 1974 [2007]. "Por uma História do Homem Negro." In *Eu Sou Atlântica: Sobre a Trajetória de Vida de Beatriz Nascimento*, edited by Alex Ratts. São Paulo: Imprensa Oficial do Estado de São Paulo and Instituto Kuanza.

Nascimento, Beatriz. 1989 [2018]. "Transcrição do Documentário Orí [1989]." In *Beatriz Nascimento. Quilombola e Intelectual. Possibilidade nos Dias da Destruição*, edited by União dos Coletivos Pan-Africanistas, 326–340. São Paulo: Editora Filhos da África.

Nascimento, Beatriz. 1992 [2018]. "Por um Território (Novo) Existencial e Físico [1992]." In *Beatriz Nascimento. Quilombola e Intelectual. Possibilidade nos Dias da Destruição*, edited by União dos Coletivos Pan-Africanistas, 413–430. São Paulo: Editora Filhos da África.

Núñez, Geni. 2021. "Monoculturas do Pensamento e a Importância do Reflorestamento do Imaginário." *Revista ClimaCom. Diante dos Negacionismos Ano* 8 (21): 1–7.

Núñez, Geni. 2023. *Descolonizando Afetos. Experimentações sobre outras Formas de Amar*. São Paulo: Planeta do Brasil.

Oliva, Nathalia. 2019. "Brasil tem onda de feminicídios no início do ano, com mais de 100 casos em 1 Mês." *IG*, April 2.

Radford, Jill. 1992. "Introduction." In *Femicide. The Politics of Woman Killing*, edited by Diana Russell and Jill Radford. New York, Toronto, and Oxford: Twayne Publishers, Maxwell Macmillan International.

Rajagopal, Balakrishnan. 2003. *International Law From Below. Development, Social Movements, and Third World Resistance*. Cambridge: Cambridge University Press.

Rich, Adrienne. 1995. *On Lies, Secrets, and Silence. Selected Prose 1966–1978*. New York and London: W. W. Norton & Company.

Rizki, Cole. 2019. "Latin/x American Trans Studies: Toward a Travesti-Trans Analytic." *TSQ: Transgender Studies Quarterly. Duke University Press* 6 (2): 145–155. https://doi.org/10.1215/23289252-7348426.
Russell, Diana. 1992. "Preface." In *Femicide. The Politics of Woman Killing*, edited by Diana Russell and Jill Radford. New York, Toronto, and Oxford: Twayne Publishers, Maxwell Macmillan International.
Russell, Diana. 2011. "The Origin and Importance of the Term Femicide." https://www.dianarussell.com/origin_of_femicide.html.
Russell, Diana, and Jane Caputi. 1992. "Femicide: Sexist Terrorism against Women." In *The Politics of Woman Killing*, edited by Diana Russell and Jill Radford. New York: Twayne Publishers.
Russell, Diana, and Jill Radford. 1992. *Femicide. The Politics of Woman Killing*. New York, Toronto, and Oxford: Twayne Publishers, Maxwell Macmillan International.
Santana, Dora Silva. 2019. "Mais Viva! Reassembling Transness, Blackness, and Feminism." *TSQ: Transgender Studies Quarterly. Duke University Press* 6 (2): 210–222. https://doi.org/10.1215/23289252-7348496.
Segato, Rita. 2010. "Femi-geno-cidio como crimen en el Fuero Internacional de los Derechos Humanos: El derecho a nombrar el sufrimiento en el derecho." In *Una Cartografía Del Feminicidio en las Américas*, edited by R. Fregoso and C. Bejarano. México D.F.: UNAM CIIECH.
Segato, Rita. 2016. *La Guerra Contra Las Mujeres*. Madrid: Traficantes de Sueños.
Sellers, Patricia Viseur. 2009. "Gender Strategy Is Not Luxury for International Courts Symposium: Prosecuting Sexual and Gender-Based Crimes Before International/Ized Criminal Courts." *Journal of Gender, Social Policy & the Law* 17 (2).
Senado. 2019. "Preocupação Com Aumento de Feminicídios No Brasil Motiva Debate Na CDH." *Senado*, June 17, 2019.
Simpson, Leanne Betasamosake. 2014. "Land as Pedagogy: Nishnaabeg Intelligence and Rebellious Transformation." *Decolonization: Indigeneity, Education & Society* 3 (3): 1–25.
Smith, Linda Tuhiwai. 1999. *Decolonizing Methodologies. Research and Indigenous Peoples*. London and New York: Zed Books and University of Otago Press.
Stanley, Eric A. 2021. *Atmospheres of Violence: Structuring Antagonism and the Trans/Queer Ungovernable*. Durham and London: Duke University Press.
Streva, Juliana, and Iracema Dulley. 2023. "Invitation, To Exi(s)t." In *Displacing Theory Through the Global South*, edited by Özgün Eylül Iscen and Iracema Dulley. Berlin: ICI Berlin Press.
Streva, Juliana, Sarah R. Case, and Marie Petersmann. 2024. "The Inhuman as Refusal." *Critical Legal Thinking: Law and the Political* (blog). https://criticallegalthinking.com/.
Trinh, Minh-Ha T. 1992. "'Speaking Nearby:' A Conversation with Trinh T. Minh-Ha." *Visual Anthropology Review* 8 (1): 82–91.
Vásquez, Patsilí Toledo. 2009. *Feminicidio*. México: Consultoría para la Oficina en México del Alto Comisionado de las Naciones Unidas para los Derechos Humanos.
Velasco, Clara, Gabriela Caesar, and Thiago Reis. 2019. "Cai o nº de mulheres vítimas de homicídio, mas registros de feminicídio crescem no Brasil." *G1, O Globo*, August.
Vilela, Pedro Rafael. 2019. "Feminicídio: Uma inaceitável epidemia brasileira." *Brasil de Fato*, February 27.
Wekker, Gloria. 2016. *White Innocence. Paradoxes of Colonialism and Race*. Durham and London: Duke University Press.

Wynter, Sylvia. 1970s. "Black Metamorphosis: New Natives in a New World." Unpublished Manuscript, Institute of the Black World Records. Schomburg Center for Research in Black Culture, New York.
Yusoff, Kathryn. 2018. *A Billion Black Anthropocene or None.* Minneapolis: University of Minnesota Press.
Yusoff, Kathryn. 2024. *Geologic Life. Inhuman Intimacies and the Geophysics of Race.* Durham and London: Duke University Press.

Part 0

Subject-Positions: Bodies and Territories

Zero Degree

Excavating the strata upon which monocultural and femicidal systems of organization have been constructed brings us to what might be termed the zero degree. This is not a fixed point of origin but an entry into a multidimensional field – a layered terrain that requires a relational, contextualized, and rhizomatic approach. Drawing on Black geographies and critical geological studies – which argue that the histories of the past underpin the conditions of the present – this excavation seeks to uncover the structures beneath the surface of hegemonic universal narratives. As Saidiya Hartman (2008) reminds us, the act of narrating counter-histories of colonialism and slavery is inseparably linked to the project of writing a history of the present.

The notion of "zero degree" finds resonance in U.S. Black feminist scholar Hortense Spillers's (1987, 445–446) analysis of the sociopolitical order of the "New World," where colonial slavery regimes imposed a stark distinction between captive and liberated subject-positions, a distinction paralleled by the fracture between flesh and body. This critical juncture reveals the violent processes through which human beings (as well as nonhumans) were categorized and hierarchized. Ferreira da Silva (2018) also complicates the notion of the zero, exploring its multiple and simultaneous meanings: nullification, indicating the erasure of value; nothingness, referring to the absence of value; excess, denoting that which surpasses any means of measurement; and, crucially, the plenum, understood as the potential for new modes of becoming *in* and *of* the world.

Drawing from historiographic grounds, the pursuit is to unearth the often-overlooked histories of colonial monocultures and their entanglement with the hierarchical construction of identification categories shaped by Racial and Gendered ontologies of difference. Particular focus is given to the normative fabrication of White conquest-driven masculinity as a central mechanism of colonial power. Passing through the *front door*[1] of violence, this chapter

1 The metaphor of "front door" of violence was introduced in the Part –1 of this book.

DOI: 10.4324/9781003474692-2

examines the concealed histories and counter-histories of violence that underpin and sustain modern law and ontological frameworks of existence and coexistence. To trace this broader cartography, the analysis primarily engages with processes and fragmented events in Pindorama – territory now known as Brazil (Bispo dos Santos 2015) – understood within its diasporic and dialectic entanglements that co-constitute territory and temporality, here and there.

In the late fifteenth century, the colonial enterprise inaugurated a global narrative of modernity. It emerged through the colonial invasion of the region today named America and subsequently expanded to the continents now known as Africa and Asia (Gilroy 1993; Alencastro 2000; Dussel 2005). Amid territorial disputes in Abya Yala – the region now known as Latin America[2] – a series of papal bulls issued in 1493 established a demarcation line, granting Portugal control over eastern colonial possessions and Spain over western ones. This division was redefined a year later by the Treaty of Tordesillas, which secured Portuguese sovereignty over Brazil.

Modernity transcends the boundaries of the European context, involving a constitutive interplay between the so-called Old World and the New World. The colonial process, on one hand, profoundly altered the preceding European feudal system, which was defined by a hierarchical tripartition of clergy, nobility, and peasantry. This transformative shift introduced numerous categories of differentiation that carry far-reaching implications for societies and individuals.

On the other hand, an examination of the impact of European colonialism in the occupied territories of the so-called Americas and Africa unveils a multifaceted understanding of gender classifications, which can be explored through at least three distinct strands. The first strand, advanced by scholars such as Oyèrónkẹ́ Oyěwùmí in *The Invention of Women* (1997), argues that the modern gender binary was absent in precolonial societies and resulted as an outcome of colonialism, as exemplified by her study of Yoruba communities in Africa. A second strand, with authors like María Lugones (2008), extends a similar argument to Latin America. The key distinction between these two strands lies in their engagement with local historiographies: while Oyěwùmí grounds her analysis in specific African contexts, the second one does not root the analysis to the historiography of Abya Yala but instead draws significant parallels with African and Canadian studies, shedding light on the colonial imposition of gendered structures across varied geographies. The third strand, exemplified by scholars like Susan

2 The term "Abya Yala" originates from the language of the Kuna Indigenous people and refers to the territory now known as America. It encompasses meanings such as "Mature Land," "Living Land," and "Blossoming Land," offering today an anticolonial approach for renaming the continent (cf. Miñoso, Correal, and Muñoz 2014; Gargallo 2015; Curiel 2015).

Kellogg (2005), directly engages with the local historiography of Abya Yala. This perspective asserts that diverse conceptions of gender existed in the region now known as Latin America long before colonization, with variations across different geographic locations and communities.[3] It further argues that, during and after colonization, European norms sought to violently impose a homogenized understanding of gender, erasing and subordinating Indigenous worldviews.

Rather than excavating or speculating on the precolonial era, this book focuses on the period from colonization onward, examining the historical conditions and material foundations that enabled the colonial project to impose a homogenized way of living, producing, and relating. This process gave rise to a monocultural paradigm, shaped and sustained through the normativity of White conquest-driven masculinity. By tracing these developments, the book unravels the intricate and shifting articulations of Racial and Gendered ontologies of difference, acknowledging their contradictions and complexities, and offering a nuanced account of their enduring and violent entanglements across time.

The Human Script: Colonial Fractures, Separability

In the imperial context of invasion and domination, the term "colonial fracture" refers to the process through which the colonial gaze, operating geographically, ontologically, economically, and epistemically, engenders a relentless clash between the self and the other. Here, the concept of gaze extends beyond mere visual perception to encompass a broader dimension, including how colonial subject-positions impose their own way of seeing, knowing, and living upon "Others." This colonial imaginary is intricately linked to the colonial narratives of "discovery" and "encounter," authored by those who perceived these lands as a "New World," rather than by those who had long inhabited them.

Insights from anticolonial and critical Black studies, including the works of Fanon (1952), French-Tunisian writer and essayist Albert Memmi (1957), and Wynter (1970s), reveal the colonial construction of the self through the negation of the other. Within this framework, the colonial "I" asserts itself

3 For instance, the Kuna community, located in what is now Panama and Colombia, exhibited a remarkable diversity of gender roles not commonly observed elsewhere in Central America. They classified individuals as male, female, *macharetkit*, or, more frequently, *omekit*. The term *macharetkit* appears to refer to a female who transgresses traditional gender roles, encompassing tomboys or women performing typically male labor. On the other hand, *omekit* described individuals who "sometimes marry women but usually engage in sexual relations with men." Rural Kuna men often preferred rural *omekits* over their urban counterparts. Both rural and urban Kuna women held favorable views of *omekits*, with many considering any woman with an *omekit* son to be fortunate (cf. Kellogg 2005).

by simultaneously producing the colonized "not-I," positioning the latter as nonwhite, nonrational, and noncivilized. This mechanism, central to the colonial project, highlights the pivotal role of naming and categorization in shaping modern notions of the Human. Rooted in the colonial gaze, this construct is embodied by White conquest-driven masculinity, a figure that is both racialized and gendered, yet universalized as the unmarked norm of humanity.

The colonial fracture functions by separating and hierarchizing both human and more-than-human entities, driven by an endless pursuit to master and dominate the world. Through the imposition of a White supremacist human script (Wynter and Scott 2000), the colonial regime systematically denies certain modes of existence, excluding them om the category of the "Human." Instead, it enforces a Eurocentric measure of humanity as the universal standard, relegating "the rest" (Hall 1992) to the status of not human, subhuman, less than human, in other words, the inhuman (Yusoff 2018).

This division between human and nonhuman – or, as Wynter (2015) terms it, between the "selected" and "dysselected" – is not peripheral but central to the system of total violence instituted by colonial slavery. The concept of the in/human and the analytics of Raciality serve as the bedrock upon which colonialism and racial capitalism are built. This framework enforces a regime of monohumanism, exposing the underlying architecture of modern juridical and ethical norms, as well as forms of subjectivation they engender (Ferreira da Silva 2009).

Geni Núñez (2023) contends that Indigenous peoples never sought to "save" others or persuade them that their own group held the exclusive truth or the true God. Núñez emphasizes that this approach was never a part of Indigenous cosmologies, including her own Guarani worldview, which do not uphold a monocultural or monohumanist framework in which one spirituality or mode of existence must be validated through the negation of others.

In the construction of modern subject-positions, the colonial monological rationale – wherein the colonizer asserts their own civility by negating the other – profoundly reshapes perceptions of living beings, territories, and temporalities. The "Old World," self-proclaimed as rational and civilized, assumes an adultlike status, while the "New World" is relegated to a childlike, uncivilized and underdeveloped condition. Europe positions itself in a linear, developed future, while colonized lands and peoples are confined to a primitive past. This unidirectional trajectory between self and other envisions a progressive path in which the other must assimilate to mirror and become the self. Existence becomes possible only through the transformation of the other into the self – by developing the "primitive," civilizing the "uncivilized," whitening the nonwhite, normativizing the "nonnormative." In other words, it creates separability and difference to justify the need of integration, homogenization, and extermination.

The colonial fracture manifests through intricate layers of separation and negation. This study explores how colonialism enforces a White conquest-driven masculinity, characterized by an extractivist regime rooted in property accumulation, dispossession, labor division, and a patriarchal conception of family, centered on monogamy and cisheteronormativity. These colonial and postcolonial structures of femicide are both shaped by and constitutive of modern legal frameworks and ideas of justice.

Colonial "Justice"

The categories of "colonizer" and "colonized" in the context of colonial slavery, as well as "settler" and "native" within settler-colonialism frameworks, have been central to the analysis of colonial regimes and their afterlives. These concepts have been critically explored by the scholarship referenced here, all of which falls under the broader umbrella of anticolonial, countercolonial, decolonial, or postcolonial studies.

African American sociologist, historian, and activist W.E.B. Du Bois identified "the problem of the color-line" (1903, 9) as the foremost challenge of the twentieth century. The formulation of the color-line delineates the boundary in which the separation between the colonizer and colonized was established, a distinction underscored by the epidermal categorization of White and Black. At this preliminary stage of analysis, the critique of colonialism predominantly engages with the Racial ontology of difference, without presenting a nuanced analysis on the interconnections with gender.

In *The Colonizer and the Colonized* (1957), Memmi examines the enduring legacies of colonization. Memmi contends that the social and corporeal forms of identification of the colonizer and the colonized were shaped by three interconnected components. First is the assertion of difference from the colonizer toward the colonized; second, the integration of these differences into a linear historical narrative, in which one culture is deemed superior and more advanced than others; third, the exploitation of the colonized for the benefit and privilege of the colonizer. While Memmi's analysis primarily focuses on the African context, particularly Tunisia, I argue that these elements are equally resonant in the colonial history of Latin America.

During the first years of colonial invasion, the Portuguese Empire refrained from enacting any legislation to regulate the "interactions" between Portuguese colonizers and Indigenous peoples.[4] Officially, Portuguese colonial authorities adhered to Iberian provisions that formally prohibited

4 The term "interactions" is placed in quotes because, as Aimé Césaire critiques in *Discourse on Colonialism*, the engagements between colonizer and colonized can only be understood as "the complete absence of human contact" (1950, 41).

slavery. However, a significant exception existed in the form of the "just war." In practice, colonial authorities exploited the broad and ambiguous interpretation of "just war" to justify virtually any action against Indigenous peoples, driven by their self-interest. Consequently, despite the absence of explicit legal frameworks, Indigenous peoples were dehumanized and objectified from the very beginning of colonization in Brazil (Schwartz 1973; Wehling and Wehling 2004; Loveman 2014).[5]

By examining the instrumental interpretations of the vague notion of "just war," this analysis scrutinizes the foundational contours of the modern concept of justice. The indeterminate aspects of legal discourse and its gaps were manipulated to rationalize and legitimize exploitation, predicated on the denial of humanity from Indigenous subjects. In other words, legal interpretations and provisions served as instruments to create, endorse, and perpetuate the Racial ontology of difference.

Drawing on Martinican poet, author, and politician Aimé Césaire's (1950) call to analyze the effects of colonization on both the colonized and the colonizer, and guided by Fanon's assertion that "[a]ll forms of exploitation resemble one another" (1952, 64–65), this study unravels the often overlooked entanglements of colonialism and Gendered ontology of difference by focusing on the construction of a *White conquest-driven masculinity.*

Blame-Shifting: Dress Code and Legal Normativity

In 1492, during the early months of the invasion of the Americas, Italian navigator Christopher Columbus wrote letters describing his perspective on the landscape of the New World. These accounts not only detailed the geographic space but also included emphatic descriptions of Indigenous women's bodies, noting their systematic efforts to protect themselves from male colonizers. A few years later, Pero Vaz de Caminha, a scrivener in the Portuguese colonial mission, provided a detailed account of the Portuguese arrival in what is now called Brazil. While he briefly mentioned male nudity, Caminha notably fixated on female nudity, providing explicit descriptions, including details of their sexual organs.

Before presenting the transcription of an excerpt from Caminha's letter, originally addressed to D. Manuel I, I briefly explain the dual meaning of the Portuguese word *vergonha*. While the term literally translates to shame, it was also commonly used during that period as a euphemism for sexual

5 Unlike the Iberian colonies that adopted the "encomienda" system, Brazil implemented a system of slavery. Under the encomienda system, Indigenous people were coerced into labor under harsh and abusive conditions, while also being required to pay taxes to the Empire (Alencastro 2000).

organs. Below the original passage, I provide a translation to highlight its nuanced and ambiguous usage:

> *E uma daquelas moças era toda tingida de baixo a cima, daquela tintura e certo era tão bem feita e tão redonda, e sua vergonha tão graciosa que a muitas mulheres de nossa terra, vendo-lhe tais feições envergonhara, por não terem as suas como ela.*
>
> And one of those girls was all dyed from the bottom up, and she was so well-built and so round, and her very gracious *vergonha* [sexual organ] would make many women from our land [Portugal], after seeing such features feel *envergonhada* [ashamed], for theirs [sexual organ] not being as hers [Indigenous woman's sexual organ]. (my translation)

Caminha exploits the dual meaning of *vergonha* to depict the sexual organs of Indigenous women, drawing comparisons with those of Portuguese women. Both accounts reveal the pervasive objectification, fetishization, and oversexualization of female bodies and lives (Kellogg 2005).

In a letter from 1549, Portuguese priest Manuel da Nóbrega requested the dispatch of clothing to cover the *vergonhas* (sexual organs) of Indigenous peoples subjected to forced Christianization (Núñez, Oliveira, and Lago 2021). Instead of addressing the pervasive sexual violence inherent in the colonial project, the Jesuits proposed a dress code as a "solution" to conceal Indigenous women's nudity (Vainfas 1989). This approach strategically shifted the burden of colonial violence from White men onto Indigenous women, framing their bodies as the source of moral and sexual corruption.

Thus, the colonial campaign against nudity operated as a central pillar of the colonial project, addressing multiple ideological and social objectives. Nudity was framed as a marker of savagery and animalistic behavior, signifying a deviation from the presumed trajectory toward civility, Christianity, and humanity. Furthermore, it was construed as a disruptive element that threatened the Catholic enforcement of monogamous norms within colonial society (Núñez 2023), a point that will be examined in greater depth later in this chapter.

This mechanism of blame-shifting persists in contemporary cases of sexual violence and femicide, where women's clothing is often cited to justify the violence inflicted upon them. The colonial narrative exonerated White "civilized" men by attributing their "natural" and "uncontrollable" sexual impulses to the visibility of women's bodies, particularly those deemed uncivilized or Other. Consequently, gender-based violence became normalized, deeply entangled with constructs of virility, heterosexuality, and White conquest-driven masculinity, perpetuating a legacy of patriarchal and racialized domination.

Colonial legislations, such as the Brazilian First Constitutions of the Archbishopric of Bahia from 1707 (*Constituições Primeiras do Arcebispado da Bahia*), illustrate how dress codes were used as tools to enforce Gendered ontology of difference within colonial society. Beyond the general colonial mandate to conceal nudity, this legislation introduced specific binary gender regulations concerning dress. For instance, one provision imposed a fine of one hundred crusaders on men who wore "women's clothing," a rule strictly enforced to maintain gender normativity in public spaces. Depending on the severity of the perceived transgression, subjects could even face expulsion from the Archbishopric of Bahia. This regulation stands as one piece of the tangible vestiges of how colonialism directly shaped Gendered ontology of difference through legal, economic, and aesthetic mechanisms.

The Criminal Code of the Empire (1830) provides another example of how dress codes were enforced in accordance with the colonial standards of "morality and good manners" (Article 280), reflecting and reinforcing a cisgender binary. This legislation was employed to impose gender normativity while criminalizing nonbinary and nonnormative gender expressions. In *Ensaios sobre raça, gênero e sexualidades no Brasil (Séculos XVIII–XX)*, Brazilian social anthropologist Jocélio Teles dos Santos (2013) examines the rigorous enforcement of this law, which resulted in numerous arrests and legal accusations.

Santos' analysis of police reports highlights the disproportionate targeting of marginalized groups within colonial society, including the poor, beggars, sex workers, washerwomen, seamstresses, and individuals racially categorized as Black, "parda," or "cabra." These reports, alongside gendered dress codes, reveal the intricate and multifaceted nature of the Racial ontology of difference in Brazil. This system goes beyond the simplistic binary of Black and White, encompassing a broader spectrum of racial categorizations. As Teles dos Santos (2013, 12–13) explains:

> In 1772, the population subdivision of Piauí revealed the existence of nine categories: White, Black, Red (Indigenous of any nation), mulatto, mestizo, mameluco, caful, cabra, curiboca. While "mulatto" retained the same meaning as previously mentioned [referring to the offspring of a horse and a donkey, as well as to individuals resulting from interracial relationships, i.e., "the child of a Black person with a White person, or vice versa, or of a mulatto with a White person up to a certain degree"], "cabra" was used for the child of a Black person and a mulatto, while "caful" referred to the child of a Black person and an Indigenous person. Notably, the term "mestiço" was used to refer to "one who participates in White, Black, and Indigenous," a category that functioned as a repository for the many mixtures, including those that were difficult to classify within colonial frameworks.

Moreover, these colonial records make evident that individuals who contested and defied gender norms have always existed throughout history. Long before the emergence of contemporary terms such as *cuír*/queer, nonbinary, drag, transgender, and travesti, such individuals were earlier labeled by the Brazilian press as "transformers" (*transformistas*) or "man-woman" (*homem-mulher*).

One of the earliest documented cases, dating to 1591, is that of Xica Manicongo, the first African person denounced during the Inquisition's visitation to Salvador and later recognized as the first *travesti* known in Brazil. Manicongo was an enslaved person from West Africa living in the city of São Salvador – now Salvador, the capital of Bahia – who is referred to in colonial records by their baptismal name, Francisco Manicongo. As detailed by historian and anthropologist Luiz Mott (1999), Xica Manicongo was accused of defying the gender norms of the time by refusing to wear male attire. The colonial report recounts:

> [Manicongo] is reputed among the Black people of this city to be a *sodomite*, and after hearing this reputation, he was seen wearing a wrapped cloth, as is customary in his homeland of Congo for those who are *sodomites*. Furthermore, the informant stated that he knows, from his extensive time and experience in the lands of Angola and Congo, that it is customary among the gentile Black people for *sodomites* – those who partake in the nefarious sin and serve as passive women – to wear a wrapped cloth with the ends tied at the front, creating an opening. These individuals are called *quimbanda* in the languages of Angola and Congo, which means passive sodomites.

Xica Manicongo lived under a colonial regime in which both social norms and legal codes strictly forbade disruptions of gender roles. Under the *Ordenações Manuelinas* (1512–1603), the penal code in force at the time, sodomy was classified as *lesa-majestade* (a crime against the sovereign) and was punishable by execution through public burning. Those convicted faced not only death but also the confiscation of their property by the Catholic Church, along with the hereditary stigma of infamy, which extended to their descendants for three generations.

Accused of sodomy, Manicongo was coerced into relinquishing their gender identity and sexual orientation. Pejoratively labeled a "*quimbanda*, member of a gang of sodomite sorcerers" (Mott and Cerqueira 2005, 25), Manicongo is said to have adopted traditional male attire as a means of survival. Their story is marked by archival silences and contested interpretations, with the fragments of their life and death remaining subject of historical speculations (Mott 1985, 1999; Gomes de Jesus 2019; Benevides 2020).

This narrative not only highlights the resistance of dissent bodies but also underscores the gaps and erasures that define colonial archives.

Xica Manicongo's story stands as both a testament to the ancestrality of their existence and resistance, and a reminder of the complex, contested nature of historical records and colonial archives. These expressions of nonnormative performativity offer insight into the imposition of a Gendered ontology of difference, intricately entangled with racialized hierarchies. The legal enforcement of dress codes reveals a broader colonial drive toward homogenization, underscoring the persistence of practices that defied colonial normativities – practices that led to severe consequences, particularly for those occupying the most marginalized positions within colonial society.

Sexual Violence and Colonial Epistemology

Despite the enforcement of dress codes as an alledged means to regulate sexual behavior, sexual violence remained deeply entrenched within Brazil's colonial regime. Framed through the colonial myth of the allegedly "natural" and "unrestrained" sexuality attributed to female subject-positions racialized as Indigenous and Black, colonial documents demonstrate that countless acts of sexual violation were systematically overlooked and absolved by both Jesuit authorities and colonial royal courts (Schwartz 1973; Vainfas 1989).

Unlike the settler colonial regimes experienced in Turtle Island – now known as North America – where settlers established permanent residences with their families, the exploitative colonial model in Brazil operated through an extractive and transitory approach. Colonizers prioritized invasion, exploitation, and the accumulation of wealth, with the explicit aim of transferring these profits back to the Empire. This provisional arrangement also meant that colonizers' wives typically did not accompany them to the colonies.

In response to the widespread sexual violence that characterized this colonial system, the Jesuits advanced yet another "solution": the relocation of young White female orphans from Portugal to Brazil (Menezes 2013). This initiative illustrates the systematic commodification of female bodies and flesh – strongly differentiated along Racialized hierarchies, as further explored in this book – reduced to instruments for satisfying the desires of White men and consolidating their sociopolitical dominance.

These patterns of blame-shifting and normalization of violence against female subject-positions are not confined to the colonial past. Gilberto Freyre, one of Brazil's most influential sociologists, exemplifies the enduring nature of White conquest-driven masculinity within the Lusotropicalist intellectual framework. "Lusotropicalism" refers to a quasi-theory that, while reinforcing colonial discourse, portrays Portuguese colonialism as a more benign and benevolent regime compared to other European experiences of colonization. This narrative perpetuates several myths, including the colonial myth of harmonious slavery and the postcolonial rhetoric of racial democracy in Brazil (Fernandes 1972; Anderson, Roque, and Santos 2019). Freyre's major work, *Casa-Grande & Senzala*, from 1933, translated into English as

"The Masters and the Slaves" in 1946, celebrates miscegenation while concealing the enduring violence entailed in the making of Racial and Gendered ontologies of difference.

Freyre's work serves as a critical touchstone in this book, exemplifying how colonial representations of violence are perpetuated and legitimized in profoundly unsettling ways. His text not only reinforces colonial rhetoric by fetishizing subjected female subject-positions but also normalizes sexual violation through euphemistic references to it as "physical love" (Freyre 1933, 14). By adjectivizing love, Freyre separates its emotional and affectionate dimensions, reducing it to a mere physical act centered on an objectified form of "sexuality" – a term further interrogated here. While some may argue that Freyre merely documented preexisting colonial and masculinized narratives that eroticize and hypersexualize Black and Indigenous women, I contend that his work does more than uncritically reproduce these discourses. It constructs a disturbing theoretical framework that naturalizes and legitimizes sexual violence, obliterating and blurring the systemic and totalizing violence inflicted upon captive female bodies by White slaveholding men.

Freyre does not deny the inherent violence; instead, he attempts to justify sexual violation by acknowledging the "sadism" enacted by White men – deriving pleasure from inflicting pain – while perversely attributing "masochism," or a supposed pleasure in receiving violence, to captive female bodies. In doing so, he perpetuates and reconfigures the colonial gaze, cloaking its dehumanizing logic in a guise of scientific legitimacy. This framework exacerbates the fetishization and objectification of Black and Indigenous female subject-positions, grotesquely reframing violence as consensual or mutually desired. By romanticizing such brutality, Freyre reinforces the ideologies of domination and exploitation that sustain colonial power structures.

This passage symptomatically elaborates the ideological underpinnings of neocolonial regimes, foregrounding how Whiteness and conquest-driven masculinity dominate knowledge production while systematically denying the foundational role of Racial and Gendered ontologies of difference in shaping these orders of violence. The extreme violence inflicted upon captive bodies, legally reduced to property, is often euphemistically reframed by White male academic constructs as "pleasure" or "physical love," revealing the sinister entanglement of terror and enjoyment within colonial and scientific projects. These narratives not only perpetuate violent legacies but also mask them under the guise of intellectual inquiry.

In *Racism and Sexism in Brazilian Culture* (1983), Brazilian Black feminist intellectual, activist, and anthrologist Lélia Gonzalez offers a transdisciplinary analysis of how "scientific" narratives, such as those advanced by Freyre, continue to perpetuate violence against Black women in Brazil in the afterlives of slavery. Drawing on a psychoanalytic framework, Gonzalez conceptualizes this phenomenon – spanning the epistemic, ontological, juridical, economic, and political realms – as a form of "cultural neurosis" (1983, 380). A neurotic individual, as she explains, constructs mechanisms to conceal their symptoms, as this concealment affords certain privileges and alleviates the anguish of repression. This framework of cultural neurosis, manifested in works like Freyre's, not only exposes their explicit arguments but, more significantly, reveals what they seek to conceal: the reinforcement of colonial discourses surrounding White men's pleasure, which normalize and perpetuate the structural objectification, dehumanization, and pervasive violence inflicted on Black and Indigenous women.

In *Mama's Baby, Papa's Maybe: An American Grammar Book* (1987), Hortense Spillers analyzes the sociopolitical order of captivity in the United States, arguing that the institution of slavery destabilized the very framework of gender difference. Both female and male captive bodies were transformed into sites of cultural and political manipulation. Spillers identifies four key-ways in which colonial slavery inscribed meaning onto these bodies:

1) the captive body becomes the source of an irresistible, destructive sensuality;
2) at the same time – in stunning contradiction – the captive body reduces to a thing, becoming *being for* the captor;
3) in this absence *from* a subject position, the captured sexualities provide a physical and biological expression of "otherness";
4) as a category of "otherness," the captive body translates into a potential for pornotroping and embodies sheer physical powerlessness that slides into a more general "powerlessness," resonating through various centers of human and social meaning (1987, 445).

I align with Spillers in questioning whether the notion of "pleasure" can even be invoked in contexts where at least one party is not free but legally and socially reduced to property. Spillers argues that in such contexts, the term "sexuality" is deeply problematic – if not entirely inaccurate – when applied to familial arrangements within the system of enslavement. From the master's household to the enslaved enclave, terms such as reproduction, motherhood, pleasure, and desire are thrown into crisis (1987, 458).

The treatment of captive bodies marks a colonial process of objectification, wherein entrenched inequalities reinforce a dehumanizing, ungendering, and defacing project imposed upon enslaved African subjects. While gender distinctions appear even in narratives of the Middle Passage, Spillers suggests that under the brutal conditions of slavery, the captive bodies are "neither female, nor male, as both are taken into 'account' as *quantities*" (1987, 452). Ferreira da Silva builds on Spillers's insights, asserting that "the wounded captive body in the scene of subjugation is a female, but she is not a woman" (2022, 27). This nuanced framework underscores the contradictions and complexities embedded in what I term the "Gendered ontology of difference," where both processes of gendering and ungendering unfold alongside the colonial monopoly on the Human. It also encompasses the constructed definitions of womanhood and masculinity, as well as the sexualization and cisheteronormative frameworks that shape them.

This troubling framework resonates with Saidiya Hartman's concept of "enjoyment," which she defines as "the exercise of a right; the promise and function of a right, privilege, or incorporeal hereditament" (1997, 33). Within this logic, the captive bodies of Black women are appropriated as surrogates for the master's body, simulating a form of agency under a system of total domination. As Hartman explains, Black subjects were fundamentally envisioned as "vehicles for white enjoyment, in all of its sundry and unspeakable expressions" (1997, 31).

The role of law in this system is indispensable. Denise Ferreira da Silva highlights how "the juridical position of captivity (total domination) authorizes total violence, which the flesh exposes as it surfaces through skin marked by unprotection – Black skin – which permits the coercive force used to suppress the 'will' of the enslaved" (2022, 36). This juridico-economic-political rhetoric results in what Hartman terms "[t]he paternal endowments of will, voice, and humanity denying the necessary violence of racial slavery" (1997, 89).

Beyond Legal Victimhood

The role of legal discourse in determining which subject-position was entitled to protection cannot be overstated. Historical precedents underscore the need for a critical examination of legal texts to uncover latent biases and exclusions that perpetuate colonial architectures of violence. For instance, colonial legislation, such as First Constitutions of the Archbishopric of Bahia of 1707, framed "concubinage" as a punishable offense, but only under certain conditions. More precisely, this law prohibited White men from cohabiting with or impregnating "free woman" without marriage. As a consequence, female captives were situated outside the realm of legal protection. Treated as property, these subjects were regarded as nonsubjects of rights. While this provision offered limited protection to White women by regulating extramarital relationships, it left Black and Indigenous subject-positions entirely exposed to sexual violations.

This example highlights the contentious issue of defining sexual violence within legal frameworks. In *Slavery Unseen: Sex, Power, and Violence in Brazilian History*, scholar Lamonte Aidoo (2018) demonstrates how legal language was manipulated by White men to determine which subject-positions were recognized as violable. The systematic exclusion of certain bodies from legal protection perpetuated cycles of oppression and reinforced existing power dynamics. Whereas criminal law typically defines crimes based on the actions of the offender, gender-based violence has historically been framed according to the moral standards attributed to the victimized women. Within the context of colonial slavery and its aftermath, only women deemed "honest" were granted legal protection, a designation that largely applied to White women.

These precedents contributed to the construction of the stereotypical "victim." The concept of victimhood has received considerable scholarly attention, particularly in relation to its reductionist and paternalistic representation of women framed through the lens of Whiteness. This portrayal emphasizes characteristics like passivity, vulnerability, piety, purity, powerlessness, domesticity, and submissiveness, thereby consolidating an essentialized "ideal victim." In contrast, subject-positions who engage in hard work in plantations or activism or practice collective self-defense are often portrayed as "less legitimate victims" (Christie 1986; Fattah 1986; Morrison 2006; Kleinfeld 2013).

Rather than examining the actions of the offender, as is customary in criminal proceedings, discourse surrounding gender-based victimhood has historically shifted the scrutiny to the woman experiencing violence. Her lifestyle, tone of voice, and dress code are often used to assess her eligibility for legal protection. Questions such as "What were you wearing that night?" or "Why didn't you react?" – still commonly posed by male police officers and legal authorities, as discussed in Part 2 of this book – highlight the deeply ingrained sexist lens through which these crimes have been historically addressed.

This practice of victim-blaming often leads to double victimization or re-traumatization and attaches a stigmatizing label to the term "victim." This label forms a monolithic category, differentiating women who are deemed "legitimate" victims from those who are discredited. The rhetoric of the "ideal victim" or "true victimhood" ignores the contexts of actual violence. In response, this book deliberately refrains from using the term "victim," opting instead for "women victimized," "women in the context of violence," or "survivor," terms that more accurately capture the lived realities and resilience of those affected.

In contesting Lusotropicalist rhetorics, it is essential to avoid downplaying the violence inherent in the processes of colonization and the enduring colonial architectures enacted in Brazil and beyond. Unlike the products of settler colonialism manifested in the overt racism seen in official apartheid and segregation regimes, where White supremacy is eugenically tied to ideals of racial purity, Brazil exploitative colonialism exhibits a distinct form of colonial racism. As Gonzalez (1979b, 1988) argues, this region is characterized by a *racismo por denegação*, that is, racism by denial. This form of racism operates as a discursive mask for White guilt, strategically using miscegenation – a practice historically rooted in the systematic rape – to uphold the myths of racial harmony and democracy. By revisiting and rearticulating these dynamics, we expose the colonial structures that persist through the dis/possession and domination of territories, bodies, and ways of life.

Slavery1 and Slavery2

Slavery can be distinguished according to two phases in Brazil: the first moment, termed *escravidão*, and the second phase, known as *escravismo* (Alencastro 2000). Sylvia Wynter (1970s) also identifies two distinct forms of slavery in the African context: one preceding and one following the Middle Passage. Drawing on Wynter's terminology, I adapt these phases to the Brazilian context as Slavery1 and Slavery2.[6]

Slavery1 refers to the early colonial period when formal legal frameworks had yet to officially sanction the enslavement of individuals. During this phase, slavery was not considered a permanent institution but rather a legal exception, despite its extensive application to Indigenous peoples under the pretext of a "just war." The violent imposition of slavery, compounded by the ravages of Western diseases and systemic brutality, led to the genocide of a substantial portion of Amerindian populations. Historically, figures such as the Spanish Dominican Bartolomé de las Casas and the Portuguese Jesuit António Vieira, who were once defenders of Indigenous humanity, proposed the African slave trade as a "solution" to the ongoing genocide against Indigenous peoples (Schwarcz 2012a, 2012b).

Although Indigenous peoples were later officially recognized by the colonial order as "human beings," they remained commodified and dehumanized. Their status shifted from being considered less-than-human and nonsubjects of rights to being seen as humans who were obstacles to the expansion of colonial agricultural frontiers. The creation of a military unit known as *paulistas* (Alencastro 2000, 336) by colonial authorities further promoted the ongoing extermination of Indigenous populations, disrupting their ways of life and their relations with human and the more-than-human worlds – a concept now vaguely depicted as "nature."

Slavery2 marks a profound shift in which slavery evolved from a legal exception into the foundation of a vast global capitalist production system. By 1551, the Black Atlantic slave trade to Brazil had overtaken all other regions in the forced enslavement of African peoples, becoming the most extensive and enduring system of forced migration in the Western world. Between 1538 and 1888, approximately four million Africans were

6 Sylvia Wynter employs the figures of "Man1" and "Man2" to elucidate the transformation of the Eurocentric liberal monohumanist conception of humanity, tracing the shift from *homo politicus* to *homo oeconomicus* (cf. Wynter and McKittrick 2015).

forcibly transported to Brazil – a number roughly ten times greater than that recorded in the United States (Alencastro 2000; Chalhoub 2012; Schwarcz 2012b; Aidoo 2018).

By 1660, Brazil's economy had undergone rapid expansion, fueled by the large-scale production enabled by the colonial slavery regime of the plantations. Moreover, significant exports of natural minerals, particularly gold, flowed from Brazil to Europe, revitalizing European commerce and helping to catalyze industrialization (Schwartz 1973). It marked the rise of a new era of globalized, large-scale monocultural production, unleashing an unprecedented scale of ecological devastation, involving humans and more-than-humans – destructive legacies that continue to shape our world today (Bispo dos Santos 2015; Ferdinand 2021).

Under the regime of total violence that defined plantation politics, Brazil experienced an anti-Indigenous and anti-Black genocides, resulting in the highest mortality rates among enslaved Afro-diasporic subjects in the Americas. Within the first three years of transatlantic slave trade, a staggering 75 percent of captive subjects perished on the plantations (Aidoo 2018). This brutality was compounded by the colonial authorities' establishment of the *capitão do mato*, or bush captain, whose role was specifically to enforce extermination policies. These agents were tasked with the capture and killing of those designated as "runaway enslaved persons," collectively referred to as *quilombos* or *mocambos*.[7]

In her unpublished monograph, *Black Metamorphosis: New Natives in a New World*, Sylvia Wynter describes what this book refers to as Slavery2 as the "first large-scale capitalist slave trade across the Middle Passage" (1970s, 25–26). This phenomenon, Wynter argues, not only spurred the development of Europe but also directly contributed to the underdevelopment of Africa and Latin America. Her analysis resonates with the groundbreaking work of Trinidad and Tobago historian Eric Williams in *Capitalism and Slavery* (1944), which contends that the rise and expansion of Western capitalism were fundamentally intertwined with the institution of slavery. Contrary to

7 *Quilombos*, much like the *marronage*, *maroons*, *cimarrones*, *cumbes*, and *palenques* across Latin America, have historically embodied and enacted tactics and strategies of resistance and re-existence, challenging the violent structures of colonial slavery in Brazil. These acts of defiance were not merely a "vital exigency" for survival (A. Nascimento 1980, 151) but also constituted some of the most radical forms of collective organization and liberation struggles. Afro-diasporic subjects, often in confluence with Indigenous peoples, led countercolonial practices of refusal, fugitivity, and assemblage (B. Nascimento 1976b; A. Nascimento 1980; Gomes 2015; Bispo dos Santos 2015). In the face of the pervasive violence of colonial domination, they forged creative and generative sites of resistance, unsettling and transforming oppressive structures into spaces of possibility (Wynter 1970s). The notion of *quilombo* is analyzed further in Part 2, section *Beyond Representation*, of this book.

Karl Marx's characterization of slavery as a pre-capitalist stage, both Wynter and Williams posit that slavery was a cornerstone of modern capitalism itself.[8]

Williams asserted that "[s]lavery was not born of racism: rather, racism was the consequence of slavery" (1944, 7). In a similar vein, Sylvia Wynter identifies the plantation as the pivotal site where African subjects were commodified through the process of racialization, becoming what she describes as "a unit of labor power collectively labeled 'negro'" (1970s, 1). This transformation aligns with Fanon's concept of the "epidermal racial schema" (1952, 92), referring to the colonial construction of a Racial ontology of difference rooted in the categorization and hierarchization of physical features by the White colonial gaze. Contrary to the narrative of civilization, colonization is a process of "thingification" (Césaire 1950), enacted through racialization and dehumanization.[9]

As articulated by Eric Williams, and further developed by Trinidad and Tobago historian C.L.R. James (1963), Wynter (1970s), and Ferreira da Silva (2014), the reduction of colonial production to the ownership of land and people masks the economic character of the dispossession and expropriation of territories, bodies, and enslaved labor's productive capacity. On one hand, primitive accumulation forges the transgenerational concentration of property and wealth, primarily benefiting White men and, by extension, White women. On the other hand, as Ferreira da Silva (2019, 177–178) terms it, "negative accumulation" arises as its counterpart: a process of systematic dispossession and exclusion imposed on subjects racialized as Black and Indigenous.

I align with the Black Radical Tradition in asserting that conventional Marxist interpretations, which positions slavery (Slavery1 and Slavery2) outside the capitalist mode of production, fails to grasp the extent to which the expropriation of value, across past and present, is deeply inscribed within

8 Karl Marx's landmark work *Das Kapital* (1867) primarily examines European struggles and aspirations within the framework of capitalism. Colonialism is addressed only briefly, notably in the discussion of "primitive accumulation." Marx defines primitive accumulation as the historical process through which producers are estranged from the means of production, describing it as a "pre-historic stage" of capitalism. However, rather than relegating this as a mere precursor, this book builds upon Rosa Luxemburg's argument (1913) that the emergence of capitalism is fundamentally intertwined with the rise of colonial slavery.

9 Drawing on Aimé Césaire's concept of "thingification" (1950), which describes the dehumanizing reduction of individuals to mere objects, Darcy Ribeiro similarly characterized the shift from feudal to colonial regimes as a transition from the "governing of people" to the "governing of things" (1968, 152). This idea of thingification gains further elaboration when considered alongside Frantz Fanon's notion of "objectification" (1952) and bell hooks's concept of the "commodification of Otherness" (1992). Together, these frameworks emphasize how the colonial system attempts to transform human beings into commodities and objects, operating within a larger matrix of exploitation and control.

the very structures of global capital, both in blood and flesh. By revisiting the genealogy of modern capitalism, Black and critical scholarships have invoked terms such as "racial capitalism" (Robinson 1983),[10] "Plantationocene" (Haraway 2015; Haraway and Tsing 2019),[11] and "colonial capitalism" (Ferdinand 2024)[12] to underscore the material, historical, and ongoing entanglements between colonialism, slavery, and capitalism.

Labor: Racial and Gendered Ontologies of Difference

The enduring legacy of Slavery2 is crucial for understanding the colonial and neocolonial forms of violence, as well as the modes of identification based on Racial and Gendered ontologies of difference. This analysis employs a historically informed perspective on the colonial division of labor within Slavery2. While feminist political theorists such as U.K. feminist political theorist Carole Pateman (1988) and Italian feminist philosopher Silvia Federici (1998) have provided significant insights into the intersections of gender and class – particularly with regard to the sexual (social) contract and the Gendered division of labor under capitalism – a more nuanced analysis of the interplay between Racial and Gendered foundations of modern dynamics of

10 The concept of racial capitalism was notably advanced by Cedric Robinson, whose seminal book *Black Marxism* compellingly argued that the historical development of capitalism and race were inseparable. While Robinson is often associated with the theory of racial capitalism, he did not coin the term, which traces its origins to the 1970s, particularly in the work of South African scholars and activists confronting apartheid. The term was already invoked in a 1976 pamphlet from the anti-Apartheid movement, entitled *Foreign Investment and the Reproduction of Racial Capitalism in South Africa*, authored by South African historians Martin Legassick and David Hemson (cf. Kundnani 2020; Okoth 2022; Paret and Levenson 2024).

11 The term "Plantationocene," as argued by Donna Haraway and Ann Tsing, offers an alternative to the Anthropocene, focusing on the enduring legacies of the plantation system. It highlights the plantation as a multispecies system of forced labor that disrupts the natural rhythms of life, simplifying ecosystems and replacing diverse life forms with a few select ones, often through violence or coercion. This concept emphasizes the forced labor of both humans and nonhumans (plants, animals, and microbes) and critiques the ecological simplifications that underlie modern agricultural systems. The Plantationocene underscores the historical connections between the European colonization of the Americas, the capture of enslaved Africans, and the rise of plantation agriculture, a model of land and labor exploitation that continues to shape global systems today.

12 The concept of colonial capitalism, as developed by Malcom Ferdinand, argues that capitalism is inherently colonial, unfolding through the domination of new territories and peoples. Unlike the concept of racial capitalism, which focuses on racialized social divisions, colonial capitalism emphasizes the continuous colonial inhabitation of the Earth, based on the subjugation of humans and nonhumans. This framework links capitalism to the transformation of the Earth and its colonially imposed structures, suggesting that anti-capitalist politics must also envision alternative ways of inhabiting the planet.

labor is required.[13] Rather than solely addressing the construction of a patriarchal order, this discussion adopts a countercolonial and feminist approach to offer a more complex analysis of labor division. The master's house is conceptualized as a space in which Indigenous, Black, and White women coexisted, though they remained distinctly separate.

Materialist feminists have unveiled how capitalism symbolically divides the legal and economic spheres, creating a legal-economic subject while separating and opposing the public and private, as well as the political and domestic realms. In his pivotal work, *The Origin of the Family, Private Property, and the State* (1884), Prussian writer and political theorist Friedrich Engels recognizes the first division of labor as the one between men and women and asserts that it led to the earliest instances of class opposition and historical oppression. Building on this idea, Italian feminist activist Mariarosa Dalla Costa and U.S. feminist writer Selma James, in *The Power of Women and the Subversion of the Community* (1972), argue that reproductive labor plays a crucial role in this division. They contend that classical economists and policymakers have analytically and politically hidden this labor, thereby concealing that women produce a unique commodity for capitalism: the living human being, that is, "the laborer" (see also, Bhattacharya 2017).

Reproductive labor, often termed "social reproduction" within Marxist feminist discourse, encompasses the domestic tasks essential for sustaining daily life and perpetuating the workforce. This category of work includes activities such as gestation, childbirth, breastfeeding, housekeeping, cooking, and caregiving. Distinct from the so-called productive labor, reproductive labor is characterized by its isolation, invisibility, lack of remuneration, repetitiveness, and inherent exhaustion. Historically, this labor has relegated women to poorly or unpaid roles within the private sphere, limiting their visibility and political engagement. This marginalization has cast women as "nonworkers," placing them in precarious positions particularly susceptible to physical and sexual violence (Federici and Austin 1972; Davis 1983).

I examine the disparate experiences of labor among women, bringing attention to the frameworks of Racial and Gendered ontologies of difference

13 Silvia Federici acknowledges the "serious limits" of comparing the experiences of White women in the metropolis with those of Black enslaved women in the colonies but nonetheless she finds some grounds for such comparisons. She argues that the "fate of West European women during the period of primitive accumulation was akin to that of female slaves on American colonial plantations, who, especially after the abolition of the slave trade in 1807, were coerced by their masters into becoming breeders of new laborers" (1998, 89). Federici later expands her analysis to draw parallels between the experiences of West European women and those of Indigenous women, thereby deepening her examination of gendered oppression within the context of colonial and capitalist systems. While Federici's contributions are highly important, this book refrains from equating female experiences solely through a *Gendered ontology of difference*, as this could overshadow the crucial racial dimensions of subjugation. These aspects will be further elaborated in this section.

established by the colonial order. I elucidate the intersections between labor division and the colonial constructions of masculinity and femininity, which are deeply rooted in processes of dispossession, subjugation, and exploitation.

Since colonization, Amerindian and Afro-diasporic women in Brazil have been systematically subjected to perform social reproductive labor outside their own households, often with little or no compensation. Under slavery, this coerced labor was referred to as the duties of *mucamas*. Following the formal abolition of slavery, it transformed into the role now recognized as *empregadas domésticas* (domestic workers). When this labor is performed within one's own home on a full-time basis, it is typically framed as *dona de casa* or *do lar*, referring to housekeeping or housewifery. These distinctions in terminology underscore the ongoing devaluation and feminization of reproductive labor, which remains integral to the functioning of society.

The colonial monoculture regime profoundly disrupted the social and political roles of Amerindian women in the country, reconfiguring their lives and relegating them to unpaid domestic labor within both the master's household and their own communities. This reordering imposed rigid boundaries between domestic and public spheres, isolating women's labor while concealing violence and rendering their contributions invisible. As Susan Kellogg observes in *Weaving the Past: A History of Latin America's Indigenous Women from the Prehispanic Period to the Present* (2005), these colonial impositions profoundly altered Indigenous women's societal roles.

However, framing this history solely as a narrative of colonizer dominance and colonized passivity risks erasing the resistance, disruptions, and movements led by Amerindian peoples during this period. These acts of defiance, often silenced by colonial narratives shaped through the gaze of White conquest-driven masculinity, challenge reductive binaries of victimhood and oppression. Glicéria Tupinambá, an Indigenous leader, artist, activist, and researcher, critiques these omissions, urging a reexamination of Indigenous women's historical roles. She asserts:

> In the construction of the [colonial] imagination, women were always secondary, their only role was to prepare food and drink, or to serve sexually – and that isn't right! We need to be seen differently, in a new light. We are much more than how we've been portrayed, positioned, or depicted.
>
> (2022, 21)

Glicéria Tupinambá calls for research developed by and for Indigenous women, challenging colonial distortions and recovering narratives that honor Indigenous women's transformative actions and contributions throughout history.

Similar to their Indigenous counterparts, African women experienced profound upheaval and displacement, their lives uprooted as they were forcibly commodified and subjected to the horrors of the Middle Passage and their arrival in Brazil. There, they were forced into grueling labor on plantations and within the master's household, where they were often confined to domestic and reproductive labor. This enforced seclusion not only erased their contributions but also intensified their vulnerability to sexual violence, further entrenching the systemic exploitation they endured (Gonzalez 1983; Giacomini 1988).

This book acknowledges the dominant and significant contributions of U.S.-based scholarship on Afro-diasporic women's experiences under settler colonial slavery, while also seeking to foreground the insights offered by Brazilian historiography in this discussion. Through engagement with U.S. Black feminist scholarship, this book offers a nuanced analysis of both the convergences and distinctions between chattel slavery within U.S. settler colonialism and the exploitative colonial system in Brazil.

For instance, in the United States, the reproduction of Black female captives was dehumanizingly referred to as "breeding" – a term historically applied to animal husbandry. Their reproduction was regarded as economically advantageous for White slaveholders, as it ensured a self-sustaining supply of enslaved laborers (hooks 1982; Davis 1983). In contrast, within Brazil's exploitative colonial framework, the reproduction of enslaved women was often deemed unproductive and economically unviable. This perception is reflected in an 1880 publication in the journal *A Liberdade dos Ventres*, where a Brazilian slaveholder stated: "It was not worth the effort to raise them since it would only pay off after 16 years" (Giacomini 1988, 24).

This disparity stems, in part, from the differing colonial models in the United States and Brazil: settler colonialism and colonialism of exploitation, respectively. As previously mentioned, settler colonialism involved the establishment of permanent settlements, where land was occupied by families intending to create enduring communities. In contrast, Brazil's colonizers approached the land as an extractive resource – a "gold mine" – to be exploited for immediate profit, with wealth funneled back to the imperial metropole. Under this extractive logic, Brazilian enslavers prioritized the purchase of enslaved individuals over the long-term investment of raising enslaved children, whose labor would only become available years later.

In both colonial contexts, the experiences of enslaved female subject-positions in reproducing other enslaved persons were systematically denied recognition as acts of motherhood or defining features of womanhood. Despite their roles in care and reproductive labor, they were, as Hortense Spillers observes, "robbed of the parental right" (1987, 459), rendered ungendered and inhuman by colonial systems of domination. The categories of "women" and "mother" were exclusively reserved for those deemed Human within the racial hierarchies of slavery, that is, White women. In Brazil, Black enslaved female were only named as "mothers" in relation to their labor as caregivers for White children, referred to by terms like "Black mammy" (*mãe preta*) or "wet nurse" (*ama de leite*) (Gonzalez 1979a; Giacomini 1988).

Despite the distinctions between settler colonialism and exploitation colonialism, both systems institutionalized slavery as complex regimes of total violence. These regimes were underpinned by the entangled construction of Racial and Gendered ontologies of difference, which simultaneously racialized and ungendered Black female subject-position, while unracializing and gendering White women. In Brazil, however, the brutal realities of this violent history have been concealed by the perverse rhetoric of Lusotropicalism, which sought to romanticize and distort the legacies of slavery and colonization in the country.

Despite bearing the heavy burdens of systemic oppression, Black and Indigenous women forged enduring acts of resistance, defying the structures designed to erase their humanity and asserting their vitality and resilience. Lélia Gonzalez underscores how Black women's roles in social reproduction also carried subtle but potent forms of resistance, expressed in everyday acts of covert defiance and refusal. For instance, while caring for White children, Black women introduced African cultural elements into the Portuguese spoken in Brazil, reshaping the colonial language. Gonzalez coined the term *pretuguês* (1979a) – a blend of *preto* (Black) and *português* (Portuguese) – to describe this countercolonial linguistic transformation. Similarly, Indigenous languages such as Tupi have left a profound, though often unacknowledged, imprint on Brazilian Portuguese, subtly configuring its structure and enriching its cultural resonance (Rodrigues 2014; Silveira 2020). Additionally, Black women played a crucial role in preserving and transmitting African cultural traditions, including storytelling and legends, such as that of the headless mule (*mula sem cabeça*), which continue to shape the popular imagination and remain integral to Brazilian cultural identity.

Under the colonial order in Brazil, Indigenous and Afro-diasporic forms of organization and kinship were persistently subject to disruption and erasure. White enslavers wielded absolute sovereignty over the lives of enslaved persons and families, dictating whether they could remain together or face forced separation (Giacomini 1988; Reis and Klein 2011). In 1869, after over three centuries of slavery, Decree No. 1695 (Article 2) formally prohibited such separations. However, historical records reveal that this legal provision was routinely disregarded by White enslavers, who disregarded any constraints on their dominion (Giacomini 1988; Rezzutti 2018). Similarly, the "Free Womb Law" (Law No. 2040) of 1871, while purporting to define the Black family as comprising a husband, wife, and children under 15 years of age, failed to mitigate the systemic exploitation and vulnerability of Afro-diasporic families (Alencastro 2000).

Further compounding this precarity were vague and violent legal statutes, including provisions authorizing the killing of enslaved persons classified as *quilombolas* – members of *quilombos*, which were in some locations defined as groups of merely five or more runaway enslaved people. The narrow scale employed in these definitions of *quilombo* rendered even small gatherings of Black individuals vulnerable to persecution, posing significant existential threats to Black families, whether enslaved or free (cf. Nascimento 1977, 1990, 1987; Reis and Gomes 1996; Gomes 2015). These statutes demonstrate the deep contradictions and hypocrisies of modern colonial law, which functioned as a tool of systemic violence within the architecture of colonial slavery.

Heleieth Saffioti (1976), a Brazilian Marxist feminist sociologist, provides critical insight into the roles that White women played in sustaining this oppressive system of colonial slavery. She argues that, during this period, White women were primarily responsible for managing the household, a role confined to the rigidly controlled domestic sphere. Social reproductive tasks – including spinning, weaving, sewing, cooking, cleaning, gardening, animal care, and childcare – were often delegated to female captives and, at times, male captives, whom White women supervised with strict oversight. Saffioti's research indicates the political and social isolation of White women, as their confinement to the master's house severely limited their possibilities. Access to formal education and travel, particularly to Europe, were privileges reserved for White men. This economic and social marginalization, according to the author, contributed to the conservative tendencies of White women, which, in many cases, were even more pronounced than those of their male counterparts.

During the colonial period, the gendered division of labor imposed distinct roles on female subject-positions racialized as Indigenous, Black, and White, largely confining them to domestic and private spheres. Within this hierarchical framework between public and private, men and women, these women were positioned as "objects" of male desire and subjected to the control of White men. However, such a general characterization must be nuanced to account for the fragmentary and context-specific nature of slavery historiography. Variations in the experiences of these female subject-positions emerged across urban and rural settings, as well as within the vast and geographically diverse regions of Brazil. Enslaved female subjects were systematically denied recognition as women, mothers, and even as Humans, and their laboring conditions reflected the intersecting axes of racial and un/gendered oppressions.

This book acknowledges the colonial construction of subject-positions, rejecting homogenization of these experiences. Instead, it seeks to uncover the mechanisms through which colonial systems of objectification were architected and how these systems sustained the broader structures of gender-based violence. The intertwined Racial and Gendered ontologies of difference that emerged functioned as both products and instruments of colonial fractal logic, intricately linked to the racial capitalist dynamics of primitive and negative accumulation (Ferreira da Silva 2019).

The colonial notions of *mucamas*, referring to enslaved domestic workers, and *sinhás*, the White housewives in slave-owning families, have evolved into a liberal model of devalued reproductive and domestic labor, predominantly performed by women in contemporary households. In this structure, domestic work is often outsourced to *empregadas* (domestic workers), who take on the social reproductive labor historically expected of the female subject-position. Even when financially independent, most women still bear the responsibility for household management or hire another woman to delegate these tasks, thereby assuming the role of *patroa* – the woman who employs someone to handle domestic duties such as cleaning, cooking, and childcare. The relationship between *patroa* and *empregada* is deeply rooted in the exploitative dynamics of the colonial family structure, wherein the labor of Black and Indigenous captives was central to the functioning of the household. These dynamics mask the real nature of reproductive labor relations by framing the arrangement as one of familial bonds, a facade often reinforced by the statement that domestic workers are "part of the family." Such rhetoric conceals the systemic denial of labor rights to domestic workers, rendering them invisible as a working-class category and perpetuating the colonial legacies of gendered and racialized exploitation (B. Nascimento 1976; Kuznesof 1989; Pereira de Melo 1989).

There is no coincidence that domestic workers have long been one of the most marginalized sectors of the working class in Latin America, and Brazil is no exception. In 1936, domestic workers in Brazil took a pioneering step by establishing the first Syndicate of Domestic Workers in the city of Santos, São Paulo, under the leadership of Laudelina Campos de Melo, who was also a key figure in the Black Front (Chaney and Garcia Castro 1989; Kuznesof 1989; Oliveira, Conceição, and Melo 1989). In the afterlives of slavery, domestic work in Brazil has remained excluded from the same legal protections afforded to other forms of labor under the Brazilian Labor Law (*Consolidação das Leis do Trabalho*, or CLT) established in 1943. For instance, the 1988 Brazilian Constitution, which outlines 34 principles concerning workers' rights (Article 7), applies only nine of these stipulations to domestic workers. As a result, the labor conditions of domestic workers remain some of the most neglected and precarious in the country (Pereira de Melo 1989). Since the abolition of slavery in 1888, domestic work has predominantly been carried out by Black women. Many members of the upper and middle classes, mostly White, have spent their lives with full-time domestic workers, the majority of whom were poor, Black, and Indigenous women. This enduring legacy of racial and class-based exploitation continues to shape the social and economic realities of domestic labor in Brazil. However, it was only in 2015, after decades of relentless mobilization, that domestic workers achieved a historic victory: their labor rights were officially recognized through Complementary Law No. 150. This legal recognition was made possible by the 2013 Constitutional Amendment Project No. 72, under the presidency of Dilma Rousseff. This milestone marked a significant, though delayed, acknowledgment of domestic workers' contributions and struggles for justice.

Colonial Family

This section examines the critical role of law in constructing and perpetuating a patriarchal, monogamous, and heteronormative concept of family as a cornerstone of colonial society. Learning with the Brazilian context, it analyzes how the patrilineal structure of the colonial family functioned as both a socio-legal organizational unit and an effective mechanism for consolidating economic and political power through property concentration. This system of domination was embedded in networks of bloodline-based kinship and reinforced by legal frameworks designed to safeguard and sustain these hierarchies.

The term *pátria* (fatherland) derives from the Latin *pater* (father), a word that not only refers to the familial father but also more broadly to a figure of legal authority. *Pater* denotes the owner of the *patrimonium* (patrimony), symbolizing control over private property. The Latin semantics further emphasize the father's dominion over the *domus* (household), with *dominium* – rooted in the notion of "domination" – referring to his authority over both subjects and property, which were all considered part of his "family" (Chaui 2013).

Patriarchy is best understood as a historical process rooted in the institutionalization of *pátria*, that is, the dominance of men over women within both familial and societal spheres. Feminist historians such as Gerda Lerner (1986) conceptualize patriarchy as a system in which men hold authority across all major societal institutions, systematically marginalizing women from accessing power within these frameworks. Importantly, this conceptualization does not suggest that women are entirely powerless or devoid of agency. On the contrary, female subject-positions have consistently been central protagonists in movements that resist, disrupt, and reimagine the entrenched legal histories and colonial legacies of patriarchal systems. These dynamic acts of resistance and transformation are examined in greater depth in the chapters that follow.

Inheritance

In colonial Brazil, the property regime was fundamentally structured around Whiteness and patrilineal inheritance system, channeling wealth predominantly from father to son or, in some cases, from father to daughter's husband. This system of intergenerational wealth transmission underscores the central role of the family as a mechanism for property accumulation, shaped by White conquest-driven masculinity. By legally consolidating property ownership in the hands of White cismen, the colonial family became a foundational institution that orchestrated the economy of slavery and the broader frameworks of the Plantationocene.

According to the *Ordenações Filipinas* colonial code of 1603, the legal status of White women was equated to that of minors, as they were classified as "incapable" in civil matters and subjected to the guardianship of White men (II, 35, 4). Although legally recognized as subjects of rights, White women were categorized as "civilly incapacitated", which restricted their ability to inherit property, hold public office, vote, or enter into contracts without male authorization – whether from a father or husband. Despite these constraints, many White women actively navigated and challenged these limitations, employing legal strategies to assert their agency and claim inheritances from parents, husbands, or brothers, thereby carving out spaces of influence within institutional confines (cf. J. da S. Menezes 2013).

When not under the direct authority of a father or husband, White women were often confined to convents – a fate that could even befall married women in the absence of their male guardians. This patriarchal control was stratified along racial and class hierarchies, with Indigenous and Black female subject-positions mostly excluded from such spaces (Saffioti 1978; Lavrin 1986; Menezes 2013). These conditions exemplify what Silvia Federici (1998, 100) terms "legal infantilization," a systemic denial of self-determination and autonomy that characterized the subject-position of White women within the colonial legal framework.

Within this context, marriage became the primary avenue for White women to secure social standing and limited economic security, a reality driven by their lack of property rights and legal infantilization. This legal subjugation rendered White women politically and economically dependent, solidifying a condition of propertylessness that defined White womanhood through vulnerability, insecurity, submission, and compliance. It further aligned with Catholic ideals of purity, seclusion, sacrifice, and devotion, reinforcing Racial and Gendered ontologies of difference in socio, legal, and economic terms.

Throughout much of the colonial regime, Black enslaved individuals, regardless of gender, were systematically denied legal recognition as subjects of rights. As a result, they were categorically excluded from the rights to acquire or inherit property, reinforcing their complete dispossession within the legal and economic structures of slavery society. Linda Lewin's extensive study, *Surprise Heirs: Illegitimacy, Patrimonial Rights, and Legal Nationalism in Luso-Brazilian Inheritance* (2003), Volumes I and II, spanning the years 1750 to 1889, provides in-depth analysis of the legal denial of succession rights to enslaved persons. A landmark legal ruling in 1832 solidified the impossibility for enslaved persons to acquire property, establishing a jurisprudential precedent for the subsequent four decades. Notably,

Black enslaved subjects could only access the legal system if represented by "a master" or "guardian" (Azevedo 1987, 175–176; Skidmore 2010, 50).[14]

In a notable case from 1832, mentioned by Lewin, the court denied the inheritance rights of a natural child born to a Black enslaved mother and a White father. Despite the father's rare recognition of the son in his will, explicitly designating him as his heir *ab intestate*, the son was nonetheless barred from inheriting his father's property. According to the *Corte da Relação*, the high court of Rio de Janeiro, the son was legally considered an enslaved person and, as such, relegated to the status of property, rather than a subject inheritor of his father's estate.

This decision exemplifies the colonial architectural barriers that Black subjects faced in asserting their rights and pursuing justice. It provides a precise context for Ferreira da Silva's argument that "[t]he captive body (one of the referents of blackness) does not participate in the ethical scene of representation because it is fundamentally a juridico-economic object" (2022, 43).

Until 1871, Black enslaved subjects in Brazil were systematically denied the legal capacity to own or inherit property. This exclusion reflected the deeply entrenched dehumanization within the colonial legal order, connecting the possibility to own property with a full status of Human, only embodied by the White men. The enactment of the Free Womb Law (*Lei do Ventre Livre*, Law No. 2,040) in 1871, which declared that all children born to enslaved women after that date would be considered free, prompted legislators to revise some of these restrictions. Among these changes was the extension of the right to hold *peculium* – a limited form of property ownership – to enslaved individuals.[15] Yet, even under these revised laws, they were still prohibited from drafting wills, highlighting the persistent barriers to full legal agency and the enduring inequalities of the colonial legal system (Lewin 2003).

An example of the systematic violation of the rights formally granted to Black subjects, as well as the enduring resistance against colonial barriers to justice, is found in a letter written by Maria – her last name, unfortunately,

14 Luiz Gama (1830–1882), recognized as Brazil's first Black lawyer, was a pioneering advocate for the abolition of slavery and a prominent journalist. Gama's unique position as both a Black intellectual in nineteenth-century Brazil and someone who had personally endured the horrors of slavery – having been enslaved at the age of ten – shaped his tireless efforts to fight for justice. Despite his remarkable contributions as a legal strategist and his courageous advocacy in courtrooms, his name remains underrepresented in the canon of Brazilian abolitionist literature (Gama and Ferreira 2011).

15 While the Free Womb Law (1871) ostensibly freed enslaved offspring, it included provisions allowing slaveholders to reject government compensation for emancipation. In such cases, these children were classified under the legal category of *ingênuos* (naïve) and required to serve their former masters until the age of 21. This arrangement rendered the law largely ineffective, as these so-called "freed" children remained bound to the conditions of enslavement in practice (Skidmore 1976).

unrecorded – a Black enslaved woman from Recife, Northeastern Brazil. In 1881, Maria wrote to the secretary of the "New Emancipating Society" (*Sociedade Nova Emancipadora*), seeking recognition and protection for the rights of her daughters, who had been born after the enactment of the Free Womb Law. In her letter, Maria described her dire situation while asserting her claim to legal justice: "Lord, you cannot imagine what it is to live in this house, watching my master beat my three daughters and call them slaves without being able to do anything" (Azevedo 1987, 175–176; my translation).

In *Sovereignty and Society in Colonial Brazil* (1973), historian Stuart Schwartz examines the period from 1609 to 1751, offering a detailed analysis that underscores the colonial family's role in consolidating power and wealth among White men in Brazil. Schwartz explores the power dynamics of foreign magistrates who migrated to the country, highlighting marriage as a key strategy for acquiring social influence within the colony. In this framework, the family operated as a "micro-state," privatizing social relations while reinforcing both capitalist discipline and patriarchal authority.

Schwartz further explores the role of judges in solidifying the bureaucratic machinery of colonialism, revealing that many were slaveholders, with some directly involved in the slave trade. He argues that the intersection of judicial authority, bureaucratic responsibilities, and the interests of powerful elites composed a political system deeply shaped by judicial power. This colonial legacy of biased justice endures in Brazil today, a theme explored further in the final section of this book.

Cisheteronormativity

Colonial law not only institutionalized marriage but also established a framework for defining nuclear family through cisgender and heteronormative ideals. While the terms "heterosexuality" and "homosexuality" were coined only in the late nineteenth century, colonial law systems played a significant role in normalizing heterosexuality from as early as the fifteenth century. This is demonstrated in the legal regulation of marriage and the criminalization of "sodomy," both of which reinforced heteronormative definition of family. Building on the works of Monique Wittig (1978), Adrienne Rich (2003), and Ochy Curiel (2013), heteronormativity is understood here not merely as a personal sexual preference but as a social, political, and institutional structure.

The criminalization of "sodomy," broadly understood by the Portuguese Empire in the fifteenth century as sexual acts between men, represents a pivotal element of its legal and moral framework. The term "sodomy" originates from Medieval Latin *sodomia* and Ecclesiastical Latin *peccatum Sodomiticum*, meaning "sin of Sodom." This terminology is rooted in the Biblical narrative of Sodom and Gomorrah in Genesis 18 and 19, where these cities are portrayed as symbols of moral depravity.

The colonial legislations *Ordenações Afonsinas* of 1446, along with the later *Constituições Primeiras do Arcebispado da Bahia* of 1707, categorized sodomy as one of the gravest crimes, punishable by execution through burning at the stake. Between 1591 and 1620, the Portuguese Inquisition documented numerous cases of sodomy in Brazil, developing racialized terminologies to classify the accused: *somítigos* for White men, *tibira* for Indigenous men,[16] and *jimbanda* for Black men (Mott 1985, 102; Vainfas 1989, 207–208). These distinctions underscore the intersection of Racial and Gendered ontologies of difference, revealing how colonial power forged its moral, legal, and political order through the intertwined regulation of sexuality, racialization, and socioeconomic hierarchies.

Sexual acts between women were recognized much later than those between men, largely due to the phallocentric, Christian understanding of sexuality upheld by White male legislators under the colonial regime. Terms such as "homosexuality" and "lesbianism" were largely absent from the legal and cultural lexicon of the period. When female same-sex relations were addressed, they were typically subsumed under the vague charge of "improper sodomy." When such cases surfaced, they were met with severe repercussions. By the eighteenth century, the Portuguese Inquisition had documented and prosecuted women involved in same-sex relationships, sentencing them to harsh penalties, including deportation (Bellini 1987).

Monogamy and the Patriarchal Right to Kill

The imposition of monogamy is a foundational element of the patriarchal cisheteronormative legal framework that supports the colonial nuclear family. Early colonial accounts, particularly Jesuit reports, emphasize the necessity of enforcing monogamy as a Catholic "salvation," casting Indigenous relationships as "nonmonogamous" or "polygamous." These labels were deployed to depict Indigenous forms of affection and kinship as deviations from the Catholic ideal of monogamy.

As Guarani scholar Geni Núñez (2023) argues, the critique of the "monoculture of affections" imposed by colonial through monogamy is not a recent Western phenomenon but can be traced back to historical records of Indigenous ways of being, such as those of the Guarani. These characterizations became central to missionary efforts aimed at the so-called evangelization of Indigenous communities, further entrenching colonial dominance by reorganizing intimate and familial relations. Notably, between 1584 and 1586, colonial letters, including those from Portuguese priest José de Anchieta, reported that no acts

16 In this context, the 2020 novel *Tybyra – Uma Tragédia Indígena Brasileira* by Potiguar artist Juão Nyn offers a fictionalized account of the first documented instance of homophobia directed at an Indigenous person in the territory now known as Brazil.

of aggression or murder related to adultery or jealousy were observed among Indigenous peoples in the region (Núñez, Oliveira, and Lago 2021).[17]

This colonial norm is grounded in the monogamous, cisheteronormative family as the sole legitimate model of social organization. By prioritizing and institutionalizing kinship within this nuclear family framework, colonial systems not only imposed pressure upon single White women but also actively persecuted and criminalized Indigenous and Afro-diasporic subjects. Their multiple ways of being and living together – including their spiritual practices and cosmogonies – were systematically suppressed, reflecting the broader project of erasure and domination inherent in colonial rule.

The patriarchal nature of monogamy is exemplified by a colonial legislation from 1603 that not only penalized adultery but also codified the male prerogative to discipline, punish, and even kill their wives in cases of infidelity. This is precisely what the *Ordenações Filipinas* establishes in volumes 25, 36, and 38, Book V, Title XXXVIII:

> A man who killed his wife for catching her in adultery (6).
>
> If a married man finds his wife in adultery, he is *legally permitted to kill* both her and the adulterer (7), unless the husband is a peon and the adulterer is a nobleman [Fidalgo], a judge, or a person of higher rank. However, if he kills one of these aforesaid individuals upon finding them with his wife in adultery, he will not be sentenced to death, but instead exiled to Africa for a period determined by the court, depending on the status of the person he killed, not exceeding three years (1).[18]

17 The 1846 study titled *Information on the Marriage Practices of the Indians of Brazil*, conducted by the Jesuit priest José de Anchieta, analyzes the social status of women among Indigenous peoples in Brazil. This study was part of the dominant narrative of the nation supported by the Brazilian Institute of History and Geography. Observing that intimate relationships among Indigenous peoples did not involve control or domination by either men or women, Anchieta (1846, 254) noted the use of two distinct terms to describe Indigenous relationships. The term *temirecô*, translated as "partner" or "companion," does not imply gender distinctions or suggest monogamy, while *temirecô etê*, with the qualifier *etê*, was used differently from Western traditions. Instead of referring to blood-based kinship or nuclear family relationships, *etê* often acknowledged the connection of natural beings to the land, encompassing both humans and nonhuman entities such as animals and plants (Anchieta 1846, 258–259; Núñez et al. 2021, 84). Furthermore, the Guarani language, widely spoken in colonial Brazil, lacks pronouns or terms indicating possession. Rather than expressing ownership, the Guarani concept conveys companionship and the act of being-with (Núñez et al. 2021, 86).

18 Original text in Portuguese:

> *Do que matou sua mulher, pola achar em adulterio (6). Achando o homem casado sua mulher em adulterio, licitamente poderá matar assi a ella, como o adultero (7), salvo se o marido for peão, e o adultero Figaldo, ou nosso Dezembargador, ou pessoa de maior qualidade. Porém, quando matasse alguma das sobreditas pessoas, achando-a com sua mulher em adulterio, não morrerá por isso mas será degradado para Africa com pregão na audiencia pelo tempo, que aos Julgadores bem parecer, segundo a pessoa, que matar, não passando de trez annos (1).*

This legal provision extended the male right to kill beyond enslaved subject-positions – who were already legally defined as property and subjected to the total violence of slaveholders, *paulistas*, and *capitães do mato* – into the relationships between White men and White women. The law underscores the gendered and class-based distinctions of adultery. Colonial legislation granted White men the authority to use lethal force against their allegedly unfaithful wives without listening to her version or requiring any proof or evidence. This created a legal environment in which White men could inflict violence on their female partners without fear of repercussions or need for justification.

However, the right to kill the male adulterer was conditional on his class status, being permissible only if he was of equal or lower social standing than the husband. In violating such colonial male hierarchies, the punishment for the husband was exile to another Portuguese colony in Africa. Thus, in the colonial context, class, along with Racial and Gendered ontologies of difference, played a crucial role in shaping the politics of death embodied in the patriarchal right to kill.

By the seventeenth and eighteenth centuries, foreign visitors frequently expressed the high incidence of so-called passion and honor crimes, in which men violently targeted women across Brazil (Socolow 2000). This gender-based violence reflects the emergence of a modern, White conquest-driven masculinity, legally shaped by sentiments of control, ownership, possession, and authority. Property became a defining aspect of legal subject-positions, both dependent upon and reinforcing this dynamic. Consequently, the colonial racist-patriarchal order epitomized the absolute power of White conquest-driven masculinity over invaded territories and bodies.

Notably, adultery was only decriminalized in Brazil in 2005 with the enactment of Law No. 11.106/2005, which removed it as a criminal offense punishable by imprisonment. The concept of monogamy as a lifelong commitment also contributed to a delayed right to divorce, which was only legally recognized in the 1988 Constitution. Another lingering effect of the colonial imposition of monogamy is the continued criminalization of bigamy under Article 235 of the Brazilian Penal Code. Bigamy – defined as entering into a new marriage while still legally married – is still punishable by imprisonment for two to six years.

In stark contrast to Anchieta's reports from the 1580s, which noted the absence of male violence against women in Indigenous communities (Núñez et al. 2021), the enduring legacies of colonial patriarchal, cisheteronormative, and monogamous family legal structures continues to shape racial and gender-based violence in contemporary Brazil. Today, 92.9 percent of women victimized by femicide are killed by current or former male partners or family members, often driven by an inability to accept the end of a relationship or suspicions of infidelity (Fórum Brasileiro de Segurança Pública 2024, 144). The 2024 Brazilian Public Safety Annual Report records the highest number of femicides since the enactment of Law No. 13.104/2015, which defines the crime, alongside a rise in all categories of violence against women.

•

The White conquest-driven masculine structures established over territory and bodies during colonial times are not merely remnants of the past; they compose the foundations of the present. This chapter traced the colonial making of subject-positions, underscoring the central role of law in institutionalizing identity, property, labor, and family structures, all shaped by White conquest-driven masculinity. This transatlantic framework has profoundly influenced the formation of modern nation-states in the territory now known as Brazil and beyond. The subsequent chapter addresses the analysis of the macro-political grammar of nationalism, nation-states, and representative democracy.

Bibliography

Aidoo, Lamonte. 2018. *Slavery Unseen. Sex, Power, and Violence in Brazilian History*. Durham and London: Duke University Press.

Alencastro, Luiz Felipe. 2000. *O Trato dos Viventes – Formação do Brasil no Atlântico Sul*. São Paulo: Companhia das Letras.

Anchieta, José de. 1846. "Informação dos Casamentos dos Indios do Brasil." *Revista Trimensal de Historia e Geographia ou Jornal do Instituto Historico e Geographico Brasileiro* 3 (2): 254–262.

Anderson, Warwick, Ricardo Roque, and Ricardo Ventura Santos. 2019. "Introduction." In *Luso-Tropicalism and Its Discontents: The Making and Unmaking of Racial Exceptionalism*. Oxford and New York: Berghahn.

Azevedo, Celia Maria Marinho de. 1987. *Onda Negra, Medo Branco: O Negro no Imaginário das Elites – Século XIX*. Rio de Janeiro: Paz e Terra.

Bellini, Ligia. 1987. *A Coisa Obscura. Mulher, Sodomia e Inquisição no Brasil*. São Paulo: Brasiliense.

Benevides, Bruna. 2020. "No Time to Lose. Remembering Trans and Travestis Lives and Politics in Brazil. An Incomplete Timeline of an Ongoing Struggle." *Futuress. Section: Epistemic Activism* (blog), November 20. https://futuress.org/stories/no-time-to-lose/.

Bhattacharya, Tithi. 2017. "Introduction: Mapping Social Reproduction Theory." In *Social Reproduction Theory. Remapping Class, Recentering Oppression*, edited by Tithi Bhattacharya. London: Pluto Press.

Bispo dos Santos, Antônio Nego. 2015. *Colonização, Quilombos: Modos e Significados*. Brasília: Universidade de Brasília, Coordenação CNPq.

Césaire, Aimé. 1950. *Discourse on Colonialism*. Translated by Joan Pinkham. New York: Monthly Review Press.

Chalhoub, Sidney. 2012. *A Força da Escravidão. Ilegalidade e Costume no Brasil Oitocentista*. São Paulo: Companhia das Letras.

Chaney, Elsa M., and Mary Garcia Castro. 1989. "Introduction: A New Field for Research and Action." In *Muchachas No More. Household Workers in Latin America and the Caribbean*, edited by Elsa M. Chaney and Mary Garcia Castro. Philadelphia: Temple University Press.

Chaui, Marilena. 2013. *Manifestações Ideológicas do Autoritarismo Brasileiro*. Vol. 2. Escritos de Marilena Chaui. Belo Horizonte and São Paulo: Autêntica Editora, Editora Fundação Perseu Abramo.
Christie, Nills. 1986. "The Ideal Victim." In *From Crime Policy to Victim Policy. Reorienting the Justice System*, 17–30. London: Palgrave Macmillan.
Curiel, Ochy. 2013. *La Nación Heterosexual. Análisis del Discurso Jurídico y el Régimen Heterosexual desde la Antropología de la Dominación*. Bogotá: En la frontera.
Curiel, Ochy. 2015. "La Descolonización desde una Propuesta Feminista Crítica." In *Feminista Siempre. Descolonización y Despatriarcalización de y desde los Feminismos de Abya Yala*. ACSUR – LAS SEGOVIAS (Associació per la cooperació amb el Sud).
Dalla Costa, Mariarosa, and Selma James. 1972. *The Power of Women and the Subversion of the Community*. 3rd ed. London: Falling Wall Press.
Davis, Angela. 1983. *Women, Race and Class*. New York: Random House.
Du Bois, W.E.B. 1903. *The Souls of Black Folk*. New York: Dover Publications.
Dussel, Enrique. 2005. "Europa, Modernidade e Eurocentrismo." In *Colonialidade Do Saber: Eurocentrismo e Ciências Sociais. Perspectivas Latino-Americanas*, edited by Edgardo Lander. Colección Sur Sur. Buenos Aires: CLACSO.
Engels, Friedrich. 1884. *The Origin of the Family, Private Property, and the State*. London: Penguin Group.
Fanon, Frantz. 1952. *Black Skin, White Masks*. Translated by Richard Philcox. New York: Grove Press.
Fattah, Ezzat A. 1986. "Prologue: On Some Visible and Hidden Dangers of Victim Movements." In *From Crime Policy to Victim Policy. Reorienting the Justice System*, 1–14. London: Palgrave Macmillan.
Federici, Silvia. 1998. *Caliban and the Witch: Women, the Body and Primitive Accumulation*. New York: Automedia.
Federici, Silvia, and Arlen Austin. 1972. *The New York Wages for Housework Committee 1972–1977. History, Theory and Documents*. New York: Autonomedia.
Ferdinand, Malcom. 2021. *Decolonial Ecology: Thinking from the Caribbean World*. Cambridge: Polity Press.
Ferdinand, Malcom. 2024. "Terre, Capital et Racisme: Penser Le Capitalisme Colonial. Commentaire Sur 'Théoriser Le Capitalisme Racial' de Julian Go." *Marronnages* 3 (1): 56–62.
Fernandes, Florestan. 1972. *O Negro no Mundo dos Brancos*. São Paulo: Difusão Europeia do Livro.
Ferreira da Silva, Denise. 2009. "No-Bodies: Law, Raciality and Violence." *Griffith Law Review* 18 (2): 212–236.
Ferreira da Silva, Denise. 2014. "Toward a Black Feminist Poethics: The Quest(ion) of Blackness Toward the End of the World." *The Black Scholar* 44 (2): 81–97. https://doi.org/10.1080/00064246.2014.11413690.
Ferreira da Silva, Denise. 2018. "Hacking the Subject: Black Feminism and Refusal beyond the Limits of Critique." *philoSOPHIA* 8 (1): 19–41.
Ferreira da Silva, Denise. 2019. *A Dívida Impagável*. São Paulo: OIP.
Ferreira da Silva, Denise. 2022. *Unpayable Debt*. On the Antipolitical, Vol. 1. London: Sternberg Press.
Fórum Brasileiro de Segurança Pública. 2024. *18° Anuário Brasileiro de Segurança Pública*. São Paulo: Fórum Brasileiro de Segurança Pública. https://publicacoes.forumseguranca.org.br/handle/123456789/253.
Freyre, Gilberto. 1933. *Casa-Grande & Senzala: Formação da Família Brasileira sob o Regime da Economia Patriarcal*. 51st reviewed ed. São Paulo: Global.

Gama, Luiz, and Ligia Fonseca Ferreira. 2011. "Introdução: As Vozes Múltiplas de Luiz Gama." In *Com a Palavra, Luiz Gama: Poemas, Artigos, Cartas, Máximas*, edited by Ligia Fonseca Ferreira. São Paulo: Imprensa Oficial.

Gama, Luiz da. 2011. "No Álbum do Meu Amigo J.A. da Silva Sobral." In *Com a Palavra, Luiz Gama: Poemas, Artigos, Cartas, Máximas*, edited by Ligia Fonseca Ferreira. São Paulo: Imprensa Oficial.

Gargallo, Francesca. 2015. *Feminismos desde Abya Yala. Ideas y Proposiciones de las Mujeres de 607 Pueblos en Nuestra América.* Bogotá: Ediciones Desde Abajo.

Giacomini, Sonia Maria. 1988. *Mulher e Escrava. Uma Introdução ao Estudo da Mulher Negra no Brasil.* Petrópolis: Editora Vozes.

Gilroy, Paul. 1993. *O Atlântico Negro: Modernidade e Dupla Consciência.* Translated by Cid Knipel Moreira. 2nd ed. São Paulo: Editora 34.

Gomes de Jesus, Jaqueline. 2019. "Xica Manicongo: A Transgeneridade Toma a Palavra." *Revista Docência e Cibercultura* 3 (1): 250–260. https://doi.org/10.12957/redoc.2019.41817.

Gomes, Flávio dos Santos. 2015. *Mocambos e Quilombos. Uma História do Campesinato Negro no Brasil.* Coleção Agenda Brasileira. São Paulo: Claro Enigma.

Gonzalez, Lélia. 1979a. "A Mulher Negra na Sociedade Brasileira: Uma Abordagem Político-Econômica." In *Por um Feminismo Afro-Latino-Americano*, edited by Flavia Rios and Márcia Lima. Rio de Janeiro: Zahar.

Gonzalez, Lélia. 1979b. "Cultura, Etnicidade e Trabalho: Efeitos Linguísticos e Políticos da Exploração da Mulher." In *Por um Feminismo Afro-Latino-Americano*, edited by Flavia Rios and Márcia Lima, 25–44. Rio de Janeiro: Zahar.

Gonzalez, Lélia. 1983. "Racismo e Sexismo na Cultura Brasileira." *Revista Ciências Sociais Hoje, ANPOCS*: 223–244.

Gonzalez, Lélia. 1988. "Por um Feminismo Afro-Latino-Americano." In *Por um Feminismo Afro-Latino-Americano*, edited by Flavia Rios and Márcia Lima, 139–150. Rio de Janeiro: Zahar.

Hall, Stuart. 1992. "The West and the Rest: Discourse and Power." In *Essential Essays, Volume 2: Identity and Diaspora*, 141–184. Durham: Duke University Press.

Haraway, Donna. 2015. "Anthropocene, Capitalocene, Plantationocene, Chthulucene: Making Kin." *Environmental Humanities* 6: 159–165.

Haraway, Donna, and Anna L. Tsing. 2019. "Reflections on the Plantationocene: A Conversation with Donna Haraway & Anna Tsing." *Edge Effects*, June 18. https://edgeeffects.net/wp-content/uploads/2019/06/PlantationoceneReflections_Haraway_Tsing.pdf.

Hartman, Saidiya. 1997. *Scenes of Subjection: Terror, Slavery, and Self-Making in Nineteenth-Century America.* 2nd ed. New York and London: Oxford University Press.

Hartman, Saidiya. 2008. "Venus in Two Acts." *Small Axe (SX26). A Caribbean Journal of Criticism* 12 (2): 1–14.

hooks, bell. 1982. *Ain't I a Woman. Black Women and Feminism.* London: Pluto Press.

hooks, bell. 1992. *Black Looks: Race and Representation.* Boston: South End Press.

James, C.L.R. 1963. *The Black Jacobins. Toussaint L'ouverture and the San Domingo Revolution.* 2nd revised ed. New York: Vintage Books.

Kellogg, Susan. 2005. *Weaving the Past: A History of Latin America's Indigenous Women from the Prehispanic Period to the Present.* Oxford and New York: Oxford University Press.

Kleinfeld, Joshua. 2013. "A Theory of Criminal Victimization." *Stanford Law Review* 65: 1087–1152.

Kundnani, Arun. 2020. "What Is Racial Capitalism?" In *Havens Wright Center for Social Justice*. University of Wisconsin-Madison. https://www.kundnani.org/what-is-racial-capitalism/.

Kuznesof, Elizabeth. 1989. "A History of Domestic Service in Spanish America, 1492–1980." In *Muchachas No More. Household Workers in Latin America and the Caribbean*, edited by Elsa M. Chaney and Garcia Castro. Philadelphia: Temple University Press.

Lavrin, Asunción. 1986. "Female Religious." In *Cities & Society in Colonial Latin America*, edited by Susan Migden Socolow and Louisa Schell Hoberman. Albuquerque: University of New Mexico Press.

Lerner, Gerda. 1986. *The Creation of Patriarchy*. Oxford and New York: Oxford University Press.

Lewin, Linda. 2003. *Surprise Heirs: Illegitimacy, Patrimonial Rights, and Legal Nationalism in Luso-Brazilian Inheritance, 1750–1821*, Vol. 1. Stanford: Stanford University Press.

Loveman, Mara. 2014. *National Colors. Racial Classification and the State in Latin America*. Oxford and New York: Oxford University Press.

Lugones, María. 2008. "Colonialidad y Género." *Tabula Rasa, Bogotá* 9: 73–101.

Luxemburg, Rosa. 1913. *The Accumulation of Capital*. Translated by Agnes Schwarzschild. London: Routledge Classics.

Marx, Karl. 1867. *Capital – A Critique of Political Economy*. Translated by Samuel Moore and Edward Aveling, Vol. I, The Process of Production of Capital. Moscow: Progress Publishers.

Memmi, Albert. 1957 [2006]. *Decolonization and the Decolonized*. Minneapolis and London: University of Minnesota Press.

Menezes, Jeannie da Silva. 2013. *Sem Embargo de Ser Femea. As Mulheres e um Estatuto Jurídico em Movimento no Século XVIII*. Jundiaí, São Paulo: Paco Editorial.

Miñoso, Yuderkys Espinosa, Diana Gómez Correal, and Karina Ochoa Muñoz. 2014. *Tejiendo de Otro Modo: Feminismo, Epistemología y Apuestas Descoloniales en Abya Yala*. Popayán, Colômbia: Editorial Universidad del Cauca.

Morrison, Adele M. 2006. "Changing the Domestic Violence (Dis)Course: Moving from White Victim to Multi-Cultural Survivor." *University of California, Davis* 39: 1061–1120.

Mott, Luiz. 1985. "Relações Raciais Entre Homossexuais No Brasil Colônia." *Revista Brasileira de História, São Paulo* 5 (10): 99–122.

Mott, Luiz. 1999. *Dicionário Biográfico dos Homossexuais da Bahia (Séculos XVI–XIX)*. Salvador: Editora Grupo Gay da Bahia.

Mott, Luiz, and Marcelo Cerqueira. 2005. "Boletim do Quimbanda-Dudu." Boletim n. 6. Bahia: Grupo Gay Negro da Bahia. Direitos Humanos, Diversidade Sexual e Cidadania dos Afro-Descendentes.

Nascimento, Abdias do. 1980. *O Quilombismo. Documentos de uma Militância Pan-Africanista*. 3rd revised ed. São Paulo: Editora Perspectiva.

Nascimento, Beatriz. 1976a [2007]. "A Mulher Negra no Mercado de Trabalho." In *Eu Sou Atlântica: Sobre a Trajetória de Vida de Beatriz Nascimento*, edited by Alex Ratts. São Paulo: Imprensa Oficial do Estado de São Paulo; Instituto Kuanza.

Nascimento, Beatriz. 1976b [2018]. "Zumbi de N'Gola Djanga Ou de Angola Pequena ou do Quilombo de Palmares [1976]." In *Beatriz Nascimento. Quilombola e Intelectual. Possibilidade nos Dias da Destruição*, edited by União dos Coletivos Pan-Africanistas, 104–111. São Paulo: Editora Filhos da África.

Nascimento, Beatriz. 1977 [2018]. "Historiografia do Quilombo [1977]." In *Beatriz Nascimento. Quilombola e Intelectual. Possibilidade nos Dias da Destruição*, edited by União dos Coletivos Pan-Africanistas, 125–165. São Paulo: Editora Filhos da África.

Nascimento, Beatriz. 1987 [2018]. "Introdução Ao Conceito de Quilombo [1987]." In *Beatriz Nascimento. Quilombola e Intelectual. Possibilidade nos Dias da Destruição*, edited by União dos Coletivos Pan-Africanistas, 303–315. São Paulo: Editora Filhos da África.

Nascimento, Beatriz. 1990 [2018]. "A Luta dos Quilombos. Ontem, Hoje e Amanhã [1990]." In *Beatriz Nascimento. Quilombola e Intelectual. Possibilidade nos Dias da Destruição*, edited by União dos Coletivos Pan-Africanistas, 348–352. São Paulo: Editora Filhos da África.

Núñez, Geni. 2023. *Descolonizando Afetos. Experimentações sobre Outras Formas de Amar*. São Paulo: Planeta do Brasil.

Núñez, Geni, João Manuel de Oliveira, and Mara Coelho de Souza Lago. 2021. "Monogamia e (Anti)Colonialidades: Uma Artesania Narrativa Indígena." *Teoria e Cultura* 16 (3): 76–88. https://periodicos.ufjf.br/index.php/TeoriaeCultura/article/view/34439.

Okoth, Kevin. 2022. "Resistance from Elsewhere." *London Review of Books* 44 (7). https://www.lrb.co.uk/the-paper/v44/n07/kevin-okoth/resistance-from-elsewhere.

Oliveira, Anazir Maria de, Odeter Maria da Conceição, and Hildete Pereira de Melo. 1989. "Domestic Workers in Rio de Janeiro: Their Struggle to Organize." In *Muchachas No More. Household Workers in Latin America and the Caribbean*, edited by Elsa M. Chaney and Mary Garcia Castro. Philadelphia: Temple University Press.

Oyěwùmí, Oyèrónké. 1997. *The Invention of Women. Making an African Sense of Western Gender Discourses*. Minneapolis: University of Minnesota Press.

Paret, Marcel, and Zachary Levenson. 2024. "Two Racial Capitalisms: Marxism, Domination, and Resistance in Cedric Robinson and Stuart Hall." *Antipode. A Radical Journal of Geography* 56 (5): 1802–1829.

Pateman, Carole. 1988. *The Sexual Contract*. Stanford: Stanford University Press.

Pereira de Melo, Hildete. 1989. "Feminists and Domestic Workers in Rio de Janeiro." In *Muchachas No More. Household Workers in Latin America and the Caribbean*, edited by Elsa M. Chaney and Mary Garcia Castro. Philadelphia: Temple University Press.

Reis, João José, and Flávio dos Santos Gomes, eds. 1996. *Liberdade Por Um Fio. História dos Quilombos no Brasil*. São Paulo: Companhia das Letras.

Reis, João José, and Herbert S. Klein. 2011. "Slavery in Brazil." In *The Oxford Handbook of Latin American History*, edited by Jose C. Moya. New York: Oxford University Press.

Rezzutti, Paulo. 2018. *Mulheres do Brasil: História Não Contada*. Rio de Janeiro: LeYa.

Ribeiro, Darcy. 1968 [1978]. *O Processo Civilizatório. Etapas da Evolução Sócio-Cultural. Estudos de Antropologia da Civilização*. São Paulo: Vozes/Círculo do Livro.

Rich, Adrienne. 2003. "Compulsory Heterosexuality and Lesbian Existence." *Women's History* 15 (3): 11–48.

Robinson, Cedric J. 1983. *Black Marxism: The Making of the Black Radical Tradition*. Chapel Hill and London: The University of North Carolina Press.

Rodrigues, Aryon D. 2014. "Sobre a Influência das Línguas Indígenas no Português Brasileiro." *DELTA: Documentação e Estudos em Linguística Teórica e Aplicada* 30 (3): 443–446. http://doi.org/10.1590/0102-445067692919987352.

Saffioti, Heleieth. 1976. *A Mulher na Sociedade de Classes: Mito e Realidade*. Sociologia Brasileira 4. Petrópolis, Brazil: Vozes.
Saffioti, Heleieth. 1978. "The Social Position of Women." In *Women in Class Society*, translated by Michael Vale. New York: Monthly Review Press.
Santos, Jocélio Teles dos. 2013. *Ensaios Sobre Raça, Gênero e Sexualidades no Brasil (Séculos XVIII–XX)*. Salvador: Edufba.
Schwarcz, Lilia Moritz. 2012a. "As Marcas do Período." In *História do Brasil Nação: 1808–2010*, edited by Lilia Moritz Schwarcz, Vol. 3, A Abertura para o mundo: 1889–1930. Rio de Janeiro and Madrid: Objetiva and MAPFRE.
Schwarcz, Lilia Moritz. 2012b. *Nem Preto Nem Branco, Muito pelo Contrário: Cor e Raça na Sociabilidade Brasileira*. São Paulo: Claroenigma.
Schwartz, Stuart. 1973. *Sovereignty and Society in Colonial Brazil. The High Court of Bahia and Its Judges, 1609–1751*. Berkeley: University of California Press.
Silveira, Tamires Batista. 2020. "Influência do Tupi na Língua Portuguesa Falada no Brasil." *Espaço Do Conhecimento UFMG* (blog), May 7. https://www.ufmg.br/espacodoconhecimento/influencia-do-tupi/.
Skidmore, Thomas E. 1976 [2012]. *Preto no Branco: Raça e Nacionalidade no Pensamento Brasileiro, 1870–1930*. Translated by Donaldson M. Garschagen. São Paulo: Companhia das Letras.
Skidmore, Thomas E. 2010. *Brazil: Five Centuries of Change*. 2nd ed. New York and Oxford: Oxford University Press.
Socolow, Susan Midgen. 2000. *The Women of Colonial Latin America*. 2nd ed. New York: Cambridge University Press.
Spillers, Hortense J. 1987. "Mama's Baby, Papa's Maybe: An American Grammar Book." *Diacritics, Culture and Countermemory: The "American" Connection. The Johns Hopkins University Press* 17 (2): 64–81.
Tupinambá, Glicélia (Célia). 2022. "An Indigenous Woman Troubling the Museum's Colonialist Legacy: Conversation with Glicéria Tupinambá." Translated by Pedro Marco Gonçalves. *Museum International. Towards Decolonisation* 74 (3–4): 10–23.
Vainfas, Ronaldo. 1989. *Trópico dos Pecados. Moral, Sexualidade e Inquisição no Brasil*. Rio de Janeiro: Editora Campus.
Wehling, Arno, and Maria José Wehling. 2004. *Direito e Justiça No Brasil Colonial: O Tribunal da Relação do Rio de Janeiro (1751–1808)*. Rio de Janeiro: Renovar.
Williams, Eric. 1944. *Capitalism and Slavery*. Chapel Hill: The University of North Carolina Press.
Wittig, Monique. 1978. "The Straight Mind." In *Out There: Marginalization and Contemporary Cultures*, edited by Russell Ferguson, Martha Gever, Trinh T. Minh-ha, and Cornel West, 51–57. Cambridge, MA: MIT Press.
Wynter, Sylvia. 1970s. "Black Metamorphosis: New Natives in a New World." Unpublished Manuscript, Institute of the Black World Records. Schomburg Center for Research in Black Culture, New York.
Wynter, Sylvia, and Katherine McKittrick. 2015. "Unparalleled Catastrophe for Our Species? Or, to Give Humanness a Different Future: Conversations." In *Sylvia Wynter. On Being Human as Praxis*, 9–89. Durham and London: Duke University Press.
Wynter, Sylvia, and David Scott. 2000. "The Re-Enchantment of Humanism: An Interview with Sylvia Wynter." *Small Axe: A Caribbean Journal of Criticism* 8: 119–207.
Yusoff, Kathryn. 2018. *A Billion Black Anthropocene or None*. Minneapolis: University of Minnesota Press.

Part 1

Colonial Racial-Patriarchal Order: Nation-State and Democracy

Re-membering

The political-juridical architecture of femicide operates across two interrelated scales within the *colonial racial-patriarchal order:* the subject-position and the nation-state. While the previous part focused on the micro-scale, examining modern modes of individual categorization and the institutionalization of the colonial family as foundational to the legal enablement of femicide, this chapter shifts to the macro-scale. It interrogates the broader institutional structures that shape the neocolonial nation-state and its promises of protection, equality, and citizenship.

At first glance, this exploration may seem to diverge from the book's central focus on femicide. Yet rather than a detour, this chapter traces the deeper strata upon which femicidal violence is naturalized and disavowed. It asks: What forms of memory, narration, and forgetting underwrite the legal and political frameworks that conceal systemic gendered and racialized violence? How is the colonial racial-patriarchal order reconfigured and masked in the universalizing language of nationhood and democratic progress?

To address these questions, the chapter expands its analytical scope, tracing the entanglements between private and public, family and nation, human and citizenship. It reveals how the dismemberment of the Human – the fragmentation of bodies and subjectivities through colonial logics – prefigures the emergence of the citizen within the modern nation-state.

The act of narrating History, in this context, becomes a political and epistemological battleground. As Haitian American anthropologist Michel-Rolph Trouillot reminds us, "history" refers both to the sociohistorical process, "what happened," and the narrative construction of that process, "what is said to have happened" (1995, 2–3). This duality is key to understanding how the narrative of law operates within the state to construct myths of origin and belonging that render violence invisible or normalized.

Within this framework, the chapter excavates how national myths are manufactured by the *colonial racial-patriarchal order*, through erasures,

DOI: 10.4324/9781003474692-3

obliterations, and liberal fictions of equality and freedom. Drawing on French literary theorist and philosopher Roland Barthes (1957), myth is understood here as a mode of discourse that deliberately distorts historical processes and causality, presenting them as static, self-evident, and natural. Expanding this critique, Édouard Glissant warns that myths carry "a hidden violence" (1990, 50) that disrupts relationality: they sever the links of filiation and negate the other's existence as a condition of relation.

Central to this process is what the U.S. cultural theorist and literary scholar Lauren Berlant terms "public paramnesia." Adapted from clinical terminology, paramnesia refers to a distortion of memory involving the misremembering of events or experiences that never occurred. Berlant deploys this term to address a political condition in which "a substitution for traumatic loss or unrepresentable contradiction that marks its own contingency or fictiveness while also radiating the authority of insider knowledge that all euphemisms possess" (1997, 48). This erasure, she argues, replaces the complexity of historical trauma "with a magical and consoling way of thinking that can be collectively enunciated and easily manipulated, like a fetish" (Berlant 1997).

By foregrounding these epistemological and institutional dynamics, this chapter examines how the colonial racial-patriarchal order is not merely a residual past but also a persistent and adaptable architecture encoded in the very foundations of the nation-state. Through this lens, what may appear as a departure from femicide is in fact a necessary inquiry into the discursive and structural conditions that sustain and normalize its ongoing presence. The expansion from the intimate scale of the body and family to the structural scale of the nation-state allows for a fuller understanding of how subject-positions and kinship formations are projected onto, and embedded within, institutional forms that sustain colonial violence under the guise of liberal democracy.

Nation, Nationalism

Conceived as a contemporary expression of patriotism and "fatherland," the concepts of the nation-state and nationalism have been characterized by historians and political theorists as an artificial and historical form of community that emerged around the 1830s (Hobsbawm 1990; Chaui 2013; Loveman 2014).

In this section, I analyze three of the most influential references of nationalism and modern nation-states: the conference delivered at the Sorbonne entitled *Qu'est-ce qu'une nation?* by Ernest Renan (1882) and the books *Nations and Nationalism* by Ernest Gellner (1983) and *Imagined Communities: Reflections on the Origin and Spread of Nationalism* by Benedict Anderson (1983). Rather than offering a conventional literature overview, my aim here is twofold: first, to delineate the distinctions between nationalism and racism as depicted in the canon, while highlighting the marginalization of gender;

and second, to propose a different approach that moves beyond established scholarly frameworks.

In his lecture *Qu'est-ce qu'une nation?*, Ernest Renan critiques the traditional conception of a nation, which, at that time, was conceived as a natural formation of groups sharing common ancestry, race, language, religion, and interests within a specific territory. He challenges this ethnic-centric perspective, deeming it a significant error. Renan argues that it "confounds the idea of race with that of the nation and attributes to ethnographic, or rather linguistic, groups a sovereignty analogous to that of actually existing peoples" (1882).

According to Renan, the mentioned elements – common ancestry, race, language, religion, and interests within a specific territory – are insufficient to fully explain the modern nation. This inadequacy stems from their inability to account for the sense of belonging to a larger community that extends beyond the nuclear family. Here, the nuclear family is associated with an ethnic definition of the nation, while the broader community and the sense of belonging are linked to its political dimension.

When considering ethnic and political interpretations of the nation, it might be helpful to examine the etymological roots of the word. The term "nation" originates from the Latin noun *natio*, denoting birth or origin. Initially, a nation was defined as a collective of individuals born in the same territory, or from the same mother. The social body was perceived as an extended form of the nuclear family. Before transforming into a political concept, the terminology of "nation" primarily referred to Indigenous communities, African and Jewish peoples (Hobsbawm 1990; Chaui 2013), or as Renan puts it, to "ancient tribes and cities" viewed as extensions of the family (1882).

By questioning the link between nationhood and race, Renan suggests that what distinguishes various forms of modern nation is not the dynastic notion of pure races but rather the fusion of diverse populations. Within a Eurocentric historiography, this fusion is framed in his work, notably due to the limited presence of women from the same racialized group. As Renan states, "[t]his fact was itself the consequence of another important particularity: that the Franks, the Burgunds, the Goths, the Lombards, and the Normans had very few women of their race with them" (1882). This is the only moment in his lecture where a gender differentiation is mentioned.

Despite the nearly complete absence of engagement with a Gendered ontology of difference or an intersectional approach to nationhood, the author focuses on differentiating nation from race. To this end, Renan examines the "sense of belonging" to a nation, which he characterizes as both a "feeling of sacrifice" and a "great solidarity," based on two main components. First, the sense of belonging encompasses the feeling of sharing a "legacy of memories," that is, a shared ancestral heritage. Here, Renan argues that forgetting is an essential element in nation-building, serving to obliterate the fact that "[u]nity is always brutally established" (1882). Historical investigations, in contrast, would threaten the integrity of nationhood by revealing that acts of violence have frequently underpinned the formation of political entities.

Second, the sense of belonging encompasses the "desire to live together," which is perceived not merely as a historical gesture but as an ongoing, reiterated commitment in the present. This continuous implicit consent is metaphorically described as a "daily plebiscite," with the common will serving as the sole basis for the legitimacy of the nation. Thus, the formation of the nation-state involves both ethnic, also known as cultural dimension – rooted in a shared heritage – and political dimension – embodied by a daily plebiscite. The author adopts a favorable view of this model of national organization, considering it as "the guarantee of liberty, a liberty that would be lost if the world had only one law and one master" (Renan 1882). Later in this chapter, I revisit the modern political lexicon of legitimacy, consent, and equality in greater depth.

The European discourse on modern nationhood and nationalism experienced a significant revival almost a century after Renan's lecture in 1882. In 1983, *Nations and Nationalism* by Ernest Gellner and *Imagined Communities* by Benedict Anderson were published.[1]

In *Nations and Nationalism*, French anthropologist and historian Ernest Gellner conceptualizes nationalism as a political principle that merges political and national entities into a "congruent unit" (1983, 7). Gellner's analysis regards nationalism as the legitimizing foundation of modern politics, where ethnic boundaries no longer intersect with political borders. Instead, the theory of political legitimacy under nationalism, as he sees it, involves a parasitic relationship established between nation and state.

According to Gellner, a nation is typically defined either culturally, by the shared cultural traits of its members, or voluntaristically, by the mutual recognition of rights and duties associated with a common social membership. This perspective echoes Renan's discussion of ethnic and political dimensions. While Gellner underscores that nationalism inherently requires cultural homogeneity – asserting that "[h]omogeneity imposed by objective, inescapable imperative eventually appears on the surface in the form of nationalism" (1983, 39) – he contends that neither cultural nor voluntaristic definitions alone suffice to fully grasp the modern configuration of the nation-state.

Moreover, Gellner suggests that discussions on nationalism should begin with German sociologist, jurist, and historian Max Weber's conceptualization of the legitimate monopoly of violence. Despite the Eurocentric nature

1 Eric Hobsbawm (1990) notes a nearly one-hundred-year gap between Renan's conference in 1882 and the next significant publications on nationalism. According to Hobsbawm, a fruitful period in nationalism scholarship emerged after the 1970s, though the historical reasons for this gap remain unclear.

of this assumption, Weber's framework has significantly shaped scholarly analyses of the nation-state, influencing studies not only in Europe but also in Latin America (Saffioti 1976; Centeno 2013). Weber defines the ideal type of the state as a "human community which (successfully) lays claim to the monopoly of legitimate physical violence within a certain territory" (1919, 310). To understand the composition of the modern nation-state, one must consider the delineation of territory and population, the establishment of a bureaucratic apparatus, and the enforcement of this monopoly of violence.

In this framework, the Weberian concept of *Herrschaft* is particularly noteworthy. The German term *Herrschaft* combines *Herr*, a male title analogous to "mister" or "master," with the suffix *schaft*, which denotes a category or state of being, similar to "-ship" in English. It can be literally translated as "masculine mastership," encompassing notions of both domination and rule, a concept that strongly resonates with the previously articulated idea of White conquest-driven masculinity. However, in Weber's analysis, *Herrschaft* extends beyond the monopoly of violence to include the legitimacy that underpins such control, which is precisely the focus of this part's analysis.

Like many theories on nation and nationalism, Weber's sociological analysis neglects the deep-seated connection between colonialism and the formation of nation-states, overlooking critical issues related to legitimacy and violence. Rather than attributing the global emergence of nation-states solely to events in the so-called global North, such as the French Revolution, it is essential to recognize the pivotal role of colonialism in the Americas as a historical milestone in the creation of the modern nation-state. The period from 1830 to 1920 marked not only the proliferation of nation-states across Europe but also the simultaneous establishment of the first nation-states in Latin America, forged through anticolonial struggles for independence (Anderson 1983; Quijada 2000). This interconnected process underscores the need to situate the rise of nation-states within a global and relational framework, challenging narrow narratives that confine their origins within European history alone.

For instance, while Gellner acknowledges the context of imperialism and colonialism, his analysis remains entrenched in a framework that perpetuates Western colonial perspectives. He characterizes the "conquest" of Latin America as motivated by "good old-fashioned non-commercial rapacity," attributing it to "economic and technological superiority, and not a military orientation" (Gellner 1983, 43). Such framing reinforces the colonial narrative of inherent "superiority" and obscures the violent realities of conquest and exploitation.

In contrast to this perspective, Anglo-Irish political scientist and historian Benedict Anderson (1983), our third key reference, offers a markedly different interpretation of colonialism, emphasizing its formative role in shaping modern notions of nationhood. Anderson argues that colonialism expanded cultural and geographic horizons, reshaping people's imaginations of human possibility and the configurations of collective identity that underpin the concept of the nation-state. His approach underscores the transformative interplay between colonial practices and the emergence of national consciousness, moving beyond Manichean notion of superiority.

In *Imagined Communities*, Anderson identifies three pivotal and unprecedented conditions arising from the colonial regime that profoundly influenced the formation of the modern national order. First, the vast expansion and varying geographic conditions on either side of the Atlantic made the gradual integration of populations into larger politico-cultural units nearly impossible. Second, the large-scale migration of White European settlers to the Americas, coupled with the military, economic, and technological dominance over colonized peoples, led to the violent imposition of European colonial rule. Finally, the imperial metropoles established complex bureaucratic and ideological systems designed to perpetuate colonial structures. In this context, he highlights colonial racism as a significant element in the formation of empires, intertwining dynastic legitimacy with national communities (1983, 150).

Anderson introduces the concept of "amnesia" as a political characteristic inherent to nation-building, paralleling the human tendency to forget. The author identifies three key institutions profoundly shaped by the colonial context: the census, the map, and the museum (1983, 163). These institutions have played a significant role in shaping and recording both colonial and national History. Echoing Renan's argument, Anderson suggests that such selective forgetfulness is integral to the construction of national memory, narrative, and identity.

Similar to the other authors just discussed, Anderson also draws a distinction between nationalism and racism. He argues that racism is fundamentally rooted in fear and hatred directed toward "the Other," tracing its origins to class-based ideologies rather than national ones (1983, 149). In contrast, nationalism is tied to traditional notions of family, characterized by self-sacrificial love and solidarity (1983, 141–144). Anderson frames nationalism and racism as products of different political affections, capturing their dualistic nature through the binary oppositions of fear/love, hatred/solidarity, and class/family. He suggests that racism tends to sustain local repression and dominance, while nationalism functions as a rhetoric to justify foreign wars.

Although the interpretations of Renan, Gellner, and Anderson differ, they ultimately converge around a dichotomy that separates and opposes racism and nationalism. Notably, there is a significant lack of comprehensive examination into the intersection of these constructs, particularly regarding their overlapping material and historical dimensions from the periods of colonial slavery to anticolonial independence in Latin America (Balibar and Wallerstein 1988; Berlant 1997; Goldberg 2002). As French philosopher Étienne Balibar aptly remarks, "[t]he connection between nationalism and racism is neither a matter of perversion nor a question of formal similarity, but a question of historical articulation" (1988, 50). Furthermore, these perspectives scarcely address the intimate historical relation between the modern nation-state and the Gendered ontology of difference.

While I recognize the substantial contributions of these scholars to the discourse on nationalism and the nation-state, my goal is not to simply revisit the established frameworks that have traditionally overlooked or erased the historical context of colonial slavery from discussions on the formation of the modern nation-state. Instead, I propose a nuanced approach that excavates the historical layers intertwining nation-making, racism, and sexism. In particular, the following sections investigate how White conquest-driven masculinity has not only influenced the colonial construction of subject-positions but also shaped the transition from empire to the independent republican framework of "citizenship" in Brazil. This analysis seeks to uncover the enduring legacies of colonial hierarchies in the formation of nation-state and its sociopolitical structures.

Politics of Silencing/Speakability

Contesting the canonic lexicon of "forgetting" (Renan 1882) and "amnesia" (Anderson 1983), which are often depicted as natural, organic, and necessary processes, I introduce the concept *politics of silencing/speakability* in the process of nation-building. This term captures the deliberate, constructed, and biased production of narratives and myths. These narratives and myths operate through the systematic marginalization, obliteration, and annihilation of ways of sensing, knowing, and existing in the world otherwise. According to Trouillot (1995, 26), silence permeates the process of historical production at four crucial stages. First, is the "fact creation," involving the formation of historical and academic sources of valid knowledge. Second, "fact assembly" refers to the establishment of official archives. Third, "fact retrieval" encompasses the crafting of narratives. Fourth, "retrospective significance" involves the erasure of stories and histories that are not aligned with hegemonic perspective in the final construction of the official History. In the upcoming sections of the book, I examine the interplay of these four modalities of silencing within the context of Brazilian nation-building.

In the midst of the formal abolition of slavery in 1888, Brazilian colonial authorities were deeply concerned about the absence of a cohesive and unified populace – an essential component for forging a national identity. The historiography of Brazil offers a compelling lens for examining the tension between the violent fractures of colonialism and the drive for unity of nationalism.

Notably, Rio de Janeiro stands as the only instance in which a European empire established its capital or metropole within the territorial bounds of its colony. This unusual configuration resulted from the Portuguese royal court's flight from the Napoleonic invasions in Portugal, relocating from Lisbon to

Rio de Janeiro in 1808. The move brought significant transformations to the city. From 1808 to 1822, the empire centralized its administrative apparatus in Rio, which became a hub for foreign visitors, including diplomats and ambassadors from around the world. European travelers, such as Arthur de Gobineau, Louis Couty, and Louis Agassiz, chronicled their experiences through diaries, letters, and fieldwork notes. Together, their works contributed to an archive steeped in White supremacist ideologies, positioning them as early proponents of social Darwinism and advocates of so-called scientific racism (Skidmore 1976).

Furthermore, it is important to contextualize that by 1931, Brazil's population was approximately five million, with estimates indicating that up to one-third, or even half, of the population consisted of Afro-diasporic enslaved subjects. Consequently, a substantial segment of society was formally excluded from the notion of "the people" (Azevedo 1987; Pereira 2016).

The subsequent sections explore the mechanisms through which the *politics of silencing/speakability* have shaped the construction of the nation-state and the "citizens" within the colonial racial-patriarchal order.

Monologue

In a letter dated October 11, 1492, Cristóvão Colombo made observations about Amerindian peoples and their manner of speaking. He stated, "[t]hey must be good and skillful servants, for I notice that they immediately repeat what we say." By exposing his imperial intentions, he added, "If it pleases Our Lord, I will take six of them from here for Your Majesties when I depart, so that *they may learn how to speak*" (Colombo 1492; emphasis added).[2]

In addressing the politics of silence/speakability, language becomes a major feature. Language serves not only as a tool for expressing the world but also as a vehicle for creating words and worlds. The invaded territory of Brazil, as discussed in Part 0, was home to a diverse array of spoken languages, a result of the unprecedented mobility catalyzed by modern colonialism and Black Atlantic slavery. This linguistic tapestry encompassed numerous Indigenous and African languages, including Yoruba, Jê, Caribe, Tupi, Guarani, Kikongo, Umbundu, Fon, Nheengatu, and Kimbundu. Among these languages, Tupi was the most commonly spoken one in Brazil until the 1750s (Costa e Silva 2011).

2 My translation from the original in Portuguese: *Devem ser bons serviçais e habilidosos, pois noto que repetem logo o que a gente diz . . . Eu, comprazendo a Nosso Senhor, levarei daqui, por ocasião de minha partida, seis deles para Vossas Majestades, para que aprendam a falar* (Colombo 1492).

In 1757, colonial authorities decreed Portuguese as the sole official language of Brazil, prohibiting the public use of any other language. The imposition of a monolingual regime by the Empire, contrasting with prevailing multilingualism of the colony, served as a tool for consolidating colonial power. In line with Colombo's assertion that Indigenous people should "*learn how to speak*," colonized subjects were cast as existing outside the boundaries of Western rationality. This rhetorical and juridical framing rendered them incapable of true interlocution, reducing them to the status of children presumed to lack the capacity for meaningful speech. By contrast, the colonizers positioned themselves as rational, authoritative "adults" capable of speech, reinforcing hierarchical binaries of power and personhood.

A unified language stands as one of the foundational elements in the formation of a nation-state. In this context of nation-building, the conditions for enunciation come to encompass much more than mere syntax or grammar. The act of *mastering* a language implies, above all, "assuming a culture and bearing the weight of a civilization" (Fanon 1952, 1–2), and in this way, becoming a participant in the "world expressed and implied by this language" (Fanon 1952).[3]

Lélia Gonzalez's work is crucial for unpacking the colonial process of infantilization that operates through the monopoly of language and the conditions of enunciation. Gonzalez (1988) displaces the psychoanalytic notion of the *infans* to address colonial forms of infantilization related to both racism and sexism. The term *infans* originates from the Greek term *phèmi*, meaning "I speak," combined with the Latin prefix "in," denoting negation, which signifies the absence of speech. Hence, the semantics of *infans* refer to the subject who has not yet acquired language, symbolized by the image of a babbling baby still incapable of articulating words.

Despite being physically present, the *infans* are spoken for by adults who perceive them as lacking reason, as objects of the conversation, as some one who does not access language. The condition of enunciation is thus dichotomized between those with the ability to speak – adults, that could be translated in the present work as White male colonizers – and those without – *infans*, or everyone pushed outside of the colonial monopoly of the Human.

3 In *The Invention of Women* (1997), which explores colonialism and gender discourses in Yoruba studies, Oyèrónkẹ́ Oyěwùmí emphasizes how language reflects patterns of social interactions, hierarchies, interests, and concerns. Yoruba, along with Bantu and Ewe-Fon languages, played significant roles in linguistic migrations and influences in the region now known as Brazil (Gonzalez 1988). Oyěwùmí argues that the absence of gender-specific categories in a language indicates the limited role of gender in shaping social categories, as demonstrated in Yorubaland. She illustrates this by noting that the lack of Yoruba terms equivalent to English words like "son," "daughter," "brother," or "sister" signifies the absence of gender-based social roles. Instead, the Yoruba terms "Egbon" and "aburo" refer to siblings based on age rather than gender (1997, 158).

Consequently, the *infans* are not recognized as the subject of their own discourse; instead, they are spoken about and, in this way, re-presented by those who possess the monopoly of the conditions for enunciation.

In this manner, Gonzalez exposes how colonized and racialized subjects, have been subjected to infantilization – a process that erases, invalidates, and suppresses their speech. This colonial apparatus is not based on a phylogenetic factor, as is the case with children, but rather emanates from the colonial racial-patriarchal order that monopolizes the conditions of enunciation. Hence, infantilization operates not in relation to an incapacity to speak. Infantilization operates as a mechanism of denial in hearing other voices, which constitutes one of the facets of what I refer here to as the *politics of silencing/speakability*.

In *Plantation Memories* (2008), Portuguese interdisciplinary artist and writer Grada Kilomba investigates everyday racism in Germany. Drawing upon two fundamental elements of psychic organization in Freudian theory – aggression and sexuality – Kilomba argues that the White subject-position represses and projects both elements, aggression and sexuality, onto Black existences. This mechanism of denegation enables the self-assertion of White subjects as the "civilized" and "decent," while simultaneously erasing the colonial genealogy of oppression. Furthermore, she systematizes infantilization (2008, 42–43) as one of the five modalities of colonial racist repression and projection, alongside primitivization, decivilization, animalization, and eroticization. Kilomba's work demonstrates the translocality of Lélia Gonzalez's conceptualization of infantilization, encompassing not only Brazil but also global entanglements of racism and sexism.

Lauren Berlant, provides a complementary facet of the process of infantilization. The author draws back to Alexis de Tocqueville, in his work *Democracy in America*, to emphasize how citizens are encouraged to love the nation as they love their own families while "democracies can also produce a special form of tyranny that makes citizens like children, infantilized, passive, and overdependent on the 'immense and tutelary power' of the state" (1997, 27). According to Berlant, such a public paramnesia contributes to the creation of an "infantile citizenship." The infantile citizen has faith in the nation "based on a belief in the state's commitment to representing the best interests of ordinary people, [which] is also said to be what vitalizes a person's patriotic and practical attachment to the nation and to other citizens" (1997, 27–28).

Drawing on the historical conditions of enunciation, during the First National Congress of Colonial Anthropology in Porto, Portugal, in 1934, Eusébio Tamagnini, the founder of the Portuguese Society of Eugenic Studies, asserted that colonized populations encountered "serious difficulty in learning the language of the colonizer, leading to a 'corruption of the forms and alteration in the meaning of most words'" (Matos 2013, 138). Instead of reiterating the colonial of the conditions for enunciation, as suggested by the referenced eugenic framework, I situate this disruption as a manifestation of everyday practices of resistance enacted by Indigenous and Afro-diasporic subjects.

Epistemic violence inherent in the colonial monologue does not imply an absence of countercolonial resistance in any way. Gonzalez emphasizes how camouflaged everyday resistance, particularly carried out by Black women, challenges the passive and submissive stereotype that serves as the basis for the myths of harmony and racial democracy. As mentioned, Gonzalez (1979b, 1983) emphasizes that the underground resistance carried out by Black women has resulted in the Africanization of the Portuguese language in Brazil, a transformative process referred to as *pretuguês*.

Black women engage in subtle acts of epistemic resistance, continually disputing and reinventing the connections between words and worlds. Lélia Gonzalez names this strategy as *rasteira* (1983) and Édouard Glissant refers to it as *detour* (1990). Through the oral history of tales, proverbs, sayings, and songs, creole languages were invented and performed as a *detour* in the Caribbean context. Similar to the notion of *pretuguês*, creole refers to the act of contesting, reinventing, and subverting the colonial language. Once again, we observe the translocal nature of anticolonial movements and the political strategies enacted by those subjugated by the colonial order, in challenging the colonial borders of nation-states while reconnecting struggles and subjects across political geographies.

This epistemic countermovement can be understood in conjunction with what Frantz Fanon identifies as one of the elements for eradicating the "degrading and infantilizing structures" (1958, 102) established through colonization. According to Fanon, decolonial liberation would entail the complete dismantling of the colonial system and encompasses the eradication of the oppressor's language, the abolition of departmentalization, and the dissolution of the customs that perpetuate the formerly colonized population's entanglement with the cultural, ontological, epistemic and ideological aspects imposed by the colonizers (1958, 105).

Myth 1: Harmony

I revisit three institutional mechanisms outlined by Anderson (1983) that were shaped by and have shaped the colonial invention of the nation-state: the census, the map, and the museum. Each proposes a distinct mode of hegemonic archive, whether documenting populations, spaces, narratives, monuments, and images. Such documents are "kept and classified under the title of the archive by virtue of a privileged topology" (Derrida 1995, 10), imbuing them with an intentional type of national authority and legitimacy.

In the intersection of the census, map, and museum, Brazil established the Institute of History and Geography (IHG) in 1838 with the aim of creating the official narrative for the nation. In 1844, the institute launched a contest titled "How to Write the History of Brazil?" Surprisingly (or not), a Bavarian subject named Karl von Martius (1794–1868) won the contest. Von Martius proposed writing Brazilian History as an "unrivaled mix of peoples and colors," resulting from the "unique blending" of Indigenous, White, and Black subjects (Rowland 2003, 370; Miskolci 2013, 21–22; my emphasis).

Rather than advocating for a "pure race," as dictated by Eurocentered White supremacist ideology, von Martius's proposal aligns with what Ernest Renan would later describe as the "fusion of diverse population" (1882), a key aspect of the modern nation-state. The narrative of harmony and *mestiçagem* (miscegenation) became the milestone for the creation of Brazilian national identity, referred to as *brasilidade*. This foundational myth of the Brazilian nation underscores the cynicism inherent in such a national narrative – one that is conveniently and unilaterally fabricated by the colonial gaze of history.

The book *História Geral do Brasil* (*General History of Brazil*) was published in two volumes between 1854 and 1857 by the diplomat Francisco Adolfo de Varnhagen, who has been considered as "the father" of modern Brazilian History. Varnhagen, deeply aligned with Dom Pedro II, the second and last monarch of the Empire of Brazil, collaborated with the IHG to establish a unified national narrative. In his work, Varnhagen (1857) glorifies the Portuguese colonization and its influence on the formation of Brazil as a nation.

The myth of harmony, epitomized by the celebration of *mestiçagem*, is not merely a romanticized fiction of racial fusion; it is a calculated epistemic and political project. As discussed in Part 0, this orchestrated myth occludes the sexual economies that underpinned colonial slavery, where un/gendered female captives, racialized as Black and Indigenous, were classified as property to be owned by White men, in a grotesque convergence of domination and desire. Such ideological neurosis that Lélia Gonzalez (1983) aptly diagnoses: a national psyche in denial, repressing its violent origins while reasserting the privileges of White masculinity.

I present two historical examples that illustrate the pervasive circulation of this myth through various social devices and apparatuses in the making of the modern nation. In 1880, the Brazilian Society Against Slavery released a manifesto reinforcing the rhetoric of harmony, asserting that "until today, slavery could not create any racial hatred among us" (Schwarcz 2007, 29; my translation). Similarly, in 1881, the newspaper *Província de São Paulo* published the following statement: "We, Brazilians, do not distinguish between races. The slaves [sic] of today, through their future skills and education, will be equal to the masters of the past, and as undifferentiated citizens, both will collaborate toward the nation's greatest prosperity"

(Schwarcz 2007). Who is included in this "we"? Who is implied in this "us"? Who holds the authority to speak *for* the collective that constitutes the national body of the people?

As discussed in Part 0, subjects racialized as Indigenous and Black were positioned at the bottom of the Racial ontology of difference. Amerindian people were essentialized by the White gaze as a fixed entity – pure, naive, good, and honest. The imagery of a distant Indigenous ancestor was hypocritically instrumentalized as a symbol of *brasilidade*, a national myth of common origin in which everyone belonged to the same extensive family, even as the genocide against Indigenous communities persisted (Costa e Silva 2011). European painters commissioned by the Portuguese Empire often portrayed Indigenous subjects with lighter skin tones in numerous works used to decorate the *Palácio Imperial* (Imperial Palace). Even when adopting the national rhetoric of miscegenation, the ultimate objective remained the same: Whiteness.

Despite having the largest population of African descendants outside of Africa, the colonial construction of Brazilian national memory attempted to erase the Afro-diasporic central role in its nation-building. The paramnesia imposed by the politics of silencing/speakability was so abrupt and contradictory that, just one year after the formal abolition of slavery – a regime that endured for nearly four hundred years – the 1889 Republican anthem declared: "We do not believe that slaves [sic] have ever existed in such a noble country!"[4] Once again: Who is considered entitled to speak *for* the collective encapsulated in the national people?

It is crucial to critically contest the use of "we" in such assertions. For subjects racialized as Indigenous and Black, the reality of slavery was not merely a belief but a lived experience, passed down through generations. Their very existence, memories, stories, and bodies constitute forms of living archives of slavery and its afterlives. In this context, the "we" invoked by the republic anthem exposes a deep divide between those included in, and those excluded from the national idea of "the people." This "we" delineates the boundary between those who could speak, deny, forget, or misremember the legacy of colonial slavery, and those who bore its wounds, were rendered unspeakable, and whose voices and memories were systematically silenced.

In pursuit of a national development model centered on "order and progress," the Brazilian White male elite attributed the country's perceived "backwardness" to its "racial mixture." Based on the nation's racist and misogynistic foundations, the state officially implemented a Whitening

4 From the original in Portuguese: *Nós nem cremos que escravos outrora / Tenha havido em tão nobre país!*.

project.[5] In 1911, the director of the Brazilian National Museum, representing the country at the First International Racial Congress in London, openly reinforced the White supremacist ideology underpinning Brazil's project of nation. He asserted, "It is logical to assume that, at the start of the new century, the mestizos will have disappeared in Brazil, coinciding with the parallel extinction of the Black race among us" (Skidmore 1976, 64). Similarly, Brazilian eugenicist Artur Neiva declared, "In a century, the nation will be White" (Skidmore 1976, 269).

Another crucial aspect of the rhetoric surrounding "the people" and the infantilized citizenship embodied in the collective "we" – where a few speak on behalf of the entire nation – lies in the institutionalization and instrumentalization of census data, numbers, and statistics. It is important not to view the census as a mere objective and neutral representation of reality, as national rhetoric often suggests. Instead, I align with political and historical sociologist Mara Loveman's assertion that the census is "both a stake and an instrument of politics. Census categories, in turn, are political products" (2014, 8–9).

In *National Colors: Racial Classification and the State in Latin America* (2014), Loveman analyzes how national statistical censuses became strategic mechanisms for ethnic and racial classification in Latin America. Emerging in the mid-nineteenth century, these institutions were instrumental in advancing projects of "modernization," encompassing the administrative consolidation of the modern state, cultural efforts to forge national unity, and scientific endeavors aimed at producing demographic data as foundation for national "progress." Loveman highlights how these three dimensions – state-building, nation-making, and the scientific framing of development – converged within the operations of central statistical agencies, positioning them at the heart

5 While the Whitening project in Brazil gained prominence following the formal abolition of slavery in 1888, its implementation began much earlier. For example, as early as 1808, the colonial regime offered financial incentives for White Europeans to migrate to Brazil, including free land. Swiss immigrants, predominantly Catholic and French-speaking, established the first colonies in Bahia in 1808, followed by another colony in Nova Friburgo in 1820. In 1824, the first German colony was founded in São Leopoldo, south of Rio Grande do Sul. Between 1811 and 1830, nearly seven thousand Germans immigrated to Brazil, mainly from Hesse, Prussia, Saxe, Württemberg, and Oldenburg. Spanish and French migrants also followed this trend until the early nineteenth century (Costa e Silva 2011). Following the end of slavery, the national project of Whitening was institutionally and legally endorsed for several decades. For instance, the Brazilian Constitutional Law of 1934 stipulated in Article 121, Paragraph 6, that immigration was to be regulated to ensure "ethnic integration" and "physical and civil aptitude of the immigrant," limiting it to an annual cap of 2 percent of the national population. On September 18, 1945, President Getúlio Vargas promulgated a decree, Law No. 7967, to complement the previous constitutional law, establishing that immigrants should be admitted with the aim of "preserving and developing the ethnic composition of the population," defined as having the "most desirable characteristics of European descent" (Skidmore 1976, 275–277).

of the so-called modernization efforts. These agencies did not merely categorize citizens; they actively shaped the calculative logics that underlie systemic violence – a framework I conceptualize as the *mathematics of violence* (Part 1) – embedding these classifications within the broader architecture of state power and control.

In the nineteenth and early twentieth centuries, Brazilian national censuses served not only as tools for population documentation but also as instruments for advancing the eugenic project of Whitening the nation. The first national census of 1872 distinctly divided its data into two tables: one for the free population and another for the enslaved subjects, mirroring the fragmented sociopolitical fabric of the nascent nation. Following the formal abolition of slavery in 1888, subsequent censuses consolidated these tables into a single dataset, symbolizing an aspiration for national unity. However, rather than abandoning racial classification altogether, Brazil's census authorities of the time produced racial statistics that emphasized widespread miscegenation. This approach reinforced the central myth of racial democracy, which portrayed the mixed-race population as emblematic of a society devoid of racial discrimination.

Myth 2: Independence

Confronting the colonial mythologies embedded in the fabric of modern nation-building, I raise the question: What, then, does the concept of independence entail? The Etymology Dictionary (2017) traces the term "independent" back to the seventeenth century, describing it as an individual who is self-sufficient and does not rely on external sources for sustenance. Nevertheless, it is well acknowledged that living beings inevitably depend on external factors for survival, including both human and nonhuman relations. The political use of the concept of independence is often associated with the pursuit of emancipation, agency, and autonomy, which enable subjects and collectivities to exist free from the control of others.

The Latin etymology of "emancipation" combines the prefix *ex-* (out or away) with *mancipare*, a verb derived from the noun *mancipum*, referring to possession or property. This term's roots in legal and paternalistic authority, specifically the control exerted by the *pater familias* over the household and property, underscore how emancipation, at its core, is tied to the assertion of autonomy from paternal control and its mechanisms of objetification. However, within the modern political lexicon, both "independence" and "emancipation" extend beyond an individualistic act. Emancipation now frames the broader political anticolonial struggles for liberation, enslaved people's fight for freedom, as well as feminist movements advocating for gender equality. Similarly, independence transcends the mere developmental transition from childhood to adulthood, encompassing collective, embodied, and territorial liberation from external forms of domination. As Guyanese historian and activist Walter Rodney notes, "The achievement of any of these aspects of personal development is closely tied to the state of society as a whole" (1972, 3).

Frantz Fanon further deepens our understanding of this complexity within the context of anticolonial struggles, asserting that independence does not inherently lead to a profound political transformation. He writes: "History teaches us that the anticolonial struggle is not automatically written from a nationalist perspective" (Fanon 1961, 97). Fanon's insight underscores the need to critically examine how anticolonial struggles, initially aimed at liberation, have often been co-opted by dominant Western discourses surrounding nation-statehood and independence, ultimately transforming the promise of freedom into a new form of control.

In the context of Brazil, the discourse of independence masked the persistence of colonial structures of power under a new guise. Instead of marking a break from the past, independence symbolized a shift from one form of dominion to another, that is, from colony to monarchy, from the control of the father to the control of the son. Contrary to the popular emancipation envisioned by anticolonial struggles, Brazil's declaration of independence resulted in what has been termed "double colonization" or "recolonization" (Pereira 2016, 150; Rowland 2003), which, far from liberation, continued to suppress the widespread uprisings led by Afro-diasporic subjects and Amerindian peoples.

On September 7, 1822, Dom Pedro, the son of the Portuguese emperor Dom João and, at the time, Brazil's Prince Regent, officially declared the country's independence and assumed the throne as the emperor of the newly independent nation.[6] However, neither individual nor political independence can be reduced to a singular event; such a reductionist perspective is precisely what colonial narratives sought to obfuscate. Independence is instead a protracted and multifaceted process characterized by persistent acts of radical transformation. In Brazil, these movements continued well beyond the formal declaration of independence in 1822, as evidenced by major uprisings and revolts before and after this date. Movements like the Mâles (1835), the Cabanagem (1835–1840), the Farrapos or Farroupilha (1835–1845), the Sabinada (1837–1838), the Balaiada (1838–1841), the Praieira (1848–1849), and the Canudos (1896–1897), all underscore the enduring, irreconcilable tensions that shaped Brazil's nation-building process (Gonzalez 1979a; Chaui 2017).

In *Decolonising International Law* (2011), Sundhya Pahuja examines how international law has solidified the nation-state as the primary and exclusive framework for colonized territories to achieve independence. Although

6 At the close of 1821 and the outset of 1822, the Portuguese royal family decided to return to Portugal, leaving Dom João's son, Dom Pedro, to govern the colony as Prince Regent (*Príncipe Regente*) (cf. Schwarcz 2006, 2012a).

Pahuja's analysis focuses on the mid-twentieth century decolonization struggles, her arguments provide a critical lens for assessing earlier independence movements, including those in Latin America. By underscoring the duality of international law, encompassing both its imperial and counter-imperial dimensions, Pahuja contends that the radical aspiration of liberation from colonial domination has historically been constrained within the developmentalist paradigm of the nation-state. The author demonstrates how foundational concepts of international law, such as the nation-state and sovereignty, were not merely applied but actively constructed through legal discourse, shaping the contours and limits of what independence could mean within this framework.

Building on Pahuja's argument, while international law provided a framework and legal language through which anticolonial claims could be articulated, it simultaneously undermined their transformative potential. By framing independence solely within the confines of nationhood, it compelled colonized territories to adopt the colonial epistemology. This framework classified them as peripheral, underdeveloped, backward, and part of a constructed "Third World," thereby ensuring that their independence remained tethered to colonial logics rather than breaking free from them.

In the same direction, in *Imperialism, Sovereignty, and the Making of International Law* (2004), Antony Anghie contends that international law, through its methodologies and frameworks, perpetuated mechanisms of othering, thereby facilitating the rise of a new form of empire. Consequently, international law not only legitimized colonial exploitation but also established significant barriers to any potential reparation for those subjugated and wounded by colonial slavery regimes. Scholars such as Anghie and Pahuja have emphasized the pivotal role of colonialism in shaping international law, including the development of the doctrine of sovereignty within the context of colonial encounters. Building upon this critical scholarship, the following sections explore the interconnectedness of constitutional law and colonialism, aiming to extend the analysis beyond the confines of international law.

Colonial Pact: The Constitutional Law

The emergence of nation-states marked a significant transformation in the institutionalization of colonialism, shifting from imperial structures to a new system of mandate, borders, sovereignty, and governance. This transition was characterized by the adoption of contractual, liberal, and constitutional frameworks, which redefined the mechanisms of power and control (Hall 2010).

The 1824 Constitutional Code serves as the foundation of Brazil's constitutional order. To fully grasp its significance, it must be understood within the broader historical context, particularly the transformative events that followed the arrival of the Portuguese royal family in 1808. At that time, Brazil was navigating a complex transition from its status as a colony under the absolutist rule of Portugal to an "independent" state formally designated as the Empire of Brazil (*Império Brasileiro*). This transitional period saw the convening of the first Constituent Assembly on June 3, 1822, under the leadership of José Bonifácio de Andrade e Silva. However, the declaration of independence on September 7, 1822, did little to resolve the deep-seated political tensions that continued to shape Brazil's emergent state. Escalating political discord, coupled with repression of popular insurgencies, culminated in D. Pedro I's dissolution of the Constituent Assembly on November 12, 1823 (Garcia 2024). This episode in Brazil's early constitutional history underscores the complex interplay between the aspirations of nation-building and the contradictions inherent in the enduring legacies of colonial governance.

Following this dissolution of the Constituent Assembly, D. Pedro I established a new Council of State tasked with drafting a constitutional project. The resulting draft, presented in December 1823, was nominally subject to review by municipal chambers prior to its ratification – a process that ultimately never took place (Garcia 2024). Nonetheless, on March 25, 1824, D. Pedro I *unilaterally* promulgated Brazil's first Constitution. Despite the rhetoric surrounding the establishment of a "new order," the Constitutional Code of 1824 was conceived and enacted solely by the former colonial authority.[7] Far from reflecting the "general will of the People," this expedited process mirrored the practices of absolutist monarchies (Garcia 2024, 70). These continuities, rather than ruptures, reveal the enduring legacy of colonial structures on the postcolonial state.

Article 1 of the 1824 Constitution proclaims: "The Empire of Brazil constitutes the *political association* of all Brazilian citizens. They form a free and independent nation that rejects any other form of union or federation that undermines its independence." The concept of "political association," paired with the ideals of freedom and independence, aligns closely with the foundational principles of social contract theory. Within this framework, the emergence of constitutional law in Brazil can be interpreted through the social contract's central premise: the collective transfer of certain individual rights to a sovereign authority, presumed to be trusted and transcendent. This arrangement encapsulates what Lauren Berlant (1991, 12) describes as a "juridico-utopian promise," that is, a pledge of individual protection through incorporation into the symbolic political realm of citizenship.

7 At that time, Brazil's primary legal framework still relied on the *Ordenações do Reino* (Laws of the Kingdom), a compilation of Portuguese legal codes dating from 1446 to 1603 (Schwartz 1973; Lewin 2003; Menezes 2013).

Social contract theories, as articulated by Thomas Hobbes (1588–1679), John Locke (1632–1704), and Jean-Jacques Rousseau (1712–1778), were developed during the European colonial expansion and the transatlantic slave trade in the Caribbean and Latin America. Their accounts often traced a linear evolution of a so-called primitive state to civilized political communities, which was framed as a transition from the "state of nature" to the "civic state," and from customary norms to the formal rule of law.[8] In doing so, they reinforced Eurocentric conceptions of progress and civilization anchored in the constitutional pact, embedding hierarchical and racialized assumptions into the very foundations of modern political theory.

As French anthropologist Pierre Clastres notes, "the emergence of the State resulted in a significant typological division between Savage and Civilized man, creating an insurmountable gap where everything was transformed as Time transitioned into History" (1974, 200). This classification is more than descriptive; it imposes a value system that positions Europe as the global ideal of civilization. By universalizing its own context, colonial monoculture, monolanguage, and monologue portray the European model of existence as an inevitable and linear development for all societies worldwide.

Carole Pateman (1988), a British feminist and political theorist, introduced a significant shift in the interpretation of social contract theory by foregrounding its fundamentally patriarchal structure. She argues that the social contract is underpinned by what she terms a "sexual contract," a tacit agreement that secures male domination and representation, established not by men in general, but exclusively by White cismen. Pateman further identifies a racial dimension to this structure in what she calls the "slave contract," which legitimizes the subjugation of Black people and naturalizes White male supremacy (1988, 221).

Building on this critique, Jamaican philosopher Charles W. Mills (1997) proposes the concept of "racial contract," which addresses White supremacy as an enduring political system that extends well beyond the period of legal slavery. Mills characterizes the racial contract as a colonial agreement through which White supremacy is globally institutionalized, enacted through the purported consent of individuals who perceive themselves as equals: White men. Whether or not this consent is explicitly given, all White subjects are beneficiaries of it. Within this framework, the phrase "we, the

8 During the late sixteenth and seventeenth centuries, social contract theories emerged to explore and speculate on the origins of society, the establishment of social sovereignty, and the perpetuation of inequalities. In Thomas Hobbes's seminal work, *Leviathan* (1651), he argues that the need for a political pact arises from the inherent fear of violence in the "state of nature" (Hobbes 1651, 79), a hypothetical pre-social stage marked by a constant state of war of everyone against everyone. The social pact, in turn, is according to him what made it possible to create a civil state – a political association where laws are established and fear is no longer justified (1651, 84).

people" resurfaces as an analytical entry point, revealing how Western constitutional discourse has historically invoked a universal subject that in fact designates "we, the white people" (Mills 1997, 1–3).

This book underscores the critical need to acknowledge the often-overlooked dimensions of sexual and racial contracts in the formation of modern nation-states and liberal democracies, as a means of unearthing the contemporary politics of femicide. As analyzed in Part 0, these contracts are deeply intertwined with the cisheteronormative pact (Wittig 1978; Preciado 2002; Rich 2003; Curiel 2013) and other forms of colonial normativity. Together, they compose what is referred to here as the colonial racial-patriarchal order.

Representative Democracy

In the wake of the formal abolition of slavery in 1888, the Brazilian monarchy collapsed, giving way to a republican regime the following year. This political transformation necessitated a new framework to legitimize neocolonial institutions, one that could replace the coercive and so-called transcendent authority of the imperial monarch. In this context, the Republican Constitutional Code sought to establish a new mythology of political legitimacy: representative democracy.[9]

The concept of modern democracy has sparked extensive debate across contemporary political and legal spheres, encompassing diverse forms such as representative, republican, socialist, liberal, radical, imperialist, direct, social, participatory, anarchic, deliberative, and plebiscitary, among others. For some, democracy represents the ultimate achievement of so-called modern and developed nations, a value to be universally promoted and refined. For others, democracy remains a Western construct, one that has yet to be fully realized, even in Europe (Brown 2015).

Rather than exploring the myriad interpretations and iterations of democracy, my focus here is on the emergence of representative democracy and its entanglement with the colonial racial-patriarchal order. Specifically, I examine how this form of governance intersects with the constructs of representation and citizenship, revealing the enduring legacies of colonialism within democratic frameworks.

The new political legitimacy was anchored in a democratic system, as reflected in the language of the constitutional preambles. Unlike the Brazilian Monarchical Constitutional Code of 1824, which asserted that the emperor

9 Influenced by the federalist movements in the United States, the Brazilian Constitutional Code of 1891 not only established the republican system but also introduced a presidential regime with four-year terms and a federal regime that granted greater autonomy to the states, provided they did not contradict the Federal Constitution (cf. Quijada, Bernand, and Schneider 2000; Wood 1995).

had the "unanimous acclamation of the peoples,"[10] the Constitutional Code of 1891 emphasized the representation of the collective will through the inclusive "we": "We, the representatives of the Brazilian people, gathered in a Constituent Congress, to establish a free and democratic regime."[11] This foundational principle has been consistently upheld, including in the current Constitution of 1988, which begins with: "We, the representatives of the Brazilian people, gathered in a National Constituent Assembly to establish a Democratic State."[12] In other words, we are all implicitly bound by the social contract embodied by the constitutional code.

Influenced by the social contract framework, the notion of the "sovereign people" emerged as the cornerstone of postcolonial political authority. In this paradigm, citizens delegate a portion of their rights to elected representatives. The legitimacy of liberal democracy is fundamentally anchored in the national concept of a shared or common will, often interpreted as the will of the majority. It is essential to critically examine the concepts of majority and minority, rather than reducing them to mere descriptions of reality.

The transition from plantation slavery to waged labor reconfigured the Lusotropicalist myth of harmonious slavery and the "good [sic] slave" into a narrative portraying Black subjects as bad, criminal, unqualified, and unprepared for citizenship. This reframing places the onus of social mobility squarely on Black subjects while simultaneously absolving the White population and neocolonial institutions of accountability (Gonzalez 1979b). It erases and attempts to forget their responsibility for addressing structural inequalities, perpetuating systemic denial of reparative justice and reinforcing racial hierarchies.

The rhetoric of "unpreparedness" for citizenship has long served to marginalize and exclude certain groups from the collective "we" that constitutes the national will, effectively silencing their participation in political processes and representation. Within the framework of liberal democracy, these subject-positions are then legally recognized as free; they are politically rendered materially and politically incapable of exercising this purported freedom, embodying what has been termed the "infantilized citizen" (Gonzalez 1988; Berlant 1991).

A critical yet frequently overlooked dimension of this exclusionary discourse is its Gendered ontology of difference. The persistent challenge lies in

10 My translation from the original text: *Dom Pedro I, por Graça de Deos, e Unanime Acclamação dos Povos, Imperador Constitucional, e Defensor Perpetuo do Brazil* (1824, preambule).

11 Original text: *Nós, os representantes do povo brasileiro, reunidos em Congresso Constituinte, para organizar um regime livre e democrático, estabelecemos, decretamos e promulgamos a seguinte* (1891, preambule).

12 Original text: *Nós, representantes do povo brasileiro, reunidos em Assembleia Nacional Constituinte para instituir um Estado Democrático* (1988, preambule).

historicizing and learning with the political mobilizations of Indigenous, Black, and queer women and dissent bodies within the formation of modern nation-states and liberal democracies – systems traditionally constructed as paternalistic, White conquest-driven masculinity's model or civilization. Their struggles unsettle such paradigms, offering other frameworks for reimagining political belonging and sovereignty – a theme further analyzed in Part 2 of this book.

Despite the constitutional rhetoric of popular sovereignty, the Brazilian Republic was established through a forceful top-down intervention by the military. The coup resulted in the replacement of the emperor, Dom Pedro I, with the military general, Deodoro da Fonseca (1889–1891). This transition underscores the profound disparity between legal discourse and political reality, particularly in its connection to the legacy of White conquest-driven masculinity – historically marked by acts of conquest, domination, and coercion (Miskolci 2013).

The modern concept of representation merges two distinct traditions: liberal and democratic. Political liberalism, with its focus on principles such as the rule of law, the separation of powers, and the protection of individual freedoms, intersects with the democratic tradition, which champions ideals of equality and popular sovereignty. Thus, liberal democracy forges a novel form of authority by synthesizing the notions of collective will and political representation (Hall 2010).

One significant aspect of the transition from monarchy to liberal democracy is the separation of church and state, which introduces a clear distinction between the private and public spheres. In absolutist regimes, the ruler and the state – the private and the public – were often conflated. In contrast, liberal democracies delineate between public institutions and the individuals who occupy them. The public realm theoretically encompasses entities directly owned, organized, or administered by the state, while the private sphere includes all areas beyond direct state control, such as the personal, domestic, and intimate domains (Pateman 1988; Olsen 1990; Bartlett 1990; McClure 1992; Mills 1997). In practice, these binary categories have reinforced the association of White men with the political and public spheres of representation and authority, while simultaneously maintaining women relegated to the private and domestic spheres, where they remain passively represented and spoken for.

Property ownership played a pivotal role in shaping and legitimizing the "new" legal and political regime (Bhandar 2012). Just before the formal abolition of slavery in Brazil, electoral laws were strategically reformed. In 1881, the minimum income requirement for voting was raised, resulting in only 1 percent of the population being eligible to vote or participate in elections (Mattos 2012; Costa e Silva 2011). This reform reinforced the notion of "unpreparedness," a label imposed on those historically barred from property ownership. In this colonial context, where property ownership was a prerequisite for political and legal recognition, the term "citizen" effectively became an abstract designation reserved for White men.

Following the formal abolition of slavery in 1888, eligibility criteria for citizenship began to include literacy requirements. Despite the legal ideal of equality, this change meant that fewer than 5 percent of the population could vote or hold public office (Mattos 2012; Segato 2010). The requirement for citizenship was thus updated to target those historically excluded from the educational system – again, the majority of the population. Literacy emerged as a new mechanism for perpetuating colonial politics of silencing/speakability, shifting the basis of political and civil rights from property ownership to literacy, thereby continuing to reserve these privileges predominantly for White men.

The figure of the "citizen" in this colonial racial-patriarchal order reflects the roles historically embodied by the signatories of the social contract – father, husband, plantation owner, and slaveholder. Argentine political theorist and philosopher Ernesto Laclau's assertion that "if democracy is possible, it is because the universal has no necessary body and no necessary content" (1992, 35) underscores the legal fiction that underpins democratic ideals. While Laclau's theoretical argument is compelling, the historical grounds of colonialism reveals that the so-called universal legal subject has consistently been embodied by a very specific and identifiable group: White men. Liberal democracy, with its abstract rhetoric of equality, freedom, and sovereignty, perpetuates myths of equality, racial democracy, and meritocracy. In this narrative, Black, Indigenous, queer, and female subject-positions are superficially acknowledged as "equal before the law," yet without any material transformation of the social structures that sustain inequality.

First Wave

The relationship between law, antiracist struggles, and feminist movements has long been fraught with ambivalences and paradoxes, particularly since the emergence of modern democracies (Williams 1987; Smart 1989; Cusicanqui 2010). Central to these tensions is the demand for rights, especially the right to vote and hold public office, which catalyzed what has come to be known as the first wave of feminism. This period marked the rise of feminism as a mass political movement, characterized by its focus on securing legal and political equality for women (Fraser 2009, 101–103).

In her groundbreaking work, *A Vindication of the Rights of Woman* (1796), British writer Mary Wollstonecraft uses the language of rights to advocate for women's access to education. Employing the rationalist terminology of the eighteenth century, Wollstonecraft argues that "men, in general, seem to employ their reason to justify prejudices, which they have imbibed, they can scarcely trace how, rather than to root them out" (1796, 16).

Wollstonecraft's vindication has inspired women worldwide, including Brazilian educator, translator, and philosopher Nísia Floresta. In 1832, Floresta wrote *Direito das mulheres e injustiça dos homens* (*Women's Rights, Men's Injustice*), a text seen as a translation of Wollstonecraft's work. Furthermore, in 1838, Floresta founded Brazil's first school for women, Colégio Augusto, in Rio de Janeiro (Rezzutti 2018, 167–168). The advocacy for education rights eventually led to demands for voting rights, a cornerstone of modern democracy.

Under Brazilian law in 1881 (Decree 3029, Article 2, para. 10), any person with a "scientific or literary diploma from any legally recognized faculty, academy, school, or institution, national or foreign" was formally eligible to vote. Despite meeting these criteria, Isabel de Sousa Mattos, a White woman from the elite, was denied the right to vote in 1885. Mattos became the first woman in Brazil to legally reclaim the right to vote, though her political achievement was nullified by the new legislation of the Republican regime in 1889.

In 1911, Leolinda de Figueiredo Daltro, along with other women, founded the Female Republican Party in Brazil. They aimed to expose the paradox of being able to form an official party while being denied the political right to vote or hold public office (Rezzutti 2018). In 1922, Diva Nolf Nazário attempted to register as a voter, arguing that the legal text (Article 70 of the 1891 Constitution) referred to "all citizens" in an abstract and universal sense, and should, therefore, include both men and women. However, her request was rejected by the court, which directly argued that women's roles were confined to the domestic sphere and not the public or political life. Nazário's appeal from 1923 highlighted how the culturally ingrained sexism within the judiciary system effectively denied women full citizenship.

Through persistent political pressure, the right to vote was eventually granted to women in certain regions of Brazil via municipal laws in 1927. Celina Guimarães Viana and Julia Alves Barbosa became the first women registered as voters in Brazil. In 1928, Luísa Alzira Teixeira Soriano was elected mayor of Lajes in the state of Rio Grande do Norte, becoming the first female mayor in Latin America (Rezzutti 2018).

This chapter explores the feminist suffrage movement within the context of both anticolonial struggles and civil rights movements, complicating its genealogy and emphasizing the limits of rights-based mobilizations within the nation-state framework. By reexamining feminist suffrage as part of civil rights struggles, the chapter interrogates the ways in which such movements, while expanding political participation for some, often neglected the excludent structures they aimed to challenge. In particular, the feminist pursuit of suffrage was framed within the transition from "unpreparedness" to the liberal ideal of "effective citizenship" (McClure 1992, 109–110), a strategy that prioritized inclusion within existing legal frameworks, rather than addressing the deeper, systemic injustices that defined the Racial and

Gendered ontologies of difference within colonial and neocolonial architectures of power. This alignment with the nation-state framework, as well as the tendency to universalize a White, cisheteronormative conception of womanhood, obliterates the genealogies, needs, and lived realities of Black, Indigenous, and queer women.

Lélia Gonzalez's critique, written during Brazil's re-democratization in the late 1970s,[13] highlights the failure of mainstream feminist movements to recognize the intersection of race and gender in shaping women's oppression (Gonzalez 1979a). Liberal feminism, even as it challenged patriarchal structures, neglected the entanglement of *colonial racial-patriarchal order* that underpinned both state institutions and gendered subjectivity. This limitation is exacerbated by the nation-state's exclusive role in political action and citizenship, which, by confining emancipatory struggles to its frameworks, solidified the racial and gendered hierarchies it ostensibly sought to dismantle.

Drawing back on the introduction of this chapter, the concept of "public paramnesia" becomes crucial in understanding how the nation-state constructs and perpetuates its narratives of progress and inclusion. As Berlant (1997) describes, public paramnesia functions as a form of collective forgetting, where the contradictions and traumas of colonial histories are substituted by euphemisms and constructed memories of unity and harmony. This selective memory obscures the legacies of exploitation and racialized violence, while maintaining the authority of dominant discourses that claim to represent "insider knowledge." The feminist suffrage movement, though framed as a step toward equality, becomes an example of this public paramnesia that obliterates ancestral mobilizations of women for liberation.

Thus, the feminist movement's alignment with the nation-state's liberal framework reflects a broader mechanism of forgetting, where the promise of emancipation, though ostensibly radical, is co-opted into the logic of the very structures that maintain Racial and Gendered ontologies of difference. The state's version of "independence" and "emancipation," framed as progress toward full citizenship, masks the colonial and neocolonial continuities that shape the afterlives of slavery. Public paramnesia, in this sense, operates as a tool of nation-building, silencing the histories and struggles that do not conform to its idealized vision of progress.

•

This book shifts from the liquid paradigms established by liberal feminist waves to the grounded practices cultivated by women in grassroots movements in Brazil. The next Part analyzes how countercolonial-feminist praxis

13 Brazil was under a civil-military dictatorship from 1964 to 1985, which was succeeded by a period of re-democratization from 1979 to 1988. This process included political amnesty, restoring a multiparty system, and the promulgation of the 1988 Constitutional Code.

fosters *choreographies of survival* that create modes of existence and action that contest, refuse, and reinvent entrenched colonial legacies within the legal order. Through acts of re/de/composition and radical world-making, these movements challenge the solidified structures of *colonial racial-patriarchal order*, unsettling their foundational grounds and reimagining possibilities for liberation, redress, and justice otherwise.

Bibliography

Anderson, Benedict. 1983. *Imagined Communities. Reflections on the Origin and Spread of Nationalism*. Revised ed. London and New York: Verso.
Anghie, Antony. 2004. *Imperialism, Sovereignty and the Making of International Law*. Cambridge Studies in International and Comparative Law. New York: Cambridge University Press.
Azevedo, Celia Maria Marinho de. 1987. *Onda Negra, Medo Branco: O Negro no Imaginário das Elites – Século XIX*. Rio de Janeiro: Paz e Terra.
Balibar, Étienne. 1988. "Racism and Nationalism." In *Race, Nation, Class: Ambiguous Identities*, edited by Étienne Balibar and Immanuel Wallerstein. New York and London: Verso.
Balibar, Étienne, and Immanuel Wallerstein. 1988. *Race, Nation, Class. Ambiguous Identities*. New York and London: Verso.
Barthes, Roland. 1957. *Mythologies*. Translated by Annette Lavers. Vintage Classics. London: Penguin.
Bartlett, Katherine T. 1990. "Feminist Legal Methods." *Harvard Law Review* 103 (4).
Berlant, Lauren. 1991. *The Anatomy of National Fantasy*. Chicago and London: The University of Chicago Press.
Berlant, Lauren. 1997. *The Queen of America Goes to Washington City. Essays on Sex and Citizenship*. Durham and London: Duke University Press.
Bhandar, Brenna. 2012. "Disassembling Legal Form. Ownership and the Racial Body." In *New Critical Legal Thinking. Law and the Political*, edited by Matthew Stone, Illan rua Wall, and Costas Douzinas. London and New York: Birkbeck Law Press, Routledge.
Brown, Wendy. 2015. *Undoing the Demos: Neoliberalism's Stealth Revolution*. New York: Zone Books.
Centeno, Miguel Angel. 2013. "Max Weber and the Latin American State." In *Fondo de Cultura Económica y el Centro de Investigación y Docencia Económicas (CIDE)*. Marx Weber: una mirada iberoamericana.
Chaui, Marilena. 2013. *Manifestações Ideológicas do Autoritarismo Brasileiro*, Vol. 2. Escritos de Marilena Chaui, Belo Horizonte, São Paulo: Autêntica Editora, Editora Fundação Perseu Abramo.
Chaui, Marilena. 2017. *Sobre a Violência*, Vol. 5. Escritos de Marilena Chaui. Belo Horizonte: Autêntica Editora.
Clastres, Pierre. 1974. *Society Against the State*. Translated by Robert Hurley. 6th ed. New York: Zone Books.
Colombo, Cristóvão. 1984. *Diários da Descoberta da América: As Quatro Viagens e o Testamento [1492-1504]*. Translated by Milton Persson. Porto Alegre: L&PM.
Costa e Silva, Alberto da. 2011. "População e Sociedade." In *História do Brasil Nação: 1808–2010*, edited by Lilia Moritz Schwarcz, Vol. 1, Crise Colonial e Independência 1808–1830. Rio de Janeiro: Objetiva.

Curiel, Ochy. 2013. *La Nación Heterosexual. Análisis del Discurso Jurídico y el Régimen Heterosexual desde la Antropología de la Dominación*. Bogotá: En la frontera.
Cusicanqui, Silvia Rivera. 2010. "Ch'ixinakax Utxiwa: A Reflection on the Practices and Discourses of Decolonization." In *Ch'ixinakax Utxiwa. On Practices and Discourses of Decolonization*, translated by Molly Geidel, 46–70. Cambridge: Polity Press.
Derrida, Jacques. 1995. *Archive Fever. A Freudian Impression*. Translated by Eric Prenowitz, Vol. 25. Diacritics 2. The Johns Hopkins University Press.
Dietz, Mary G. 1987. "Feminism and Theories of Citizenship." *Daedalus, Learning about Women: Gender, Politics, and Power* 116 (4): 1–24.
Etymology Dictionary. 2017. "Independence." In *Online Etymology Dictionary*. https://www.etymonline.com/word/independence.
Fanon, Frantz. 1952. *Black Skin, White Masks*. Translated by Richard Philcox. New York: Grove Press.
Fanon, Frantz. 1958. "Decolonization and Independence." In *Toward the African Revolution*, translated by Haakon Chevalier, 99–105. New York: Grove Press.
Fanon, Frantz. 1961. *The Wretched of the Earth*. Translated by Richard Philcox. New York: Grove Press.
Fraser, Nancy. 2009 [2010]. *Scales of Justice. Reimagining Political Space in a Globalizing World*. New York: Columbia University Press.
Garcia, Emerson. 2024. "A Constituição de 1824 e o Constitucionalismo Contemporâneo: Pontos de Inflexão." *Revista Do Ministério Público Do Estado Do Rio de Janeiro* 91 (March): 67–81.
Gellner, Ernest. 1983. *Nations and Nationalism*. Oxford: Basil Blackwell.
Glissant, Édouard. 1990. *Poetics of Relation*. Ann Arbor: The University of Michigan Press.
Goldberg, David Theo. 2002. *The Racial State*. MA: Blackwell.
Gonzalez, Lélia. 1979a. "A Mulher Negra na Sociedade Brasileira: Uma Abordagem Político-Econômica." In *Por um Feminismo Afro-Latino-Americano*, edited by Flavia Rios and Márcia Lima, 49–64. Rio de Janeiro: Zahar.
Gonzalez, Lélia. 1979b. "Cultura, Etnicidade e Trabalho: Efeitos Linguísticos e Políticos da Exploração da Mulher." In *Por um Feminismo Afro-Latino-Americano*, edited by Flavia Rios and Márcia Lima, 25–44. Rio de Janeiro: Zahar.
Gonzalez, Lélia. 1983. "Racismo e Sexismo na Cultura Brasileira." *Revista Ciências Sociais Hoje, ANPOCS*: 223–244.
Gonzalez, Lélia. 1988. "Por um Feminismo Afro-Latino-Americano." In *Por um Feminismo Afro-Latino-Americano*, edited by Flavia Rios and Márcia Lima, 139–150. Rio de Janeiro: Zahar.
Hall, Stuart. 2010. *Sin Garantias. Trayectorias y Problemáticas en Estudios Culturales*. Popayán: Instituto de Estudios Peruanos; Instituto de Estudios Sociales y Culturales, Pensar. Pontificia Universidad Javeriana; Universidad Andina Simón Bolívar, Sede Ecuador.
Hobbes, Thomas. 1651. *Leviathan, or the Matter, Forme, & Power of a Common-Wealth Ecllesiasticall and Civill*. London: Andrew Crooke, at the Green Dragon in St. Pauls Church-yard.
Hobsbawm, Eric. 1990. *Nations and Nationalism since 1780. Programme, Myth, Reality*. 2nd ed. Cambridge: Cambridge University Press.
hooks, bell. 2004. *The Will to Change. Men, Masculinity, and Love*. New York and London: Atria Books.
Kilomba, Grada. 2008. *Plantation Memories. Episodes of Everyday Racism*. 5th ed. Münster: Unrast.

Laclau, Ernesto. 1992. "Universalism, Particularism and the Question of Identity." *Emancipation(s)* October (61): 83.
Lewin, Linda. 2003. *Surprise Heirs: Illegitimacy, Patrimonial Rights, and Legal Nationalism in Luso-Brazilian Inheritance, 1750–1821*, Vol. 1. Stanford: Stanford University Press.
Loveman, Mara. 2014. *National Colors. Racial Classification and the State in Latin America*. Oxford and New York: Oxford University Press.
Matos, Patrícia Ferraz de. 2013. *The Colours of the Empire. Racialized Representations during Portuguese Colonialism*. Translated by Mark Ayton. European Anthropology in Translation. Oxford and New York: Berghahn Books.
Mattos, Hebe. 2012. "A Vida Política." In *História do Brasil Nação: 1808–2010*, edited by Lilia Moritz Schwarcz, Vol. 3, A Abertura para o mundo: 1889–1930. Rio de Janeiro and Madrid: Objetiva and MAPFRE.
McClure, Kirstie. 1992. "On the Subject of Rights: Pluralism, Plurality and Political Identity." In *Dimensions of Radical Democracy. Pluralism, Citizenship, Community*, edited by Chantal Mouffe. London: Verso.
Menezes, Jeannie da Silva. 2013. *Sem Embargo de Ser Femea. As Mulheres e um Estatuto Jurídico em Movimento no Século XVIII*. Jundiaí, São Paulo: Paco Editorial.
Mills, Charles H. 1997. *The Racial Contract*. Ithaca and London: Cornell University Press.
Miskolci, Richard. 2013. *O Desejo da Nação: Masculinidade e Branquitude no Brasil de Fins do XIX*. São Paulo: Annablume.
Nogueira, Octaciano. 2012. *1824*. 3rd ed., Vol. 1. Constituições Brasileiras. Brasília: Senado Federal, Subsecretaria de Edições Técnicas.
Olsen, Frances. 1990. "The Sex of Law." *Feminism and Critical Legal Theory: An American Perspective* 18. International Journal of the Sociology of Law.
Pahuja, Sundhya. 2011. *Decolonising International Law: Development, Economic Growth and the Politics of Universality*. Cambridge: Cambridge University Press.
Pateman, Carole. 1988. *The Sexual Contract*. Stanford: Stanford University Press.
Pereira, Luisa Rauter. 2016. *O Povo na História do Brasil. Linguagem e Historicidade no Debate Político (1750–1870)*. São Paulo: Paco.
Preciado, Paul. 2002 [2018]. *Countersexual Manifesto*. New York: Columbia University Press.
Quijada, Mónica. 2000. "Nación y Territorio: La Dimensión Simbólica del Espacio en la Construcción Nacional Argentina. Siglo XIX." *Revista de Indias* LX (219): 373–394.
Quijada, Mónica, Carmen Bernand, and Arnd Schneider. 2000. *Homogeneidad y Nación. Con un Estudio de Caso: Argentina, Siglos XIX y XX*. Madrid: Consejo Superior de Investigaciones Científicas. Centro de Humanidades. Instituto de Historia.
Renan, Ernest. 1882. *Qu'est-Ce Qu'une Nation*? Presented at the conference delivered at the Sorbonne on March 11th, 1882, Paris.
Rezzutti, Paulo. 2018. *Mulheres do Brasil: História Não Contada*. Rio de Janeiro: LeYa.
Rich, Adrienne. 2003. "Compulsory Heterosexuality and Lesbian Existence." *Women's History* 15 (3): 11–48.
Rodney, Walter. 1972. *How Europe Underdeveloped Africa*. Revised ed., 1981. Washington, DC: Howard University Press.
Rowland, Robert. 2003. "Patriotismo, Povo e Ódio Aos Portugueses: Notas sobre a Construção da Identidade Nacional no Brasil Independente." In *Brasil: Formação*

do Estado e da Nação, edited by István Jancsó. São Paulo: HUCITEC, UNIJUI and FAPESP.
Saffioti, Heleieth. 1976. *A Mulher na Sociedade de Classes: Mito e Realidade.* Sociologia Brasileira 4. Petrópolis: Vozes.
Schwarcz, Lilia Moritz. 2006. "A Mestizo and Tropical Country: The Creation of the Official Image of Independent Brazil." *Revista Europea de Estudios Latinoamericanos y Del Caribe* 80: 25–42.
Schwarcz, Lilia Moritz. 2007. *O Espetáculo das Raças: Cientistas, Instituições e Questão Racial no Brasil (1870–1930).* São Paulo: Companhia das Letras.
Schwarcz, Lilia Moritz. 2012. "As Marcas do Período." In *História do Brasil Nação: 1808–2010*, edited by Lilia Moritz Schwarcz, Vol. 3, A Abertura para o mundo: 1889–1930. Rio de Janeiro and Madrid: Objetiva and MAPFRE.
Schwartz, Stuart. 1973. *Sovereignty and Society in Colonial Brazil. The High Court of Bahia and Its Judges, 1609–1751.* Berkeley: University of California Press.
Segato, Rita. 2010. "Femi-Geno-Cidio como Crimen en el Fuero Internacional de los Derechos Humanos: El Derecho a Nombrar el Sufrimiento en el Derecho." In *Una Cartografía del Feminicidio en las Américas*, edited by R. Fregoso and C. Bejarano. México D.F.: UNAM CIIECH.
Skidmore, Thomas E. 1976 [2012]. *Preto no Branco: Raça e Nacionalidade no Pensamento Brasileiro, 1870–1930.* Translated by Donaldson M. Garschagen. São Paulo: Companhia das Letras.
Smart, Carol. 1989. *Feminism and the Power of Law.* London and New York: Routledge.
Trouillot, Michel-Rolph. 1995. *Silencing the Past. Power and the Production of History.* Boston, MA: Beacon Press.
Varnhagen, Francisco Adolfo de. 1857. *A Historia da Independencia do Brasil. São Paulo: Melhoramentos.* São Paulo: Melhoramentos.
Weber, Max. 1919. "The Profession and Vocation of Politics." In *Weber: Political Writings*, edited by Peter Lassman and Ronald Speirs, 7th printing 2010, 309–369. Cambridge: Cambridge University Press.
Williams, Patricia J. 1987. "Alchemical Notes: Reconstructing Ideals from Deconstructed Rights." *Harvard Civil Rights – Civil Liberties Law Review* 22 (2): 401–433.
Wittig, Monique. 1978. "The Straight Mind." In *Out There: Marginalization and Contemporary Cultures*, edited by Russell Ferguson, Martha Gever, Trinh T. Minh-ha, and Cornel West, 51–57. Cambridge, MA: MIT Press.
Wollstonecraft, Mary. 1796. *A Vindication of the Rights of Woman: With Strictures on Political and Moral Subject.* 3rd ed. London: J. Johnson, no 72. Paul's Church Yarf.
Wood, Ellen Meiksins. 1995 [2003]. *Democracy against Capitalism. Renewing Historical Materialism.* Cambridge: Cambridge University Press.

Part 2

Seeding a Politics of Vitality: Countercolonial-Feminist Praxis and the Limits of Justice

Marielle Franco

On March 14, 2018, Marielle Franco was murdered in Rio de Janeiro, together with her driver Anderson Gomes, in a scene of political femicide. While it may seem redundant to specify "political" femicide – since, as explored earlier in this book, femicides are entrenched in political-juridical architecture of violence – here, I refer explicitly to the realm of institutional politics. Marielle was an elected politician, serving in the Legislative Assembly. In 2016, amid the political turmoil of Dilma Rousseff's impeachment, Franco became the fifth most-voted candidate for Rio de Janeiro's city council, serving from 2017 until her tragic death in 2018.

Marielle Franco described herself as a "Black woman, mother, and favelada" (2018, 118). Raised in Complexo da Maré, the largest favela in Rio de Janeiro, she pursued a degree in social sciences at the Pontifical Catholic University of Rio de Janeiro (PUC-Rio), the same university where I later earned my bachelor's degree in law. Notably, Lélia Gonzalez, whose work features prominently throughout this book, served as a professor and head of the Department of Sociology at PUC-Rio until 1994. While our journeys through this institution unfolded at different times and within distinct disciplines, I find it profoundly resonant to reflect on the shared transtemporal space we occupied, even as our subject-positions and experiences remained distinct.

During her mandate, Franco presented 116 proposals and 16 bills, addressing a range of urgent social issues. Among these were initiatives to launch campaigns against sexual harassment and violence on public transportation (PL 417/2017), to designate a "Day of the Fight against Homophobia, Lesbophobia, Biphobia, and Transphobia" in the official calendar (PL 72/2017), to provide free public technical assistance for designing and constructing social housing for low-income families (PL 642/2017), and to establish childcare centers day and night (PL 17/2017), among others (cf. CMRJ 2017; AMAERJ 2018). As the spokesperson for the Women's Committee, she played a crucial role in overseeing efforts to monitor and hold accountable

DOI: 10.4324/9781003474692-4

instances of police and military violence, as well as other abuses of power in Rio de Janeiro.

I vividly remember the moment I first learned of Marielle Franco's death – it felt like a physical blow to my chest, accompanied by a punch to my stomach. I had closely followed her work, particularly her fight against racism, police violence, and militias in Rio de Janeiro, with admiration. Her political femicide affected me emotionally and physically, disrupting my hormonal balance and reverberating through my body like a molecular strike. In search of solace and a way to mourn from faraway, I immersed myself in interviews, protests, and demonstrations, longing to become part of a collective grieving.

Her campaign slogan, "I am because we are," encapsulated the African philosophy of Ubuntu, which emphasizes the deep interconnectedness, mutual dependence, and relational fabric that binds all beings.[1] Franco infused this ethos into her political practices, advocating for a Black feminist governance model grounded in collective and grassroots actions. She pursued her mandate collaboratively, firmly believing that "the (political) mandate of a peripheral, Black, favela woman must be woven together with social movements and organized civil society" (Franco and Fenizola 2020).

The day before her assassination, Marielle posted on Twitter: "Another young man has been killed, potentially by the Military Police. Matheus Melo was leaving church. How many more lives must be lost until this war ends?" (2018b; my translation). The following day, she spoke at an event

1 Ubuntu, a philosophy rooted in the African proverb *umuntu ngumuntu ngabanye bantu* (a person is a person through other people), articulates an ethic of interconnected humanity. Emerging from African communities in what became South Africa, it poses profound questions about ethical relations, particularly in the context of colonialism's dehumanizing legacy. Its global prominence grew under Archbishop Desmond Tutu's leadership of South Africa's Truth and Reconciliation Commission (TRC), where he emphasized Ubuntu's relational ethos while acknowledging the difficulty of translating it into Western frameworks (Gordon 2014; Ramose 2014; Cornell 2014; Cornell and Marle 2015; Tamale 2020; Chigumadzi 2021). Central to Ubuntu is the inseparability of *ukuhlawula* (atonement through reparations) and *ukubuyisa* (restoring relationships), highlighting that forgiveness demands tangible acts of contrition. However, as scholars like Drucilla Cornell (2014) and Panashe Chigumadzi (2021) note, Ubuntu's radical potential has often been undermined in the South African context. The TRC's recommendations for reparations and Tutu's proposal for a wealth tax on White South Africans were ignored, reflecting a broader pattern of commodifying Ubuntu while severing it from its transformative demands for justice (Cornell 2014; Cornell and Marle 2015; Chigumadzi 2021). This erosion of Ubuntu's ethical accountability parallels the dispossession of Black South African peoples from their land. For White South African settlers (*Abelungu*) to become *Abantu* (people of Africa), they must address this historical injustice, beginning with land restitution. Only through *ukubuyisa ngokuhlawula* – restoring relationships through reparations – can a shared future be built, anchored in Ubuntu's principles of justice, mutual recognition, and ethical restoration (cf. Chigumadzi 2021).

titled "Black Female Youth Moving the Structure" (*Jovens Negras Movendo a Estrutura*). As she and her driver, Anderson Gomes, departed the venue, they were brutally assassinated in their car in the heart of Rio de Janeiro. Her haunting question reverberates still: How many more lives must be lost until this war ends?

In the wake of March 14th, 2018, I resolved to pack my belongings and return to Brazil, driven by a need to grieve closer to, listen to, and learn with women active in grassroots movements. My journey began in Rio de Janeiro, my birthplace, continued through Salvador, proceeded to Manaus, and ultimately circled back to Rio.[2] Each of these cities offers a unique lens on the everyday choreographies of survival, mobilization, and collective resistance that strive to transform enduring regimes of violence.

These conversations unfolded during the politically charged lead-up to Brazil's national elections in October, a moment that would culminate in the election of a far-right president. Yet this period was also marked by powerful articulations and fractures, movements explored further in this chapter. Between May and June 2018, as Rio de Janeiro and Salvador weathered their rainy season and Manaus entered the peak of tropical summer, I walked through these cities and encountered not only the intense heat and humidity, especially the Amazonian *mormaço*, but also a profound sense of interpersonal and political warmth. This warmth went beyond the physical, fostering

2 The selection of Rio de Janeiro, Salvador, and Manaus was based on their distinct historical formation and the particular ways grassroots feminisms have been articulated in each city. (i) Rio de Janeiro, the capital of the state of Rio de Janeiro, is located in southeast Brazil. In the 1730s, its port became the primary entry for slavery, receiving two-thirds of all slave ships arriving in Brazil. Remarkably, Rio is the only city in modern history where a monarchy established its empire within a colony. In 1808, fleeing Napoleon's invasion, the Portuguese royal family moved from Lisbon to Rio, transforming it into the center of a pluricontinental Lusitanian Empire. This shift brought Portugal's embassies and consulates to Rio, turning it into a transatlantic hub for European diplomats (Schwarcz 2007, 2012; Miskolci 2013; Campello 2018). Today, it is Brazil's second most populous city, with over seven million residents. (ii) Salvador, the capital of the state of Bahia in northeast Brazil, was the first capital of Brazil, founded in 1549. From 1678 to 1830, Salvador received nearly 30 percent of all slave ships arriving in Brazil. Along with Rio de Janeiro, these two cities accounted for almost one-third of all slave ships coming to the Americas (Florentino, Ribeiro, and Domingues da Silva 2004). Salvador has been central to Afro-diasporic resistance and the formation of Afro-Bahian heritage, expressed through practices such as *Candomblé*, *capoeira*, and culinary traditions like *acarajé* and *abará*. Today, Salvador has the largest Black population in Brazil, making it the city with the largest African-descended population outside of Africa. (iii) Manaus, the capital of the state of Amazonas in north Brazil, is located along the Negro River in the heart of the Amazon rainforest. The city, founded in 1669 as a Portuguese fort to deter Dutch and Spanish expansion, was named after the Indigenous Manaós people. The rubber boom led to significant population growth, making Manaus the seventh-largest city in Brazil. Today, it remains the most populous city in Amazonas, with over two million inhabitants.

a feeling of kinship and mutual care that resonated in the shared spaces and conversations.

As I traveled across Brazil, I engaged in conversations with 35 activists, listening to their life stories, political articulations, and ongoing strategies for resisting and creating other ways of living in this world. The women I met welcomed me into their homes and care spaces, sharing not only their personal histories and political insights but also inviting me into their circles of friendship, activism, and political engagement. They offered sweetened coffee with cake, invited me to join them in *mutirões* (collective initiatives providing community services like feminist legal assistance), *festa junina*, art exhibitions, theater performances, concerts, political events and discussions, and even birthday gatherings. The warmth of these kinships lingers with me.

While some initial and entirely justified questioning of my positionality and research intentions emerged, there was also a shared recognition of the importance of academia – embodied in my role as legal researcher – to listen to their everyday experience and knowledge, a crucial epistemic dimension of their multifaceted struggles. This work aims not merely to document these experiences but to blur the traditional boundaries between empirical engagement and theorization, boundaries that restrict activists to practice while safeguarding academics to theory. I observed that many of these activists are deeply engaged in terminological debates and conceptual choices, entwining their practices with their own modes of theorization – a theme that recurs throughout this chapter.

While most participants identified as feminists, particularly as intersectional or antiracist feminists, the term "feminism" was also occasionally questioned and, at times, rejected for feeling distant from their political lexicon. These tensions surfaced most strongly in discussions where feminism was perceived as Western, mainstream, and liberal – primarily focused on the experiences of White, cisgender, heterosexual women. The struggles and movements these women engage in embody radical and plural approaches to women's struggles and feminisms, as they seek to challenge and dismantle the entangled structures of colonial violence.

The notion of the *encruzilhada* (crossroads) provides a helpful framework for understanding the dynamic movement that arises from interconnected processes, where performative practices, theorizations, and worldviews intersect and collide. As Leda Maria Martins (2003) explains, in Nagô Yoruba philosophy and Bantu cosmologies, the *encruzilhada* is considered a sacred intermediary space that connects different systems and realms of knowledge. It is often depicted as a cosmogram, illustrating a radial space characterized by centering and decentering, intersections and deviations, texts and translations, as well as confluences and alterations. As a result, the idea of a fixed center is dispersed, continuously shifting through acts of improvisation.

At the meeting point of *encruzilhada*, I frame the varied experiences of the women in grassroots movements with whom I engaged as forms of countercolonial-feminist praxis. Aware of the complexities and potential constraints inherent in attempting to collectively name these movements, I emphasize that their life stories, struggles, and positionalities defy any monolithic or essentialized categorization; this term seeks, instead, to honor that multiplicity. Their mobilizations resonate with a countercolonial-feminist framework, converging to confront and unsettle the colonial racial-patriarchal order in all its intricacies. This framework interweaves antiracist, queer, Black, Indigenous, lesbian, bisexual, trans, travesti, non-ableist, class-conscious, and critical feminist movements, amplifying a collective articulation that remains fluid, transformative, and historically entangled.

In the sections that follow, I explore the importance of a cross-disciplinary and critically engaged methodology, conceptualized here as deep listening within multimodal legal ethnography. This approach unfolds into an exploration of political ecologies of the seed (*semente*) and their connections to what I term a *politics of vitality*, rooted in struggles enacted in resistance to, within, and beyond the law. The following section highlights radical legal praxis and generative redress as radical pathways to transformative justice. In the final sections, I address the inherent limitations of representation and engage with countercolonial theories and practices of lawmaking and unmaking.

Legal Ethnography Otherwise: Deep Listening

While decolonial and postcolonial scholarship has extensively examined issues of enunciation and speakability, particularly in the foundational works of Chandra T. Mohanty (1984) and Gayatri C. Spivak (1988), this section shifts the focus to consider the dynamics of listening – especially within legal methodologies, investigations, and research practices. Who has historically been heard in legal discourse? This question has been only tentatively addressed in legal scholarship, where listening is largely relegated to procedural acts in courtrooms, such as bearing witness, testifying, reporting crimes, or conducting interrogations. Traditional legal research typically limits the act of listening to the analysis of authoritative texts (legislation, doctrine, and jurisprudence); when interviews are conducted, the focus is on legal practitioners such as judges, lawyers, and other "experts."

In this book, I advocate for an expansion of the law's "ears" by adopting transdisciplinary approaches that bridge law with multimodal anthropological and sociological methodologies. This shift invites legal scholarship to engage actively with lived experiences and everyday *choreographies of survival* (as conceptualized in Part –1), recognizing these as vital sites for reimagining law. By broadening the scope of legal inquiry, we enrich its potential to comprehend, with embodied sensitivity, the social worlds it seeks to address and redress.

Since the 1970s, U.S. composer and writer Pauline Oliveros has developed practices centered on the concept of "deep listening," which distinguishes the automatic, passive, or involuntary act of hearing from the intentional and attentive act of listening. Deep listening, as Oliveros describes, is a lifelong process that cultivates an embodied perception of sonic environments, encouraging active engagement with both internal and external soundscapes. She explains, "The more I listen the more I learn to listen. Deep Listening involves going below the surface of what is heard" (Oliveros 2005). In this way, listening is a dynamic interplay that transforms both what is heard and the listener themselves – a phenomenon she terms the "listening effect" (Oliveros 2022). This transformative potential is further explored in her concept and book *Quantum Listening*, defined as the simultaneous practice of listening in multiple ways, a method that reshapes perception while being continually shaped by the act of listening itself. Such an approach entails a profound sensitivity to sonic landscapes, enhancing awareness, fostering creative collaboration, and encouraging improvisation (cf. Oliveros 2005; 2022).

Listening, as an intentional act, allows stories and voices to resonate within our bodies and theories, creating a polyphonic and generative dialogue. Grada Kilomba describes listening as "an act of authorization towards the speaker. One can only speak when one's voice is listened to" (2015, 194). However, listening does not necessitate complete comprehension of another's thoughts. Instead, it demands a deliberate effort to engage with both the substance of what is shared and the forms through which it is expressed. In this way, listening becomes a practiced commitment to encountering another's world without seeking mastery or authority over their experience.

In the social sciences, however, listening to and learning from lived experiences is often mediated through methodologies such as interviews, fieldwork, and ethnography. Yet within these scientific frameworks, listening is frequently reduced to a one-directional act. The researcher, cast as a supposedly neutral and objective observer, extracts information from the interviewee, who is treated primarily as a source of "qualitative data." These methods tend to confine listening to the task of validating pre-established research questions or theoretical assumptions, framing it as nothing more than a tool for "data collection." This reductive approach, deeply entrenched within colonial and Whiteness-informed genealogies, left me increasingly unsettled in the process of conducting interviews within the parameters of "scientific" research. I became acutely aware of the discipline's reliance on a narrow methodological lexicon, one that asserts itself as the only legitimate language through which scholarly authority and expertise can be claimed: *a language of the mastery*. Beneath this façade of objectivity lies a deeper discomfort: the paradox of striving to do critical, decolonial, feminist, and antiracist research while still operating within tools historically shaped by the very institutions I sought to question. Tools that privilege detachment over relation and extraction over collaboration, and that continue to uphold knowledge hierarchies rather than foster translocal and generative forms of dialogue.

This entrenched practice of studying "the other" through ethnographic observation traces back to the colonial era, when European travelers documented encounters with the so-called New World. Figures like Arthur de Gobineau, a French aristocrat who journeyed to Brazil and became a leading proponent of scientific racist theories, exemplify this legacy (Gobineau 1967, 1990; Skidmore 1976; Streva 2018). These accounts, historically presented as universal and authoritative, set a precedent for speaking *about* and *on behalf of* others. Within this paradigm, law became a crucial instrument for constructing and sustaining the colonial order (as discussed in previous chapters), while anthropology assumed the role of a voice – indeed, at times, *the voice* – of the colonized. This modern interlocutory role was anything but neutral; it served the material and ideological objectives of Empire, aligning with specific mechanisms of domination designed to appropriate land and resources, essentialize "difference" in colonized territories, and govern the populations subjected to colonial rule (Said 1989; Paine 1989; Smith 1999; A. Simpson 2014).

Drawing on Aimé Césaire's assertion that "colonization = thingification" (1950, 42), colonial practices of commodification also constitute and are constituted by Western scientific disciplines. This book has examined these dynamics in relation to the politics of silencing/speakability, monologic knowledge production, and the epistemic violence of infantilization. In this context, economic, and political regimes of violence operate in conjunction with an epistemic dimension that objectifies and silences countercolonial praxis.

In Brazilian social sciences, Black and Amerindian writers and activists have critically contested these dual processes of silencing and the objectification of their lives as mere subjects of academic inquiry. The social scientist, poet, and politician Guerreiro Ramos (1957) offered a sharp critique of this tendency, denouncing how sociology often reduces Black subjects and movements to static, essentialized "themes" of study. Ramos coined the termed *negro-tema* (Black-theme) to describe how academic frameworks structurally position Black subjects and communities as mere topics or fields of investigation, perpetuating colonial projects of subjugation.

In contrast, Ramos proposed the concept of *negro-vida* (Black-life), a recognition of Black subjects as dynamic agents, actively shaping and engaging with the world in its complexity. His intervention calls for a shift away from objectifying frameworks and toward an acknowledgment of the fullness of life, experience, and creativity that resists reductive categorizations. This critique remains vital today, challenging the epistemic and institutional practices that perpetuate the marginalization of Black and Indigenous epistemologies within academic discourse.

Western social sciences have long operated through what has been termed "epistemic extractivism" (Cusicanqui 2010; Grosfoguel 2016; Mombaça 2021a) – a concept reflecting the extractive logic of colonial resources exploitation, now applied to academic research practices. The epistemic extractivism disregards the theoretical frameworks, contexts, and lived experiences through which racialized subject-positions and subjugated groups, create their own knowledge and ways of theorizing the world; because "when we theorize, we make a claim in and about the world" (McGranahan 2022). Sandra Muñoz, a Black queer[3] feminist activist from Salvador and one of my interlocutors, powerfully critiques this extractivist approach in interviews with activists, asking me: "Who are these women speaking in our name at the City Council, writing books about us? They come here, take our stories, write a book, and don't even come back to say, 'Hey, I'm talking about you,' you know?" (2018).

Taking these critiques seriously, and with the full consent of my interlocutors to use their names openly, this work challenges the conventional practices in the social sciences of anonymizing or assigning pseudonyms to participants, which are often framed as measures of protection. Intellectual authorship holds immense value within academia, where scholars are routinely cited for their ideas. However, this purported dialogical collaboration often falters when it comes to oral exchanges with interlocutors perceived as non-academics. In such instances, there exists a pervasive tendency to anonymize, alter, or even omit their names, despite their explicit consent to be publicly acknowledged. This practice perpetuates the detrimental binary between theory and ethnography, whereby academics are recognized as legitimate producers of knowledge, while activists or marginalized subjects are reduced to mere empirical data. Geopolitically speaking, theory has been historically located within the knowledge produced in the so-called global North, while ethnographic realities have been reduced to case studies and empirics often located in the global South. While frequently justified under the guise of protective ethics, I argue that such measures can also serve as a paternalistic means of erasing the vital contributions of those involved in knowledge production.

The decision to omit names in collaborative scholarship underscores a disparity: the designation of someone as an "author" or an "activist" often determines whether they receive credit for their contributions. U.S. cultural

3 Sandra Muñoz has described herself using the slang term *viada*, the feminine form of *viado*. Originally meaning "deer," *viado* has historically been used in Brazil to refer to gay men. Here, Muñoz queers the term to situate herself as a nonnormative subject, as a dissent body.

anthropologist Erica Weiss provocatively asks, "What happens when we choose to see these two practices as a unified system of citation and anti-citation, of contextualization and misdirection, and perhaps even of attribution and appropriation?" (2021). The "politics of anti-citation," as Weiss terms it, perpetuates infantilizing and extractivist dynamics, a critique examined in earlier chapters.

British-Australian feminist writer and activist Sara Ahmed reminds us that "citation is how we acknowledge our debt to those who came before; those who helped us find our way when the way was obscured because we deviated from the paths we were told to follow" (2017, 17). Citation, in this sense, is not merely an academic convention but an ethical practice of recognizing intellectual and epistemic labor. Canadian scholar of Black studies Katherine McKittrick echoes this sentiment, arguing that a thoughtful citation practice "asks that we think about the epistemological grounds through which we theorize and imagine and name liberation in our referencing practices" (2021, 27).

For McKittrick, citation is not about mastering knowledge or consolidating intellectual authority but about sharing how we come to know. She writes,

> This cites and sites a genre of humanness that emerged from but is not solely defined by plantocratic logics of dispossession: the works cited, what we tell each other about what we know and how to know, contain *how to* refuse practices of dehumanization.
>
> (2021, 27–28)

Thus, the citation project embraced here goes beyond acknowledgment; it fosters an exchange of thoughts and ideas that nourish a terrain of struggle. It creates space to imagine alternative futures, resisting dehumanization and advancing liberation through collective intellectual and creative engagement.

Subject-positions marginalized within Racial and Gendering ontologies of difference are often spoken about rather than engaged with – what Trinh Minh-Ha incisively terms "scientific gossip" (1989, 68). Such a mode of discourse enforces a semantic distance between the writer and their research subjects, thereby securing a position of mastery for the speaker. This practice facilitates the speaker's ability to "appropriate, own, and demarcate" (Trinh 1991, 12) their sovereign intellectual territory, while relegating the "other" to a mere object of investigation or extraction. In academic discourse, the ethics of citation demand acknowledgment of those whose insights shape our work.

In theorizing from a place of dialogue and understanding ethnography as a grounded theory, I frame my interlocutors as theory-makers, referring to them in the same manner as authored scholarship – citing their full names, in keeping with Lélia Gonzalez's emphasis that Black subjects be referred to by both first and last names (apud Bairros 1999). This engaged stance, as the anthropologist Sophie Chao points out, "recognizes the complex, transforming, and praxis-based interpretive frameworks through which our interlocutors, as active knowledge producers, understand, explain, and evaluate the nature of, and relationship between, local realities and global forces" (2023).

Since the 1980s, feminist, queer, and critical Black studies have consistently challenged the academic assumption that theory is objective, abstract, and universally authored by disembodied voices (cf. J. Acker, K. Barry, and J. Esseveld 1982; Gonzalez 1983; Haraway 1988; Harding 1993; Mombaça 2021c). Rather than dismissing the importance of theorization, my aim is to ask: How can we theorize otherwise? How can the practice of listening cultivate a polyphonic mode of writing that neither speaks *for* nor *about* others? This reimagining begins with recognizing theorization as an intrinsically collective and relational endeavor in knowledge production.

In *Interviewing Women: A Contradiction in Terms* (1981), Ann Oakley critiques traditional social science interviewing through her experience interviewing women, arguing that the researcher cannot stand outside the research process but is, rather, a woman engaging with other women. Oakley offers three pivotal feminist shifts to the masculinized methodology of social science interviews. First, she urges a departure from extractivist approaches that reduce interviewees to mere data sources, instead advocating a more attuned, relational engagement. This transformation redefines the interviewer's role "from being a data-collecting instrument for researchers to being a data-collecting instrument for those whose lives are being researched" (1981, 48–49). Second, she highlights the role of interviews in amplifying women's conditions in the world as we know it, considering relevant the documentation of narratives historically relegated to the margins. Last, Oakley stresses the importance of considering the interviewee's perspective during the interview process. Instead of mechanically adhering to a predetermined list of questions, she proposes that interviewers should listen to the issues and questions that matter to the interviewee. This approach fundamentally shifts the interview format from a monological and unilateral question-answer to a dialogical interaction.

From a critical Black and feminist perspective, Lélia Gonzalez (1983) underscores how one's positionality profoundly shapes interpretations of racism and sexism, while denouncing the persistent objectification and infantilization of Black subjects by White academia. Similarly, Patricia Hill Collins (1986) explores the distinctive standpoint of the "outsider within," particularly relevant when Black women research and articulate their own experiences. This outsider status, Collins argues, provides a space for self-definition and self-valuation, essential for Black women's survival. She observes, "Black female experience has been spent coping with, avoiding, subverting, and challenging the workings of . . . white male insiderism" (1986, 26). Later, Donna Haraway (1988) popularizes the concept of positionality and standpoint theory, highlighting that all knowledge is inherently situated.

Outside the realm of academia, the historical and enduring structural barriers to voice and self-representation resonate deeply, as recounted by nearly every activist woman with whom I engaged. Perpétua Suni Kokama, also known as Perpétua Cerqueira, an Indigenous ciswoman activist from the Yukaka community in the Amazon, shared with me her struggle against entrenched gendered silencing:

> It was always the men who spoke, right? I grew up with the custom of staying silent. At meetings, we would only see husbands, fathers, and brothers speaking . . . not the women. Women are always in the kitchen, taking care of things. (2018)

Reflecting on her journey into grassroots activism, Cerqueira emphasized the ongoing efforts to establish an Indigenous section within her political party, underscoring the transformative power of articulating one's own positionality: "I speak because I live it" (2018).

Multimodal methods in legal anthropology foster a space for experimentation and creative scholarship, in which I position *choreography* as a practice-centered way to understand the body as a site of knowledge. Historically marginalized within Western discourse, the body has often been overshadowed by abstract, universalist ideals epitomized by the White male figure. When nonnormative bodies enter the politics of speakability, particularly in activist, political, and academic spaces, their marginalization becomes central. As Guarani Indigenous leader, activist, and researcher Sandra Benites (2018) told me, the Western education system "doesn't have much of a dialogue with these different bodies, which are several bodies, different bodies that have another way of seeing the world, or even another way of positioning themselves." She recalls the disorientation she felt upon moving from the Guarani Nhandewa community to Rio de Janeiro, where academic discussions on rights lacked resonance with her embodied experience: "I don't find myself in this place . . . it feels like I'm without a body . . . as if we were not productive, as if our bodies were machines." Reflecting on her grandmother's teachings on caring for the female body and health, especially during menstruation, she recalls, "In her own way, my grandmother was a feminist. She always said that Guarani Indigenous women have a voice, a voice within the community" (2018).

Here, the counterpart of listening entails attentive engagement with a rich tapestry of polyphonic sounds, images, gestures, silences, and memories, considered in their complexity and entanglements. It requires that we view the body not merely as a site of representation but as the locus where knowledge is inscribed – transmitted through gestures, movements, choreographies, and soundscapes (Fanon 1952; B. Nascimento 1989; Martins 1997). Beatriz Nascimento profoundly observed, "Memory is the content of a continent, of its life, history, and past. As if the body were the document" (1989, 333).

This work moves beyond the conventional primacy of the visible and observable that has long defined the ethnographic gaze. Instead, it adopts a multimodal and embodied approach to legal anthropology, one that engages with the incommensurability among text, sound, and image – a perspective introduced earlier in the *mathematics of violence* and through the metaphor of the *front door* (Part –1). By challenging entrenched academic hierarchies that privilege text-centric traditions as the ultimate markers of epistemic authority in law and anthropology, this approach reimagines the possibilities of knowledge production. It foregrounds a more-than-textual mediation of sensorial experiences, choreographies involving images, movements, words, and sounds, culminating in the experimental documentary *Women in Movement* (2020), with further details provided at the end of this book.

In practice, my research eschewed rigid, detached questionnaires in favor of adaptable, sensitive methods that respected my interlocutors' availability, perspectives, life paths, geographical contexts, and expectations. Recorded dialogues began with an open invitation for participants to introduce themselves, sharing personal stories, including their paths into activism and grassroots movements. None responded in distant or abbreviated terms. Instead, they granted me the privilege of listening to the vast scope of their storytelling, encompassing lived memories, acts of world-making, ongoing struggles, and visions of futures yet to come. As Trinh reminds us, "The more ears I am able to hear with, the farther I see the plurality of meaning and the less I lend myself to the illusion of a single message" (1989, 49).

Unrecorded conversations unfolded organically, typically commencing with informal greetings upon my arrival at each meeting point. After introducing myself, I was often asked about my research project. In these moments, I aimed to articulate my research concerns, emphasizing the dialogical nature of our interaction and inviting participants to pose questions freely. It was at this juncture that I sensed my interlocutors would either embrace or refuse to engage in dialogue. This refusal is particularly significant as a methodological concern, as it reflects what the anthropologist Audra Simpson terms "sovereignty" and "jurisdictional authority," encapsulating "the right to speak and, in this case, to not speak" (2014, 104–105).[4] Fortunately, they generally welcomed the conversation, guiding it in ways that best served their interests and priorities.

4 Leanne Betasamosake Simpson (2014) acknowledges that sovereignty, as conceived within Western frameworks, is often seen as an inherently "inappropriate concept," a critique rooted in Gerald (Taiaiake) Alfred's argument that it is grounded in singular authority, Western domination, and imperialism, and is foreign to Haudenosaunee and other Indigenous philosophical traditions. However, Simpson also contends that sovereignty remains a critical term within the context of settler colonialism, a persistent structure of Indigenous dispossession and the denial of that dispossession. In this context, sovereignty becomes a language capable of conveying essential processes and intentions in ways that others can understand. Her analysis thus addresses both the juridical and textual dimensions of sovereignty, linking jurisdiction over texts with the act of writing – or, more precisely, with the imperative to write in particular ways. For this reason, Simpson asserts that sovereignty still matters, but in ways that give rise to alternative ethnographic forms, particularly one of refusal.

Despite framing our interactions relationally, there were moments when I felt less like an interviewer – a position I deliberately sought to avoid – and more like a psychoanalyst, a role I had not intended to assume. This sensation gave rise to two distinct impressions. On one hand, I recognized the emotional labor and political significance of listening, a process I actively engaged in alongside my interlocutors, whose expressions also carried healing and therapeutic dimensions. On the other hand, the psychoanalytical role felt both appropriate and misaligned, as I was an active participant in the dialogue. I explicitly invited my interlocutors to ask personal and political questions to me whenever they wished, establishing a relational dynamic that diverged from the "blank screen" traditionally associated with psychoanalysis. I sensed that, at times, they refrained from posing questions, while at other moments, they probed my views on contentious issues in Brazil – such as political affiliations, racial quotas, and social privilege – as well as more personal inquiries into my subject-position, sexual orientation, and activist commitments. In this context, I endeavored to prioritize their voices and concerns, not as a psychoanalyst, but as a listening-sharing researcher.

The issue of speakability, particularly for Indigenous women who have migrated from rural communities to urban settings, is intricately tied to the structural barriers to accessing education in the nation's official language, Brazilian Portuguese. Sandra Benites (2018), a native Guarani speaker, did not begin learning Portuguese until she was 27, a consequence of inadequate public education policies and the precarious infrastructure available to her community. Her work as a translator and her research in Indigenous school education involve navigating what she refers to as the "language of the White," a struggle echoed by numerous Indigenous activists I encountered. This multifaceted experience is examined further in this chapter.

The importance of listening to and resonating with one's voice is powerfully illustrated by Lívia da Silva, activist from Rede Sapatá in Salvador, who described to me the transformative moment of speaking publicly for the first time: "The microphone is power, isn't it? . . . For me, a Black lesbian woman in my late 30s, nearly 40, finally having the chance to speak up – it was magnificent! It truly changed my life" (2018). Her words capture the profound impact of being granted a platform in public political spaces.

Beyond the epistemic and ontological dimensions of listening, Maria Alice Paulino, an Indigenous ciswoman activist and leader from the Karapãna community, shared with me the emotional and political significance of being heard. She explained,

> Sometimes we feel unseen or unheard, but when people like you come from far away to listen to our stories, it gives us renewed motivation to continue the struggle. It reinforces that our fight is meaningful, both as women and as mothers. This is truly gratifying; it helps us feel less alone and undervalued.
>
> (2018)

This book then reimagines legal anthropology through sensorial, attentive, and intentional research practices inspired by Black and Indigenous studies (Smith 1999; Moten 2003; Ferreira da Silva 2013; A. Simpson 2014; Hartman 2019) and multimodal anthropology (Gerald, Collins, and Gill 2017; Westmoreland 2022). Within this framework, I frame my encounters as "conversations" rather than "interviews," emphasizing their inherently dialogical nature. Thus, my approach to legal anthropology seeks to engage both the tensions and the anticolonial possibilities inherent in critical ethnography. This involves expanding the practice of deep listening beyond the formal boundaries of courtrooms and institutionalized legal practices. By doing so, it reframes legal inquiry as a relational and dynamic process, attentive not only to official discourses but also to the choreographies of survival that challenge colonial frameworks of law and justice.

Seeding: Politics of Vitality

Many activists, particularly Black women who were running for local office, invoked Marielle Franco as a source of inspiration, as a seed, emphasizing the imperative to continue her radical legacy. Black feminists have embraced the imagery of the seed as a potent symbol, both mourning Franco's loss and celebrating her life. In this section, I expand on the notion of the seed as an agropoetic ground for collective movements that challenge the necropolitical regime by reimagining politics through the lens of vitality.

Amidst the entwined histories of femicide, ecocide, and genocide manifested in the plantation and the afterlives of slavery, the seed emerges as a potent framework for reimagining the im/possibilities of the neocolonial present and future. Departing from catastrophic narratives, the seed offers a paradigm shift toward insurgent practices and radical imaginations cultivated through countercolonial feminist ecologies. It embodies diasporic, migratory, and interspecies entanglements that disrupt colonial grounds and geographies, opening to envision life and politics otherwise. As the Brazilian artist and writer Jota Mombaça, who identifies as a nonbinary travesti of color, points out, "They've torn us apart, because they don't know that once we're in pieces, we'll spread out" (2021f, 28).

As Brazilian Black feminist physician and writer Jurema Werneck (2005) explains, the concept of *ialodê* refers to the ancestral organization of Afro-diasporic women, whose legacies resonate across generations. This enduring journey is embodied in the phrase, "our steps come from far away" (2010), situating contemporary struggles within a vast historical continuum. Figures like Dandara dos Palmares, Luiza Mahin, Aqualtune, Anastásia, Esperança Garcia, Maria Felipa de Oliveira, Tia Ciata, Tereza de Benguela, Tia Simoa, Maria Firmina dos Reis, Antonieta de Barros, Laudelina de Campos Melo, Virginia Leone Bicudo, Carolina Maria de Jesus, Lélia Gonzalez, Beatriz Nascimento, Luiza Bairros, alongside countless unnamed and unrecorded ancestors, have laid the groundwork for resistance and social transformation in Brazil. Similarly, Indigenous cosmologies underscore the collective act of walking together, learning from elders, grandmothers, and ancestors, human and more-than-human, emphasizing an intergenerational, relational ethos (Benites 2018; Paulino 2018; Galvão 2018; Núñez, Oliveira, and Lago 2021; Tupinambá 2022).

This enduring continuity of collective resistance, documented and undocumented, situates ancestrally as a rhizomatic interweaving of past, present, and future. Roberta de Pádua, a Black transwoman designer and activist with the Madame Satã Collective in Rio de Janeiro, shared with me the importance of remembering that her "ancestors fought with their lives and freedom" for her to be here. Drawing from this legacy, she envisions her own project of documenting her lived experiences as a generative act: "to compose a record, so that in the future, people like me will have something to build on; a dialogue that already exists, so they won't have to justify their existence as much as I do in my daily life" (2018). Through her words and work, de Pádua bridges the struggles of the past with the possibilities of the future, crafting a space where resilience and continuity thrive.

The political femicide of Marielle Franco catalyzed a powerful response: her legacy became a seed, continually cultivated, spread, and germinated within bodies and territories. This organic grounding ensured the enduring growth of her legacy, impervious to uprooting or interruption. Through the interconnection of living and nonliving entities, the seed symbolizes how Black feminists, alongside Indigenous, and queer women activists, transformed their anger (Lorde 1981) into a potent force of struggle, shifting from grief (*luto*) to struggle (*luta*).

A politics of vitality must not be conflated with biopolitics. As I have argued in earlier works (Streva 2016, 2017, 2018), Michel Foucault's concept of biopolitics (1975, 2008) pertains to the macropower of governmentality, which manages life through the interweaving of sovereign, disciplinary, and biopolitical mechanisms. Unlike the regulation of populations and the global processes through which power subjugates life, a politics of vitality arises from the grounded, everyday *choreographies of survival* – embodied in acts of kinship, mutual care, and political mobilization. These micropolitical rehearsals and enactments disrupt, refuse, and disorder the colonial architectures underlying modern law and democracy. The metaphor of the seed captures these insurgent practices, emphasizing the cultivation of future possibilities through quotidian action rather than reliance on the perpetually deferred promises of liberal ideologies.

Resisting the persistent romanticization of their struggles, these choreographies of resistance and refusal directly confront the "superwoman" trope, that is, a dehumanizing construct frequently imposed on Black women, portraying them as unyielding warriors, inherently strong. Scholars such as Michele Wallace (1978), Grada Kilomba (2008), and Jurema Werneck (2010) have critically interrogated this myth, which serves to deny their humanity by framing the ongoing trauma of colonialism and precarity as a form of innate resilience. This trope functions as a contemporary iteration of the un/gendering mechanisms of colonial slavery, as discussed earlier in this book (Part 0). The persistence of this dehumanizing legacy is reflected in numerous institutional and interpersonal omissions, which have direct consequences for Black women's health and well-being. These include the exacerbation of mental health challenges such as anxiety and depression, the rise of physical conditions like diabetes and hypertension, and the systematic reduction of pain management, such as anesthesia, in healthcare settings (Leal et al. 2017; Ribeiro 2020; Padro 2021).

Listening to Joyce Gomes, an Afro-Indigenous transwoman activist with the ASSOTRAM (Travestis, Transsexuals, and Transgenders Association of the State of Amazonas), the myth of inherent strength is vividly captured:

> The truth is, I'm not strong. Often, all we want is . . . to escape from all of this. But if we retreat, we remain invisible in these [public] spaces, and they will continue to proclaim, "she is the first transsexual . . ., she is still the first. . . ." Do you see? We find strength where we don't have it.
>
> (2018)

Her words reveal the exhausting labor of navigating public spaces that both demand and impose resilience, exposing the paradox of being celebrated as a trailblazer while being denied the space to express exhaustion. This relentless expectation of strength underscores the ways in which the trope of the "superwoman" continues to erase the complexities of Black women's lived realities.

A pervasive sense of exhaustion was palpable among both older and younger women activists I spoke with, highlighting the relentless demands placed on Black and Indigenous women. Edna Pinho Oliveira, a Black feminist from the *Mulheres do Subúrbio Ginga* movement, conveyed the weight of this responsibility: "Comrade, we Black women are always carrying a very heavy burden. It's heavy because it's not just about your own problems, but also the problems of other Black women who sometimes see no way forward." She continued, "The work in the periphery [of Salvador] is relentless; when your neighbor runs out of gas, she knocks on your door. . . . Here, social relations are understood differently [from the center]" (2018).

Larissa Guedes Menezes, a young ciswoman activist and lawyer also based in Salvador, echoed this sentiment, describing the social treatment of Black women as an inhuman condition: "I remind myself, I'm not alone here. I'm carrying my ancestors. I'm carrying all the women who empower me daily. And, most importantly, I'm carrying the women who couldn't be here because they are already gone" (2018). These testimonies reflect the emotional and collective burden embodied and carried across generations, revealing the intersectional weight of personal and communal struggle shouldered by Black, Indigenous, and queer women in their ongoing resistance.

In this context, the tactic of *seeding the struggle* is a vital mechanism to foster, nourish, and propagate collective action aimed at both survival and radical transformation. This approach gains urgency in the face of entrenched structural violence and the glaring inadequacies of public policy. Grassroots activism becomes an existential assertion of vital force, countering the persistent legacies of neocolonial exhaustion, precarity, and femicide. As Joyce Gomes reflected, "One of the reasons I decided to join a social movement was that, even though many things are denied to us [Black and Indigenous transwomen], at least in the association, we can count on each other" (2018).

Similarly, Edna Pinho Oliveira described the rented space of the Ginga movement as "a space that welcomes (*acolhe*) women who have a lot to say." This space goes beyond the conventional bounds of political activism, encompassing childcare, policy monitoring, professional workshops, and, crucially, emotional support. Through attentive listening and open dialogue, the movement provides a refuge for women grappling with despair.

> Sometimes they're sad, devastated, they don't want to be at home, so they come here to vent and open their hearts. . . . Afterward, they feel calmer, they leave with a new perspective, a different outlook, because we talk. It helps, doesn't it?
>
> (2018)

These movements forge what might be described as im/possible grounds for kinship – spaces where mutual support and collective resistance push back against neocolonial forms of dehumanization.

The concept of "grassroots" merges the imagery of "grass" – a living, dynamic covering of the land – and "roots," the vital channels that draw sustenance from the soil. Grassroots movements thus evoke a subterranean vitality, symbolizing capacities for germination, nourishment, and renewal that arise from below to challenge and reshape systems of dispossession, dehumanization, and erasure. In Portuguese, such movements are referred to as *movimentos de base* (base movements), emphasizing their foundational role in mobilization, emerging from the depths of colonial and neocolonial legal, socioeconomic, and political structures.

The politics of vitality draws deeply on the principles of vital force and Axé. Beatriz Nascimento links these concepts to the radical principle of *ntu*, originating in the Bantu linguistic tradition. In contrast to the Euro-modern Hegelian dialectic, *ntu* articulates a relational dynamic between the self and the other that does not rely on binary logics; a process of *being-with* rather than *being-for* the other (Nascimento 1992; Fanon 1952; Eze 2017). On a personal life-note, Nascimento's intellectual, activist, and artistic journey was tragically interrupted by femicide in 1995 (Torres 1995; Streva 2021b), a loss that underscores the urgent stakes of the struggle she theorized and embodied.

As Manuelita Carolina Machado, a feminist activist from the *Novas Felipas* movement on Itaparica Island in Bahia, articulates with me: "We are dying every day. Our death is real, it is visible" (2018). Her invocation of the plural conveys the shared and cumulative nature of violence endured by women and feminized bodies, resonating with the relational ethos of *ntu*, where the self is inextricably connected to others. Similarly, Lívia Ferreira da Silva (2018) and Laina Crisóstomo Queiroz (2018), an intersectional feminist activist, lawyer, and founder of the organization *Tamojuntas*, similarly emphasize the deeply interconnected nature of their activism, highlighting the profound toll of femicide on both individual bodies and their broader communities. In Lívia da Silva's words: "We have achieved many things, but what is happening now are the [violent] deaths. . . . Every day, one of us is dying [through murder]. . . . Every time one of us dies, it kills me too" (2018).

This concept of *being-with*, grounded in *ntu*, resonates with the metaphor of the seed, a powerful symbol of life's interconnectedness and persistence. The seed encapsulates earthy, organic forces, embodying processes of metamorphosis, regeneration, and endurance. It carries within it the potential for growth, pushing through the soil, intertwining with minerals and roots, and contributing to the revitalization of landscapes, ecosystems, and territories. In its movement, the seed has the capacity to disrupt and transform the cemented structures imposed by colonial racial-patriarchal order. The transformative potential of the seed, intertwined with the grassroots politics of vitality resonates with Sandra Benites's (2018) insight, drawing from a Guarani cosmological perspective: "our body is the very territory. We are the foundation; we are the ground. When women transform themselves, necessarily, the world is transformed." This perspective underscores the profound link between individual and collective transformation, where the body and land are inseparable sites of resistance and regeneration.

Within this agropoetic framework, environmental conditions and soil composition are vital factors influencing the seed's capacity to germinate and thrive. Still with the words shared with me by Benites reflecting on the challenges faced by a non-Indigenous woman juggling precarious informal work and raising a child in an urban context, illustrates this dynamic:

> The tendency is for [the stress] to spread to the environment she's in, but it's not her fault. It's the fault of not being able to rest, of all these things we carry, this violence we endure day in and day out, you know?"
>
> (2018)

Under favorable conditions, the seed's roots stretch out, channeling energy and nutrients through the Earth while forming dynamic relationships with other roots, plants, and entities – living and nonliving – within a multispecies ecosystem. This intricate web of interdependence fosters mutual growth and resilience, embodying a form of grassroots kinship in which every element contributes to and sustains the whole. In refusing the body-machine imposed by the landscapes of poverty, exhaustion, White supremacy and racial capitalism, recognizing the right to rest becomes a vital act of resistance (Benites 2018; Gomes 2018; cf. Hersey 2022).

Roberta de Pádua offers an inter-relational perspective on grassroots kinship: "I was not only welcomed [by the social movement], but I also opened myself up to welcome them and to build some dialogue together. Understanding myself beyond any gender, as a human being" (2018). Her reflection underscores the transformative power of mutual engagement in dismantling colonial structures of identity and belonging.

This politics of vitality is embodied, choreographed, and sustained by women across the country who cultivate countercolonial feminist kinships – inherently antiracist and queer. Building grassroots networks becomes a vital process of generating possibilities of response to the enduring of colonial architectures of dispossession, exhaustion, and violence. Through the creation of collective spaces for healing and care, these activist movements reimagine the meaning of joy in togetherness, striving not merely for survival in the face of violence but also for the pursuit of a life lived well, rooted in solidarity and mutual flourishing.

Radical Legal Praxis and the Limits of Justice

To bring legal theory and practice in conversation with Indigenous and Black onto-epistemologies, alongside countercolonial and feminist praxis, reveals profound tensions and contradictions, while simultaneously opening pathways for transformative reimaginings. Law, in conjunction with the structures of social-scientific knowledge, has played a central role in constructing and legitimating colonial landscapes of violence. Within Western paradigms, law remains bound to colonial legacies of dispossession, as discussed in previous chapters (Part 0 and Part 1).

This section engages with profound insights drawn from grassroots mobilizations, emphasizing the transformative potential of radical legal praxis. The term "radical," rooted in its etymological origin meaning "the root," is invoked here to signify lessons emerging directly from the lived experiences and strategies of grassroots movements. These countercolonial feminist mobilizations have consistently contested, resisted, and reimagined legal practices, exposing and challenging their colonial foundations while envisioning alternative frameworks of justice. Through their efforts, they offer a critique of existing redressive mechanisms, particularly in addressing and redressing the persistent violence embedded in the politics of femicide.

Before exploring the tactics and choreographies of legal dispute, it is helpful to first situate the conventional framework of modern legal systems.

Typically, the judicial system is seen as the realm where subjects of rights, whether natural or legal, interact with the state's authority and sovereignty to resolve conflicts and pursue justice. This authority is primarily represented by the figure of the judge, who is expected to adjudicate disputes impartially, with competence and objectivity, by applying the open texture of legal texts to individual cases and shaping jurisprudence accordingly. In instances of gender-based violence, the administration of justice, overseen by the judiciary, operates through a binary distinction between individuated "victim" and "perpetrator," relying heavily on punitive or retributive measures as the main means of social remedy. The legal order is constructed as the domain of safety and security, upheld by criminal law, police forces, and the carceral system. By asserting a monopoly on violence and invoking the imperative of safety, the neocolonial state fabricates an illusion of protection, based on the presumed legitimacy of police force and mass incarceration. While these narratives claim to secure a safer future, they ultimately sustain and reproduce existing power dynamics, as unpacked in Part 1 of this book.

Reparative justice remains a relatively marginal concept within European and neocolonial justice traditions. However, since the latter part of the twentieth century, alternative visions for justice have gained prominence, particularly concerning the relationship between individuals and the state. These approaches, often framed as restorative and transitional justice, mark a departure from retributive and punitive models, focusing instead on remedies that address the broader social contexts of harm. As Nigerian criminologist Biko Agozino explains, "Reparative justice differs from punitive justice by seeking how to address the wrongs done to the victimized instead of being obsessed with how to punish the offenders" (2021, 614).

In the 1990s, in the wake of post-dictatorship transitions and the broader re-democratization processes across South America, transitional justice emerged as a focal point of political and social efforts. In Brazil, Truth Commissions and Amnesty Commissions became key mechanisms investigating, documenting, and addressing institutional violence such as forced disappearances, torture, and other forms of atrocities perpetrated during the dictatorship (1964–1985). Grounded in the principles of "memory, truth, and justice," these initiatives marked a slow and gradual movement toward rebuilding democracy.

These initiatives were not spontaneously conceived but were the result of persistent advocacy by survivors and the families of those forcibly disappeared or killed by state institutions. This collective mobilization involved prolonged legal struggles, the submission of meticulously documented cases, and the preparation of human rights reports. While these dimensions will not be analyzed in detail here, as they fall outside the primary focus of this section, they underscore the extensive efforts underpinning the emergence of transitional justice in Brazil.[5] Through such initiatives, transitional justice offers an alternative vision of justice – one that foregrounds accountability, centers the voices of survivors, and seeks to repair the social fabric torn apart by state violence. This approach prioritizes community restoration and reconciliation over merely individualized punitive measures, challenging conventional retributive paradigms and advocating for a justice that acknowledges and redresses deep historical wounds.

Different from liberal reparations, the concept of redress, as adopted here, draws on Saidiya Hartman's framework (1997), which argues that efforts to address and repair the historical traumas of colonial slavery are, by necessity, always incomplete due to the enduring depth of the colonial wound. While redressive actions cannot fully restore what has been fractured, they can create pathways for a process of "re-membering" the social body, aiming to soothe the scars inflicted by repeated cycles of violence.

Building upon the critique of liberal rights discourse analyzed in previous chapters, this section now asks: What might justice become in the afterlives of slavery and within neocolonial systems that proclaim ideals of equality and liberty for all? How radical can legal praxis be in addressing and redressing the pervasive violence that structures gendered and racialized politics of femicide? These inquiries urge us to move beyond conventional frameworks, inviting us to experiment with and rehearse the transformative potential embedded in reimagining justice radically, from the ground up.

These reflections unfold through conversations with women in grassroots movements, whose persistent efforts endure despite the political-juridical architecture of femicide. In confronting such scenes of violence, we are urged to seed grounding questions: What is justice, what does it produce, whom does it fail, where does it operate, what might it yet become? (Tuck and Yang 2016). This section, then, considers how grassroots mobilizations have reclaimed justice on their own terms, reinterpreting it as both a practice and a horizon. The act of reclaiming justice embodies not only aspirations but also the disappointments tied to a concept often hollowed out by the false promises of state protection. It is a force that navigates the diverse and unpredictable paths people take, moving toward and beyond the limitations of institutional frameworks.

Reporting: Speaking and Being Heard

After experiencing gender-based violence and navigating the complexities of silencing/speakability (as discussed in Part –1 and Part 1), many women face the daunting decision of whether to report a crime to the police. Legally,

5 For more information, see Alvarez (1990); Inter-American Court of Human Rights – IACourtHR 2010; BRASIL. Comissão Nacional da Verdade 2014b, 2014a; and Teles (2015).

this process is supposed to involve being heard by a trained professional, receiving protection and psychological care, and ensuring that the perpetrator is held accountable under the law. In practice, however, the experience often diverges sharply from this ideal. One of the primary obstacles shared by the women I spoke with in attempting to report gender-based violence is the limited access to Women's Police Stations, which is hindered not only by physical distance but also by inadequate infrastructure and untrained officers. These stations are scarce, often located far from the communities they serve, and women are frequently met with resistance from male officers who discourage or even refuse to report their complaints.

The establishment of the first *Delegacia Especializada de Atendimento à Mulher* (DEAM) in 1985 was not a direct consequence of feminist demands. Nonetheless, it emerged amidst an era of heightened feminist discourse and debate concerning women's roles within state institutions. Feminist and women's groups confronted the intricate challenge of addressing violence against women, frequently questioning whether engagement in policymaking processes could yield transformative results. These debates unfolded against a backdrop of widespread mistrust in the police, particularly during Brazil's political transition, when law enforcement remained deeply associated with the repressive practices of the preceding authoritarian regime (Pasinato and MacDowell Santos 2008).

Despite these tensions and prevailing skepticism toward police institutions, the creation of the first women's police station met little overt opposition. Women's organizations across Brazil actively advocated for similar institutions in other states, yet many state governments resisted, often failing to allocate resources or implement gender-sensitive training within police forces. Over time, however, the DEAM became a cornerstone of public policy for supporting women subjected to violence. Its institutionalization reveals a complex interplay between feminist activism and state structures, illustrating how grassroots movements influenced policy despite systemic inertia and institutional constraints (Pasinato and MacDowell Santos 2008; cf. Observatório da Mulher Contra a Violência 2018; Pasinato 2017; Macdowell Santos and Pasinato 2005).

More than 30 years after these policies were introduced, the outcomes have fallen significantly short of their intended goals. In a country with over two-hundred million people, with an area spanning more than 8.5 million square kilometers, fewer than 10 percent of municipalities have a DEAM. For instance, in Roraima, a state with a population of 605,761 and a femicide rate higher than the national average, there is only one specialized police station serving the entire state (Senado 2013). In this context, activists have highlighted that accessing a DEAM can be an arduous and costly process, often physically, emotionally, and financially draining. Many survivors struggle to afford the bus fare, prompting activists to assist with transportation costs and provide emotional support by accompanying them (Muñoz 2018; Oliveira 2018; Crisóstomo 2018).

Carolina Machado recalls the experience of women on Itaparica Island who attempted to report violence at their local police station were often dismissed by officers who claimed that "This isn't the place for that. You need to go to Salvador," redirecting them to another city in Bahia. Many women were misled by this information and only the distant Women's Police Stations could register such complaints. In response, these activists have made persistent efforts, including filing complaints with the police commissioner and closely monitoring police conduct, challenging the ongoing circle of violence. As Machado stated: "We women have to solve our own problems because we are dying every day!" (2018).

Upon arrival at Women's Police Stations, women often encounter facilities that are dilapidated, neglected, and in disrepair. Beyond the absence of material resources and inadequate infrastructure, DEAMs are chronically understaffed and ill-equipped to address cases of gender-based violence with the necessary sensitivity and competence (Senado 2013). Even within these so-called gender specialized units, women are predominantly assigned to administrative roles rather than taking on the operational functions required to address such violence (IBGE 2018). As a result, these stations remain entrenched in the colonial racial-patriarchal order that continues to shape their operations. The in/justice system, in turn, perpetuates violence by reinforcing public justifications for its normalization and by shifting the responsibility for the violence onto the women who experience it.

The vital importance of being heard by a well-trained professional who understands and respects the unique context of each woman's experience of violence was a recurring theme among activists. Sandra Muñoz (2018) underscored the necessity of "understanding each woman's experience and respect their time" when creating conditions for the articulation of traumatic events. Reflecting on her own journey, she remarked, "Even though I'm a woman at the forefront, I still carry a lot inside – so imagine how a woman outside the social movement feels. It's incredibly painful." Revisiting traumas is not only emotionally burdensome but also shaped by social dynamics that retraumatize survivors, forging environments of blame-shifting, and instilling feelings of guilt. As Muñoz observed, "We're always the ones blamed, making it incredibly difficult to come forward and say, 'I was sexually assaulted.'" She emphasized that police stations must move beyond treating survivors as mere case files and instead engage with them as individuals bearing deeply personal and complex histories of trauma.

This call for reimagining how legal systems listen to women's experiences resonated in my conversation with Laina Crisóstomo. As a lawyer, Crisóstomo advocates for a feminist approach to legal practice grounded in empathy, respect, and nonjudgmental professionalism – a methodology she openly acknowledges was absent from her formal legal education and instead cultivated through lived experience. She highlights underscores the necessity of providing specialized support for women experiencing violence, emphasizing that traditional legal approaches are insufficient. As she explains,

> We cannot advocate for these women in the same way we would for anyone else, where someone walks into your office and you simply say, "What do you need? Bring these documents." No, we have to listen – truly listen to understand.
>
> (2018)

Similarly, criminologist and sociologist Lesley McMillan, in *Feminists Organising Against Gendered Violence*, stresses that legal practitioners "do not inherently know how to listen to stories of trauma; we must learn to listen to them" (2007, 171). McMillan describes "active listening" as a demanding process, especially when trauma renders these narratives fragmented or difficult to articulate. She notes,

> This culture of silence is intertwined with the notion that traumatic experiences are inherently unbelievable. When it comes to sexual and gendered violence, it is also connected to society's tendency to disbelieve women survivors. Women are painfully aware of this reality.
>
> (2007, 177–178)

From my own fieldwork, during which women often shared their stories of violence unprompted, I came to understand that listening is neither straightforward nor easy. It requires an embodied, sensitive engagement with the enduring politics of silencing perpetuated by the legal system and the colonial racial-patriarchal order that shapes dominant conditions of enunciation. Legal research and advocacy cannot be reduced to detached or purely technical procedures. Instead, they must embrace a form of active listening that acknowledges and addresses the manifold barriers women face when breaking their silence, particularly as their narratives are so frequently dismissed, disbelieved, or condemned.

In her transformative approach to legal advocacy, Laina Crisóstomo (2018) underscores how the *Tamojuntas* organization seeks to challenge the procedural dynamics of legal hearings (*oitiva*), which she describes as often feeling "police-like, investigative, even aggressive." Instead, the movement advocates for a paradigm shift toward an empathetic practice of listening (*escuta*). As Crisóstomo explains, "Listening is entirely different from hearing. It's about understanding what the story means, how it resonates within me, and how it shapes my decisions." This methodological reframing acknowledges that "judicializing the problem wouldn't heal her pain," emphasizing that meaningful redress extends beyond legal adjudication to include psychological support and reintegration into community life. "We must consider her life after violence because, for so long, her life *was* violence" (2018).

Refusal and the State

In my conversations, the theme and practice of refusal emerged as a consistent critique, especially raised by Black, Indigenous, and trans women. Interactions with law enforcement were not perceived as protective but as encounters marked by state-sanctioned violence and systemic abuse. This violence took various forms: the extrajudicial killings of their sons and husbands in favelas, pervasive sexual harassment, the denial of their social names and identities, and the armed support provided by police to farmers and agribusinesses in the invasion and dispossession of their lands. In this section, I analyze the conceptualization and manifestations of refusal within these contexts.

My conversation with Andreza da Silveira Jorge (2018), a Black feminist researcher, activist, and coordinator of the *Rede de Mulheres da Maré* – the largest favela complex in Rio de Janeiro, where Marielle Franco was raised – brought this reality into sharp relief. In this context, the police and state armed forces are seen not as protectors but as primary perpetrators of violence, harming women and their families, thus rendering the national rhetoric of public safety painfully hollow.[6] In these conditions, to whom can one safely report police violence? And how can anyone feel secure in pursuing justice when doing so necessitates disclosing their identity and location to the very institution responsible for the violence inflicted? These pressing dilemmas inform the broader exploration of Black invocations and practices of refusal, which are examined further in the next section on representation.

Indigenous leader, activist, and educator Maria Alice Karapãna, also known as Maria Alice da Silva Paulino, recounts the brutal displacement inflicted on the Karapãna community along the Tarumã Açu River, where they were forcibly removed from their ancestral lands to make way for luxury developments.

> They demolished my family's home and set it on fire, with assistance from the Military Police and hired henchmen. To this day, we still feel the effects. We could barely recover anything: broken televisions, furniture, beds, mattresses. . . . The very people who were supposed to protect us turned their backs on us
>
> (Paulino 2018),

she recalls.

This eviction case escalated to the state court of Amazonas, yet proceedings were conducted without consulting or notifying anyone from

6 The issue of police violence against Black women in Complexo do Alemão was denounced as a human rights violation within the Inter-American Human Rights System in the case *Favela Nova Brasília (Cosme Genoveva and others) v. Brazil* (2017). This case, situated within the broader context of police summary executions, highlighted the intersections of gender discrimination and sexual violence.

the Karapãna community. As Paulino underscores, "There were several hearings, but none of us were notified of them. We had no opportunity to respond: 'No, we live here! We are an Indigenous community, and we have the right to land and housing.'" This process embodies a profound disregard for Indigenous rights, where the very mechanisms of in/justice do not listen to those most impacted by their decisions. Paulino's experience further reveals that the state is not merely complicit in dispossession – it actively drives it. Under the guise of development, these colonial structures persistently attempt to erode Indigenous livability, undermining the rights to land, life, and belonging that are essential to sustaining community and resisting the relentless incursions of state violence.

Dispossession, far from an isolated incident, has long been, and remains, a primary mode of dis/engagement between Indigenous people and the colonial state, in Brazil – as addressed in Part 0 – and elsewhere.[7] In her interview *An Indigenous Woman Troubling the Museum's Colonialist Legacy* (2022), published by *Museum International*, Indigenous artist, researcher, and activist Glicéria Tupinambá shares accounts of violent police incursions into Tupinambá territories, during which resources and community-produced goods were seized, perpetually destabilizing their lives and livelihoods. Reflecting on her early understanding of the judicial system, Glicéria recalls a time when she believed that justice could be achieved through the presentation of evidence, where both sides could speak, be heard, and engage in redressive and reparative justice. However, when she and her community formally reclaimed their ancestral lands, the courts swiftly dismissed their petition, silencing their voices and denying them the opportunity to present their case.

It was only after organizing extra-legal forms of reclaim, such as a large-scale demonstration and direct actions to reclaim their land, driving out loggers and poachers while physically reasserting their presence, that the legal system began to take notice. "We stepped onto the ground, reclaimed the land, pushed out the loggers, the poachers. . . . We were taking it back," recounts Glicéria Tupinambá (2022, 15). Yet their hearing was ultimately presided over by a judge who unapologetically declared his opposition to Indigenous land claims, highlighting the entrenched biases that continue to

7 Coulthard (2014) argues that the core experience of dispossession is a central force behind the most prominent forms of Indigenous resistance to colonial structures. He contends that Indigenous struggles against capitalist imperialism should be understood not merely as conflicts over land but also as struggles deeply rooted in the land's significance as a mode of reciprocal relationship. These struggles, informed by place-based practices and knowledge systems, reveal important lessons on how to live in respectful, non-dominating, and non-exploitative relationships with each other and the environment.

permeate the legal system of in/justice. As Glicéria describes, in a translation provided in the same publication (2022, 15):

> When we get there, everyone sits down, then the judge comes and throws a bucket of cold water over us. He says: "The Tupinambá are coming to reclaim their land? I want to make something very clear to you: this jury isn't favorable to Indigenous people." And I was in shock: "What do you mean?" And this was in front of the Public Prosecution Service, in front of FUNAI [Brazilian National Foundation for Indigenous Peoples], in front of the Brazilian State. He went on: "This jury isn't favorable to Indigenous people. My father had land in Espírito Santo, which the Tupiniquim Guarani repossessed. And here, we've got the Pataxó Hã-Hã-Hãe repossessing land; there's the Pataxó down in the far south repossessing land; and now the Tupinambá come along? No . . . no, this jury isn't favorable to Indigenous people. If you want to win something, you'll have to go to Brasília [the Federal Government]. But until then . . . here, you'll lose." That's when I realized that justice, was . . . blind, you know? It was blindfolded, they only see and hear the sides [that favor them, White people].

Indigenous activists such as Glicéria Tupinambá and Maria Alice Karapãna have highlighted how "the language of the White man" and "the language of the courts" are deeply interwoven, creating a framework that compels Indigenous communities such as Tupinambá and Karapãna to engage with an exclusionary legal and linguistic system to assert their rights. This necessity to *master* a language and system designed to marginalize them illuminates a profound tension within Indigenous struggles for justice.

Indigenous and quilombola writers and activists frequently describe their endeavors as acts of translation (cf. Kopenawa and Albert 2010; Krenak 2019; Bispo dos Santos 2020; Bispo dos Santos et al. 2020; Tupinambá 2022), as previously discussed in this chapter (see section *Legal Ethnography: Deep Listening*). As Guarani activist, curator, and researcher Sandra Benites articulates, "my desire to study has always stemmed from the need to understand and to engage in dialogue" (2018).

These acts of translation encompass the sharing of Indigenous and quilombola cosmologies with the White neocolonial world, thereby challenging the dominant system of monoculture (as analyzed in Part 0) and reimagine choreographies of world-making otherwise. Benites reflects on the inherent contradictions within legal narrative and practices, which stand in stark contrast to the liberal myth that "everyone is equal before the law." She notes that there is the discourse of " 'I have a right,' but as soon as you attempt to exercise that right through your own body . . . the moment you present a different *corpus* [corporeal reality] and demand, in other words, another vision, then you start all these clashes." This generative tension leads to a profound sense of self-dispossession, as Benites explains, it "makes you feel like you don't fit in anywhere . . . . I don't find myself in that place" (2018).

Rather than merely striving for "recognition" within established legal and social frameworks, I position the translation processes enacted by Sandra Benites, Glicéria Tupinambá, and Maria Alice Karapãna as efforts aimed at cultivating im/possible dialogues that forge transformative ecologies and radical legal practices. This approach actively seeks to unsettle and dismantle the colonial foundations of dispossession. It represents a shift from *mastery* to *unmastery*, that is, a complex journey of engaging with and learning the colonial language as a means to disrupt the colonial order from within. Their multifaceted processes encompass the intersections of academic and Indigenous educational systems, artistic realms, and legal struggles, creating a dynamic space in which power relations and knowledge production are disputed and contested.

This analysis also seeks to bridge dialogues and learn *with* Indigenous praxis toward the law in what is now Brazil, by situating these within a broader framework of refusal. Indigenous feminist scholarship has increasingly theorized refusal as a nuanced and generative response to the enduring legacies of colonial slavery and settler colonialism. For instance, political anthropologist Audra Simpson's research with the Kahnawake community in what is currently Canada frames refusal as a means of exceeding the state's settler-colonial remedies and juridical mechanisms. She describes refusal as "part of the quotidian life of self-consciousness and political assertion" (2014, 107). Similarly, Simpson contrasts refusal with the concept of "recognition" of Indigenous rights, which the state often employs as a mechanism to address historical injustices. Refusal, rather than recognition, cultivates spaces where alternative modes of thought, politics, and traditions can exist critically in relation to, yet also beyond, state frameworks (2014, 2017). As such, refusal emerges as a countercolonial, generative practice a means of sustaining Indigenous ways of being that resist subsumption under state-defined identities and prescribed notions of justice.

Following Audra Simpson, the politics of recognition operates within colonial legal frameworks, often reducing to a superficial acknowledgment of rights without the meaningful redress that this notion demands. In such contexts, "recognition" serves merely to affirm the rights of Indigenous communities while overlooking the violent colonial histories that underpin statehood itself. In countries like the United States and Brazil, these states are built upon legacies of "lethal force and dispossession" and the "economic and political enslavement of particular populations" (A. Simpson 2017, 20). As a result, recognition becomes a constrained political and legal practice. In contrast, for Indigenous communities, the priority lies in being attentively heard, a necessary step of deep listening that enables the reimagining and reconfiguration of justice beyond the limits of colonial frameworks.

The Brazilian context offers a nuanced understanding of refusal, one that resists simplistic binaries of rejecting or accepting the state's authority. Pierre Clastres, in *Society Against the State* (1974), provides valuable insight into this dynamic. Clastres challenges Western narratives that portray Indigenous communities as "primitive" due to the absence of a state. Drawing from his studies with the Tupi-Guarani in Brazil, he argues that this absence does not signify a *lack*, incompleteness, or failure to develop Western technologies of state-building and economies of accumulation. Instead, it reflects a deliberate and sovereign will to *refuse* the state and the systems of production it entails. This act of refusal is not a retreat into passivity but a profound assertion of autonomy and a commitment to modes of existence otherwise.

Thus, the enduring acts of refusal encompass a wide array of strategies aimed at challenging entrenched structures of violence and imposed frameworks of recognition. In neocolonial contexts, refusal has evolved to include more nuanced approaches to engaging with the state, reimagining and transforming relationships within it. In Brazil, Indigenous women activists articulate forms of refusal that diverge from those examined by Audra Simpson in the Kahnawake community (2014, 7), where a total rejection of the state is manifested through practices such as abstaining from voting and refusing to pay taxes. The distinct historical, political, and legal realities of Brazil and Canada necessitate a context-dependent and opaque[8] approach to refusal.

In Brazil, Indigenous activists navigate both institutional- and community-based spheres, not only resisting state structures but also actively working to transform these spaces from within. As Indigenous librarian and activist Perpétua Suni Kokama (2018) and Afro-Indigenous educator and activist Marklize dos Santos Siqueira (2018), both of whom ran for office in the 2018 elections, have shared with me, their strategies encompass participating in elections, running for office, establishing Indigenous sectors within political parties, and pursuing legal claims within the judicial system, among other efforts. This political mobilization was later articulated in 2022 by the

8 The concept of opacity, as introduced by Édouard Glissant (1990), challenges the traditional Western ideal of transparency, which assumes a singular, universal truth for all of humanity. In place of this reductive transparency, there exists a powerful force of opacity – one that goes beyond merely renewing the mystery of origin. Opacity, in Glissant's framework, embraces a more intricate relational dynamic, where diverse and often marginalized elements come together without merging, fostering connections that defy oversimplification. Whereas transparency was once conceived as the mirror through which Western humanity projected its own image, it now yields to a fertile, yet indistinct opacity. This opacity, akin to silt left behind by various populations, remains largely unexplored and frequently denied or disparaged, yet its presence is undeniable, insistent, and impossible to ignore.

Articulation of Indigenous Peoples of Brazil (APIB)[9] as a strategy of *aldear* (Indigenization) of politics,[10] reflecting a conscious effort to transform formal politics with Indigenous worldviews.

The colonial epistemic order imposed the nation-state as the sole pathway to independence, as analyzed in Part 1. Within this framework, refusal manifests in dynamic practices that challenge state sovereignty, also from within. These practices transform the state into a contested space, where struggles over land demarcation, education, healthcare, and food sovereignty are fought. At the same time, they create a space where Indigenous modes of world-making continue to endure and thrive. By reconceptualizing the state as a site of struggle, these practices open new pathways for envisioning justice that transcend the limits of colonial frameworks.

An example of this nuanced engagement is found in Glicéria Tupinambá's account of a courtroom hearing concerning the land rights of the Tupinambá community. She recounts an elder from the community addressing the judge: "You [the state] have the right to refuse [our claims], but we [Indigenous people] have the right to resist" (Tupinambá 2022, 15).[11] Spoken within the confines of a legal institution, the elder's statement boldly asserts Indigenous sovereignty, surpassing the need for state recognition or validation. This moment encapsulates the grounds of refusal: the "right to refuse what has been refused to you" (Halberstam 2013, 8) – a defiant and enduring demand for justice that exists within and beyond the constraints of state-imposed frameworks.

9 In 2020, the Articulação dos Povos Indígenas do Brasil initiated its first Indigenous Campaign under the rallying cry, *demarcar as urnas* (demarcate the voting machine). This groundbreaking effort provided critical support for Indigenous candidates, offering resources for candidate registration, legal and communications advice, and strategic guidance on aligning with progressive political parties. The campaign prioritized individuals whose activism and advocacy for Indigenous rights had already earned broad recognition. Building on this momentum, APIB launched a new Indigenous Campaign in 2022, setting forth a comprehensive agenda to guide and support the candidates it endorses. These efforts mark a pivotal shift in Indigenous political mobilization, redefining how Indigenous sovereignty and representation intersect with national politics. For more information, visit https://apiboficial.org/.

10 For more information about this campaign, see https://campanhaindigena.info/aldear-a-politica/. Additionally, the powerful film *Música é arma de luta (Acampamento Luta pela Vida 2021)*, directed by Carou Trebitsch, Idjahure Kadiwéu, Lucas Canavarro, and Nana Orlandi, is available on Youtube at https://youtu.be/uLB8pSld5Fg?si=2R5KrCxPWVrL2KDn.

11 It is important to note that this conversation was not directly conducted by me, and I am not sure if she actually used the term "refuse" or if the translator chose it to represent the state's rejection of Indigenous claims.

Refusal as Generative Redress

Black, Indigenous, and queer practices of refusal in Brazil forge forms of kinship that directly confront the state's unfulfilled promises of law, challenging the deep-rooted practices of negation and dispossession. Here, I argue that refusal functions as a multifaceted and generative practice of redress, referring to the rejection of what has been historically denied, while simultaneously reinvigorating grassroots forms of *acolhimento* (welcoming).

Many activist women have shared with me how they find themselves without adequate institutional protection or support when experiencing gender-based violence or in the aftermaths of reporting it. While legislation like the Maria da Penha Law from 2006 (Brazilian Law n. 11.340) mandates the establishment of a range of support services, the reality is that police are often the only available recourse in many regions. This limitation reflects a deeper structural issue within the liberal framework addressing gender-based violence, which continues to rely on individualized, punitive, and carceral solutions.

In theory, Brazilian law has established two primary types of shelters for women: the Women's House (*Casa da Mulher Brasileira*) and the Shelter House (*Casa Abrigo*). The former is designed to offer a range of specialized services, including psychosocial support, police and judicial assistance, resources from the public ministry, economic empowerment programs, and access to transportation and childcare services. The latter is intended as a secure, confidential refuge that provides multidisciplinary support for women at immediate risk, allowing them space and time to seek safety and rebuild their lives.

In practice, the availability of shelters is severely limited. Less than 2.5 percent of Brazilian cities have any form of shelter for women experiencing violence. In states like Acre and Roraima – regions with some of the highest femicide rates in the country – no shelters exist at all. Of the 3,852 towns with populations under 20,000, only 16 have operational shelters, amounting to one shelter for every 240 towns (Campos 2017). Conditions in the few existing shelters have deteriorated over recent years, with closures reducing the number of operational shelters to a mere 74 nationwide – a strikingly insufficient figure for a country with a population of over 104 million women.

In refusing what has long been denied to them, countercolonial feminists have cultivated practices of *acolhimento* – a Portuguese term that transcends mere shelter or refuge. *Acolhimento* suggests a holistic embrace, a sanctuary where one is genuinely seen, supported, and nourished. It represents a space of mutual care and collective refuge. As Sandra Muñoz (2018) reflects,

> The shelter [*acolhimento*] began in my own home. For nearly a decade, I welcomed women with urgency and compassion, taking on many roles: lawyer, psychologist, mother. I did it all. There were times it was unbearable, and the pain was overwhelming.

The Association of Indigenous Women from the Alto Rio Negro (*Associação de Mulheres do Alto Rio Negro* – AMARN) offers a profound example of how refusal can manifest as *acolhimento*. Founded in 1984 by Indigenous women in collaboration with anthropologist Janet Chernela, AMARN was established in Manaus, the largest urban center in the Amazon. The organization emerged as a direct response to the exploitative and marginalizing conditions endured by Indigenous women migrating to the city. Many of these women found themselves employed as domestic workers under precarious circumstances, often unable to speak Portuguese, the official national language, further compounding their vulnerability.

During my visit to Manaus in 2018, several Indigenous women shared accounts of migrating to the urban setting in search of work, only to encounter exploitation and abuse. These experiences resonate with Brazil's enduring history of domestic worker activism, outlined in Part 0. The founding and ongoing efforts of AMARN embody a transformative approach to refusal – challenging systems of marginalization while cultivating spaces of collective care and economic autonomy. AMARN addresses the structural inequities faced by Indigenous women by fostering a collective space that brings together members from more than ten Indigenous groups, offering *acolhimento* (physical and emotional) and establishing sustainable income-generating initiatives to support women living in Manaus.

I met with Joana Galvão, also known as Umucipó, a Desano ciswoman activist who has been involved with AMARN since 2007. Our conversation took place at Bahserikawi, the Center for Indigenous Medicine in downtown Manaus. She detailed how AMARN not only advocates for labor rights but also offers the possibility for Indigenous women to establish community-driven economies, enabling them to break free from exploitative domestic labor. Moreover, the organization tackles gender-based violence with a nuanced and transformative approach, emphasizing structural change and fostering community resilience over punitive measures (2018).

A defining moment for AMARN came when one of its members shared to be facing life-threatening domestic violence. Rather than relying on the punitive state apparatus, the association initiated a collective, community-led response that centered on accountability and awareness building. This approach addressed the systemic roots of violence while offering immediate support. Their practice exemplifies a redressive and transformative justice – an ethic of care that emphasizes structural change and relational accountability over liberal, individualized criminalization. In this framework, justice emerges not from punishment but from collective resilience, deeply rooted in shared histories, mutual care, and a steadfast commitment to thriving beyond the constraints of colonial frameworks.

In my conversations, community-driven approaches to addressing violence emerged not only as repairing pathways for survivors but also as crucial strategies for preventing violence against women. Afro-Indigenous feminist activist and trade unionist Florismar da Silva shared how her understanding of gender-based violence as deeply structural sharpened after moving to the outskirts of Manaus, where she witnessed haunting scenes, such as "women fleeing from men wielding knives" (2018). In one residents' association meeting, she told me that a man arrived "all smiles, proudly displaying his wife's tooth in his pocket" (2018). Outraged, Florismar confronted him, and from that moment on, her home organically became a refuge for women escaping domestic violence. Reflecting on these experiences, she and her fellows began asking themselves, "What is feminism really about?" (2018). Her journey in feminist mobilizations led her into institutional roles as vice president of the Municipal Council of Women's Law, a member of the National Coordination of the Brazilian Women's Articulation, and co-founder of the Women's Solidarity Movement of Amazonas (*Movimento de Mulheres Solidárias do Amazonas* – MUSA).

Luzanira da Silva, also a MUSA co-founder and member of the Permanent Forum of Women of Manaus (FPMM), underscores the vital role of emotional and psychological support in the healing process for survivors of violence. She describes the systematic abuse, neglect, and re-traumatization that women face in police stations designated to address gender-based violence. "We reported this to the Public Prosecution, held a public hearing, yet nothing has changed. The police continue their same practices" (2018).

As criminal lawyer and activist Natália Damazio articulates, a feminist praxis that navigates both within and beyond the law is, at its core, an act of care for other women and a methodological break from masculinist norms. The White conquest-driven masculinity norm, which pervades institutional cultures, manifests in competition, domination, and aggression. Reflecting on her experience within the legal field, Damazio shares, "In my work within the [criminal law] institutional field, I navigate a highly masculine environment marked by shouting, yelling, and aggressive body language – rooted in an effort to dehumanize others as a means of self-affirmation" (2018). The challenge, then, is to resist being assimilated into this logic, to refuse adaptation to spaces clearly not designed for us. To disrupt these patterns is to transform violent legal spaces from within, disordering and reconfiguring the interactions that shape them.

Such acts of care and refusal cultivate spaces of vitality that disrupt entrenched cycles of structural violence. They emphasize a critical insight: the judicialization of harm often fails to address or alleviate suffering. As Crisóstomo observes, "it wouldn't heal her pain" (2018). Instead, legal systems frequently exacerbate harm, shifting the burden of accountability onto those most affected – particularly Black, Indigenous, queer, and transgender communities, with women bearing the brunt. Women's movements, dating back to the 1970s, have long recognized this dynamic, centering their demands not on criminal justice but on creating networks of refuge and solidarity (Pires and Souza 2020). Over time, these demands have been reshaped, and sometimes co-opted by legal frameworks, as seen in the establishment of Women's Police Station (Part 2), the criminalization of the femicide (Part –1), and the civil rights initiatives of the first wave (Part 1).

Beyond judicializing, the movement is about politicizing the wound itself. Mombaça describes this act as being "together in the midst of fracture, finding among the shards of shattered glass an improbable link, the rough trace of a collective yet to be formed" (2021e, 26). The creation of space of *acolhimento* by grassroots movements reflects this politicization – a collective inhabitation of, and transformation within, oppressive environments. How to create and sustain such spaces without the material conditions of the state?

These movements exemplify the generative forms of redress Black, Indigenous, and queer women cultivate as they embody shared, alternative ways of living and organizing. Through collective practices of world-making, they foster spaces for deep listening, mutual support, and healing, directly challenging liberal paradigms of accumulation and competition that equate justice with individualized punitive measures and incarceration. In doing so, they refuse colonial racial-patriarchal order, anchoring their resistance in interdependence, relationality, and care as foundational principles. These practices lay the groundwork for a radically different future tenses – one built on community, kinship, and the affirmation of life beyond the restrictive confines of colonial order and state-sanctioned responses.

Refusing Dehumanization

In feminist grassroots advocacy, the act of listening necessitates a radical rethinking of the legal construct of victimhood, inviting recognition of women as "whole subjects" (Crisóstomo 2018). This framework envisions redress as a process through which women "re-member" their fractured bodies, as proposed by Saidya Hartman (1997), in which the act of re-member-ing involves reconnecting the dismembered body and reclaiming the wholeness that exists before, during, and after experiences of violence. Underlying this work are the constructs of the in/human and the Racial and Gendered ontologies of difference (as discussed in Part 0), which form the scaffolding of colonialism, upholding White supremacist, male-centered, and cisheteronormative definitions of the Human. These constructs expose the foundational architecture of modern legal and ethical norms, alongside the modes of subjectivation they engender (Wynter 1970s, 2015; Ferreira da Silva 2007).

Reconfiguring the "Human" thus becomes a critical legal and political task, one that contests the colonial scripts of humanity built upon the dis-membering of captive subjects (Spillers 1987) and the construction of skins and masks (Fanon 1952). It also demands the permeation of ontological and psychological dimensions into legal practice. Legal actors – lawyers, judges, and others – are called upon to engage in a form of *deep listening* that resists reproducing the dehumanizing gaze that has historically positioned racialized and un/gendered voices, pushing them outside the boundaries of legal protection.

This defiance of colonial constructs of the Human and the work of reconfigurating humanity itself emerged in my conversations, such as the one with Charlene Borges (2018), a Black feminist public defender in Salvador. Borges describes her feminist legal praxis as one committed to affirming women as "full human beings," a task that remains profoundly challenging within Brazil's criminal system of in/justice. Despite the rights enshrined in Brazil's 1988 Constitution, systemic forms of dehumanization persist: from punitive measures that disproportionately target Black and trans women to reductive legal framings that essentialize White ciswomen as mere "victims" (as discussed in Part 0). For Borges, these dynamics reveal not only the deeply embedded gendered and racialized logics within legal institutions but also underscore the urgent need to reimagine prevailing frameworks of humanity.

The colonial and neocolonial architectures of femicide reflect a broader Racial and Gendered ontology of difference that underpins legal systems, determining whom they protect and whom they neglect or directly harm. Activists like Natália Damazio (2018) work to expose and contest these entrenched system of in/justice. Damazio highlights the legal system's disproportionate targeting of women, particularly trans women, who are often incarcerated for minor infractions, such as petty theft, but receive excessively harsh sentences. Trans women are typically held in facilities that disregard their specific needs, underscoring the systemic violence they endure. She recounts harrowing stories of mothers whose children are taken from them brutally, leaving them desperate for any information about their whereabouts. These practices do more than enforce punishment; they intensify the historical dehumanization of racialized and marginalized female subject-positions and reproduce the colonial hierarchies that constitutional legal frameworks purport to dismantle.

Reclaiming humanity, then, is not merely a theoretical gesture of inclusion but a call to re/de/composition of[12] the structural conditions through which

12 The concept of "re/de/composition," woven throughout this chapter, prompts reflection on the relationship between processes of world-decomposing and world-recomposing. Does one necessarily precede the other, or can they unfold simultaneously? These inquiries intersect with the speculative elements of Ferreira da Silva's argument, further elaborated later in this chapter. For a deeper engagement with these themes, see Petersmann (2024).

humanity has been defined under colonial slavery and its afterlives. As critical Black theorists such as Tina Campt (2019) have argued, refusal is not merely "a rejection of the status quo as livable" but also "the creation of possibility in the face of negation" (83). Within this generative frame, refusal signals an urgent need to rethink temporality, spatiality, and the very language through which politics, activism, and theory are articulated, alongside a refusal of the imposed terms through which struggle is named and recognized. It is a practice of transforming negation as a "creative source of disorderly power to embrace the possibility of living otherwise" (Campt 2019, 83). In this way, refusal becomes a generative force that unsettles the colonial foundations of the "Human," opening the possibility for other ways of being and becoming with others (cf. Streva, Case, and Petersmann 2024).

Together, these advocates articulate forms of existence, among humans and more-than-humans, that exceed and resist the constraints of the colonial order. Through insurgent practices and improvised modes of being, they challenge definitions of humanity within and beyond current frameworks of law, by setting up "juridico-economic architectures of redress" (Ferreira da Silva 2014, 85).

Reparar *the Irreparable*

How might we envision a contested system of justice and lawmaking capable of addressing the layered legacies of colonial violence and the colonial grounds of political femicide today? How might we begin to speak of repair in the face of historical and ongoing structural violence? Can we imagine forms of reparation that are both possible and "impossible" – a vision of repair that acknowledges the irreparable while striving for justice otherwise?

In Portuguese, the word *reparar* opens up a dual conceptual pathway for thinking about repair, rooted in two complementary meanings that enrich its potential. One meaning aligns with the common notion of "repair" as fixing or restoring, while the other extends to "paying attention, noticing, or observing" something previously overlooked. Although the English term "repair" shares these etymological roots, it only captures the first sense – restoring what is broken. In contrast, I propose embracing *reparar* in its second sense: an act of redress that does not seek to restore an unattainable past but instead calls us to deeply attend to silenced narratives, violent geologies, and neocolonial structures, engaging with them in a transformative manner. While the inherited debt is unpayable (Ferreira da Silva 2022), and the violence irreparable, the work of redress is ongoing and necessary.

On October 30 and 31, 2024, the long-awaited verdict in the case of Marielle Franco and Anderson Gomes was delivered in Rio de Janeiro's 4th Jury Tribunal. Through a live virtual broadcast, the public could witness the procedural and performative intricacies of the two-day trial, where a case steeped in political resonance unfolded. Federal Police delegate Guilhermo de Paula Machado Catramby concluded that the primary motive behind Marielle Franco's assassination was the political force of her activism. "Although land issues were not central to Marielle's mandate, our investigation confirmed that she and her party, PSOL, actively addressed them. They became a thorn in the side of militia interests, particularly in the West Zone," he stated (Carvalho 2024).

While male politicians from the same party had also confronted these militia strongholds, the gendered aspect of Franco's murder received minimal attention in the legal proceedings, as the crime was not even classified as femicide. Judged by a jury primarily composed of middle-aged White men – after the defense dismissed the only two women selected for service (Rodrigues, Laforé, and Oliveira 2024) – the confessed shooter and the driver, both former military police officers, were sentenced to 78 years and 9 months, and 59 years and 8 months in prison, respectively. They were convicted of double homicide with triple aggravation, the attempted murder of Fernanda Chaves (who survived the attack), and unlawful use of a cloned vehicle. In addition, the court ordered R$3.5 million in reparations, including a pension for Anderson Gomes's son, compensation for the families, and legal costs. Those suspected of ordering the crime await a separate trial before the Brazilian Supreme Court (G1 2024).

As the judge Lúcia Glioche delivered the verdict, she remarked, "Justice is sometimes slow, blind, flawed, even unjust, but it arrives. Justice arrives for those who, like the accused, believe they are beyond its reach."[13] As the sentence was announced, an undeniable wave of emotion filled the courtroom, stirring relatives and friends of Franco and Gomes. The gravity of the moment extended through the virtual broadcast, captured in the embraces, applause, and tearful faces of those present. This verdict carried profound symbolic weight, marking a moment of reckoning after years of struggle – a collective breath that, at least symbolically, suggested that justice had finally been served.

Presenting this courtroom scene serves as a gesture toward figuring the symbolic weight that rights and criminal convictions still hold in contemporary society, particularly for marginalized communities historically and continually subjected to the very violence of the legal order. This scene underscores criminal sentencing as a key corollary within the modern justice framework, a device that continues to shape our ideas of redress and accountability (P. J. Williams 1987; Tuck and Yang 2016; Pires and Souza 2020).

In *What Justice Wants*, Unangax intellectual Eve Tuck and ethnic studies scholar K. Wayne Yang compellingly describe justice as existing in the suspended space between grievance and grief; as an "unyielding of desire for redress that 'is itself an articulation of loss and longing for remedy and

13 From the original in Portuguese: *A Justiça por vezes é lenta, é cega, é burra, é injusta, é errada, é torta, mas ela chega. A Justiça chega para aqueles que como os acusados acham que jamais serão atingidos pela Justiça.*

reparation'" (2016, 8). This cyclical deferral of justice caught "between the no longer and the not yet" conveys not only the deferred promises of justice but also the relentless, collective longing for redress. While demanding legal justice in the face of state-sanctioned violence is crucial, it remains ultimately inadequate, as no legal outcome can truly reconcile the irreparable harm inflicted on those who *tombaram* (Part –1) and those who remain alive. It is a promise that can never be fully realized. Approaching justice as a discourse and practice of redress, then, invites us to engage seriously with the deep-seated desires and aspirations that shape our demands for accountability.

Legal scholar Thula Pires (2020) argues that while criminalizing certain acts may not always fulfill an anticipated social transformation, it nonetheless represents a societal recognition that these acts warrant condemnation. This acknowledgment can create a platform for expanding the discourse on protection and prevention. Pires further notes that while symbolic punishment is rightly subject to critique, the absence of criminal enforcement has its own symbolic implications, signaling who is – and is not – considered worthy of protection. Such a duality prompts a reexamination of how law and justice function within landscapes marked by historical and ongoing systemic violence.

This tension brings us to reconsider "recognition" within legal frameworks, yet in a wholly different light. In cases of femicide, criminalization has failed to meet the profound social demands surrounding gendered violence. Since the 1990s, femicide has drawn significant attention both globally and particularly across Latin America. In many contexts, public awareness of femicide preceded its legal codification rather than followed it. Though the legal classification of femicide might have increased public awareness of the issue, femicide rates continue to surge at alarming levels worldwide. Brazil ranks as one of the deadliest places for gender nonconforming individuals, grouped under the umbrella term LGBTQI+, and stands fifth globally in femicides, surpassed only by El Salvador, Colombia, Guatemala, and Russia (Laurent, Platzer, and Idomir 2013).[14]

14 In the 2019 report *Mortes Violentas de LGBT+ no Brasil*, the Grupo Gay da Bahia documented 420 deaths in Brazil the previous year attributed to "homolesbotransphobia," with 320 homicides (76 percent) and 100 suicides (24). However, data on violence specifically targeting lesbian and bisexual women, as well as gay men, remains scarce. This gap is partly due to the absence of information on sexual orientation in police records and death certificates, hindering accurate documentation (IPEA and FBSP 2019; BRASIL 2018). Additionally, the "Transrespect versus Transphobia Worldwide" project, conducted by Transgender Europe (TGEU), tracks global human rights conditions for transgender individuals, compiling data from international human rights organizations and media sources. TGEU reports that Brazil has the highest number of transgender and travesti murders in the world (TGEU 2016). Between 2008 and 2011, Brazil accounted for 39.8 percent of global murders of transgender people, with transwomen comprising the majority of victimized subjects (Instituto Patrícia Galvão 2017; TGEU 2016). For a critical perspective on the statistical discussion, see the section *Incommensurability: Mathematics of Violence* (Part I).

As discussed in the subsection on *the mathematics of violence* (Part –1), statistical data often obliterates crucial contextual and political nuances. Brazilian statistics tend to categorize female murders by gender binary, location, and municipality, revealing that the majority occur in domestic settings (IPEA 2015; IPEA and FBSP 2019; Artigo19 2018). However, such frameworks overlook essential markers like race, class, gender identity (cisgender and transgender), and sexual orientation, leaving countless instances of femicide unrecognized, omitted by the legal and statistical definitions that narrowly shape public discourse.

Yet, in part due to the proactive efforts of civil society organizations and nongovernmental groups, a more comprehensive understanding of femicide has emerged, challenging the limitations of national statistics. For instance, the *Atlas da Violência* report – produced through a collaboration between the Institute of Applied Economic Research (IPEA) and the Brazilian Public Security Forum (FBSP) – highlights a stark rise in femicide rates across Brazil. From 2007 to 2017, murders of women increased by 30.7 percent, with Black women facing a murder rate surge of nearly 55 percent during this period, while the rate for White women dropped by close to 10 percent (IPEA and FBSP 2019, 37–38). These findings illustrate that criminalization has not yet translated into meaningful protection against gendered violence, underscoring the continued influence of racialized structures of harm that differentiate whose lives are seen as grievable and whose are not (Butler 2009).

In these landscapes of violence, where criminal justice often fails to confront or redress structural legacies, Angela Davis reminds us of the need to "creatively explore new terrains of justice" (2003, 21). Marielle Franco's political and intellectual legacy exemplifies precisely this, contesting the militarization of Brazil's police and advancing an antiracist, feminist, and abolitionist vision of justice. Franco's countercolonial-feminist praxis held that defending Black women's lives is inseparable from resisting police violence and the militarization of the favelas. Her activism encompassed childcare, reproductive rights, and police accountability, all anchored in continuous dialogue with grassroots movements. Franco's approach disrupted the traditional association of criminalization with protection, especially for Black women, and instead reimagined safety through community-driven policies and structural transformation. Her life and work present a critical reconfiguration of justice itself, offering reparative, abolitionist frameworks that challenge the dominant punitive models and expand our horizons for what redress could mean (Davis et al. 2022; Augusto 2020).

Inspired by the radical calls of Marielle Franco and Angela Davis to reimagine justice and lawmaking, we might journey into uncharted territories, daring to ask more "what-if" questions that nurture other grounds for reparative (*reparar*) and redressive responses to the enduring architectures of colonial violence. In her reflections on a transformative theory of justice, Denise Ferreira da Silva argues that these speculative "what-if" inquiries are vital steps, opening pathways for decolonial justice projects that exceed the confines of "modern knowledge or its tools" (2017).[15]

What if femicide were no longer understood within a narrow, individualized framework, treated merely as a domestic crime? What if, instead, it was recognized as a complex, colonial, political phenomenon that serves as a foundational element of the modern nation-state and constitutional democracy? In this context, how might lawmaking and representative democracy address the deeply embedded and uneven distributions of violence? Furthermore, as Mombaça (2021d) suggests, what if the justice system itself – grounded in a modern-colonial narrative that upholds state neutrality and judicializes social conflicts – perpetuates a fiction that alienates subjects from their own capacities for resolution? This dynamic is reflected in the Brazilian saying, "we're going to solve this in the justice," which is often used to intimidate and treat others as adversaries, rather than fostering micro-level collective dialogue and solutions.

In a world vibrating throughout these questions, justice would not be confined to punitive retribution but envisioned as a generative force capable of addressing both individual grievances and the systemic geologies of violence embedded within the social fabric. Justice, then, reaches beyond state-controlled narratives to cultivate deeper forms of response-ability, centering practices that are both reparative and transformative. In the evocative, insurgent words of Jota Mombaça:

> In these geographies – where we have been looted and transformed into more than what they imposed on us; where we have endured pain and emerged as more than mere effects of that suffering; where we have faced imprisonment and become greater than captivity; where we have experienced brutality and risen above it – here and there, we have confronted death itself, becoming older than death and deader than dead. In that profound depth, which is not merely an external realm but is also embedded within everything, we have nurtured a life that transcends existence – a life intertwined with all things. Or, as Cíntia Guedes so eloquently expressed,

15 As Denise Ferreira da Silva argues, the act of asking "what-if" questions is closely tied to speculation, a gesture that merges thinking and imagining. "Asking 'what-if' is essential because any decolonial plan aiming at global justice – that is, the return of the full value expropriated from native lands and enslaved labor under regimes of total violence – cannot rely on modern knowledge or its tools" (2017).

which I also invoke here as an afterword: "infinite life." They will not kill us now!

(2021b, 19; my translation)[16]

Bringing together critiques of justice with the silencing often perpetuated by legal institutions, Black, queer, and Indigenous cosmologies underscore the significance of re/de/composition – forms of redress that resist negation – and community-based forms of *acolhimento* and refusal, pointing toward the *plenum* (Ferreira da Silva 2018; mentioned in Part 0) and the *corpus infinitum* (Mombaça 2021b, 19), all embedded within a politics of vitality. These frameworks envision systems that sustain ongoing processes of repair (*reparar*), drawing deeply on local knowledge and reciprocal relationships. As Leanne Simpson articulates, "we can't have resurgence without centering gender and queerness, and creating alternative systems of accountability for sexual and gender violence" (2016, 30).

In creating transnational constellations of connection, I bridge again a dialogue between Indigenous women's movements in Brazil and insights from Indigenous thinkers in Canada. Leanne Simpson's reflections on community-centered conflict resolution offer a vital approach:

> When there is conflict or something goes wrong, we have processes to hear from everyone involved. These processes allow the community of people impacted by the imbalance to learn the context of the individuals directly involved. It allows the individuals to account for themselves and their actions. It focuses on repairing and regenerating relationships and this restoration is something that happens repeatedly across scales with individuals, their interactions with plants and animals, and their families, communities, and nations. It is a supportive system of processing trauma, of taking measures spiritually, and of accounting for loss or hurt.

16 From the original:

> *Tais pistas, portanto, servem e não servem, assim como as críticas com que estão misturadas. É tudo experimento na borda das coisas, lá onde estamos prestes a dissolver as ficções de poder que nos matam e aprisionam; lá, aqui, todas essas geografias onde fomos saqueadas, e nos tornamos mais-do-que-aquilo-que-levaram; onde fomos machucadas, e nos tornamos mais do que um efeito da dor; onde fomos aprisionadas, e nos tornamos mais do que o cativeiro; onde fomos brutalizadas, e nos tornamos mais do que a brutalidade. Lá, aqui, onde fomos assassinadas, e nos tornamos mais velhas que a morte, mais mortas que mortas, e nesse fundo – esse fora que não só não está fora como está dentro de tudo -, nesse cerne em que fomos colocadas, fecundamos a vida-mais-do-que-viva, a vida emaranhada nas coisas. Ou, para ativar o presente que Cíntia Guedes me ofereceu e está registrado também aqui, como posfácio: "a vida infinita." Não vão nos matar agora!* (my translation).

> These are the same processes of Nishnaabeg diplomacy we use in conflicts internationally.
>
> (2016, 23)

Leanne Simpson's words invite us to consider justice as a regenerative practice that connects human relationships with broader ecologies, cultivating spaces where people can account for themselves and heal collectively. This approach nurtures a transformative understanding of justice as grounded in cycles of listening, repair, and restoration – a practice continually enacted across generations, species, and landscapes. Far from the isolating tendencies of punitive systems, these cosmologies broaden our sense of justice to encompass relational and ecological dimensions, where processes of redress are not reduced to state interventions but are part of everyday practices and commitments to care within and beyond human communities.

These transnational praxes offer other forms of world-making as continuous acts of resistance and creativity by those who refuse, reimagine, and re/de/compose legal and political structures. As Ferreira da Silva argues, re/de/composition involves acts of "disunifying, disfiguring, and redesigning" structures propped up by a discourse of necessity rooted in post-Enlightenment reasoning (2022, 26). Framed through my own interpretation of Ferreira da Silva's concept of re/de/composition,[17] Marielle Franco's legacy and the resonant seeds it has sown in grassroots movements become acts of re-membering and redressing the politics of femicide. Rather than interrupting her countercolonial feminist trajectory, grassroots responses amplify and collectivize it, transforming it into a vital force of seeding and cultivation. This reconfiguration unfolds through generative refusals, *acolhimento*, and practices of world-making otherwise, each aimed at unrooting, undoing, and de/re/composing the in/justice landscapes in the aftermaths of colonial slavery.

Countercolonial feminist praxis emerges not as an alternative political act but as ecologies of re/de/composition: choreographies that unsettle colonial legacies and the legalities of in/justice. By placing these issues in the soil, at ground level, these choreographies cultivate spaces for care, abolitionist ethics, and forms of justice that unlearn, unmake, and un-world the inherited geologies of violence. Here, counter-cartographies of resistance and re/de/composition emerge as the contours of a radical legal praxis, a blueprint for collective repair, and a cultivation of justice as an ongoing practice. This

17 Similar movement was made by Denise Ferreira da Silva when reading the work of Hortense Spillers. As she mentions in footnote 7: "I take liberties when borrowing from Spillers, while doing my best to remain close to her approach. When appropriating these terms, however, I am not concerned with getting at her 'meanings,' as I am not taking these terms as concepts" (2022, 27). In my case, I'm borrowing them as speculative praxis.

vision invites a radical rethinking of justice and life, grounded not merely in survival but in the continuous, expansive creation of worlds otherwise; the end of the world as we know it.

This book's engagement with femicide as part of a broader, layered geology of violence, dispossession, and precariousness neither aims to romanticize grassroots women's movements nor reduces femicide to an individualized crime. The women I spoke with often emphasized the need, at times, to turn to police or the courts in pursuit of justice. Thus, this inquiry into femicide does not dismiss the symbolic power of criminal law or its potential impact but instead calls for a more profound engagement with the structures that underpin these acts. By exploring justice as a generative redress, this book advocates for a form of redress that listens to and transforms the neglected grounds upon which these violences persist.

Beyond Representation

As Edward Said observed, "it is now almost impossible, for example, to remember a time when people were not talking about a crisis in representation" (1989, 205). The concept of representation encompasses a vast terrain, intersecting with epistemology, semiotics, psychoanalytic theory, media studies, film theory, political theory, and democratic policy studies, among others. This book engages with representation through two interconnected dimensions.

The first dimension examines the ontological and epistemic layers of representation, focusing on how modern frameworks of identity-building – the "I" versus the "not-I," the human versus the not-human – are constructed through colonial processes of essentialization, negation, and the objectification of the "Other." These dynamics have been a central thread throughout the book, shaping discussions on subject-positions (Part 0), the politics of silencing/speakability (Part 1), the methodology of listening, and the acts of refusal against the politics of recognition (Part 2).

Building on these foundations, the second dimension, discussed here, explores representation within its institutional and political context, which refers to the delegation of authority to speak or act on behalf of others. Expanding on the previous chapter's discussions of citizenship and constitutional democracy, this section situates these concepts within the framework of representation, particularly in the context of reimagining lawmaking processes through political representation. The analysis grapples with the complexities of "we, the people" and the constructs of constitutional representation, positioning these within the broader terrain of contemporary democracy. By engaging with the multifaceted layers of representation, this inquiry probes the possibilities – and limits – of political representation and lawmaking, shedding light on its broader implications for the politics of vitality.

Since the 1960s, and especially in recent decades, the disruptive mobilization of antiracist, queer, feminist, and anticolonial praxis has profoundly transformed the representational landscape through which visibility politics are navigated and contested. Predictably, debates around identity have become central to the current crises of democracy. A global resurgence of authoritarianism – driven by neoliberal agendas and far-right conservatism – has shaped electoral outcomes across diverse regions. Despite local variations, this neocolonial conservatism consistently manifests as a White conquest-driven masculinity that orchestrates systematic assaults on Black and Indigenous communities, queer and female bodies, and those within migration and displacement contexts.

At its core, we are witnessing a transnational reactionary force committed to preserving the colonial racial-patriarchal order while intensifying processes of extraction and dispossession. This force aggressively aims to interrupt and dismantle on-the-ground processes of re/de/composition and decolonial redressive praxis, violently reacting to struggles that persistently resist and rupture the hardened, wretched Earth of colonial order.

Although elections alone do not define the essence of representative democracy, they serve as a lens through which the dynamics of modern democracy can be critically assessed. It is well known that colonial racial-patriarchal order has historically shaped institutional politics, not only in Brazil but globally (IPU and PACE 2018). Brazil exemplifies the challenges of democratic representation, with one of the lowest rates of female political participation worldwide. According to *Women in Politics: 2019* report, Brazil ranked 133rd out of 191 countries for women in parliament and 149th out of 178 for women in ministerial positions (IPU and UNWomen 2017).

South America is the first region globally to surpass an average of 30 percent female representation across both parliamentary chambers. Since the re-democratization period of the 1990s, the proportion of women in lower houses across the Americas rose from 9 percent to 27 percent by 2015. The momentum for gender quotas, fueled by the United Nations Fourth World Conference on Women in Beijing in 1995, marked a turning point in the movement for gender parity. Pioneering efforts from this conference led to the establishment of a minimum quota of 40 percent female candidates, subsequently adopted by eight countries in the region – Argentina, Bolivia, Costa Rica, Ecuador, Honduras, Mexico, Nicaragua, and Panama (UNDP 2015; ECLAC 2015; IPU 2015, 2018). These advancements underscore the intricate relationship between female representation and the violent responses to it, suggesting that the two are not opposing phenomena, but rather part of the same sociopolitical struggle.

In line with the region-wide movement to criminalize femicide, nearly all Latin American countries have now integrated gender quotas into their electoral codes or constitutions. Among the 18 nations in the region, Guatemala stands as the sole exception in not adopting gender quotas (Gatto 2017). These quotas serve as affirmative action measures aimed at addressing the historical gender-based violence and inequality in political representation, while confronting the deeply entrenched White conquest-driven masculinity that constitutes institutional politics.

No other region in the world has experienced such a remarkable rise of women ascending to the highest political offices as Latin America in recent years. Figures like Dilma Rousseff in Brazil (2011–2016) and Colombia's trailblazing vice president Francia Márquez (2022), contribute to a broader legacy that includes Violeta Barrios de Chamorro, president of Nicaragua (1990–1997); Mireya Moscoso, president of Panama (1999–2004); Michelle Bachelet, president of Chile (2006–2010, 2014–2018); Kamla Persad-Bissessar, prime minister of Trinidad and Tobago (2010–2015); Portia Simpson Miller, prime minister of Jamaica (2005–2007, 2010–2016); Laura Chinchilla, president of Costa Rica (2010–2014); Cristina Kirchner, president of Argentina (2007–2015); and Xiomara Castro, president of Honduras (2022). These leaders mark a transformative shift in gender politics across Latin America and the Caribbean.

Yet, as we well know, structural transformation extends far beyond the election of a female politician. Countercolonial feminist critiques highlight the co-optation of women's representation within institutional politics, contending that such inclusion frequently serves to display a "feminine face of masculine power" (Galindo 2013, 41–42) while leaving colonial racial-patriarchal order intact. This critique is crystallized in the concept of the "femocrat" (McMillan 2007, 28), a term that reveals how women in political office may, however inadvertently, sustain rather than dismantle the very power structures they aim to contest.

In this context, Bolivian anarcho-feminist activist, psychologist, and writer María Galindo (2013) has argued that women's struggles should take place outside formal political institutions, a stance with which I respectfully diverge. While her critique of structural co-optation within institutional politics holds significant weight, I argue that disengaging entirely from these arenas risks essentializing and depoliticizing the liberatory struggles that have historically unfolded within, against, and beyond colonial architectures of power. Depoliticization here signals "the removal of a political phenomenon from an understanding of its historical emergence and the forces that produce and shape it" (Brown 2006, 15–16). This risk of detachment warrants further examination as we consider the complex interplay between activism and institutional engagement later in this section.

Globally, gender quotas have emerged as a legal intervention to address the long-standing exclusion of women from political representation. In *Quotas for Women in Politics* (2009), Mona Krook traces the expansive adoption of these policies, charting a particularly notable rise in the twenty-first century. She observes that "during the 1990s, quotas were implemented in over 50 countries, with nearly forty more joining since 2000" (2009, 3–4). Currently, more than one hundred nation-states have established gender quotas, signaling an increasing recognition of the need to recalibrate political systems through structural reforms aimed at transforming representation within traditionally male-dominated institutions.

Despite Brazil's reluctance to fully embrace the regional trend toward gender parity, the country took its first step by instituting gender quotas with Law No. 9100 in 1995. This was followed in 1997 by Law No. 9504, which introduced a 30 percent party quota for female candidates; however, the law did not require parties to meet this threshold, resulting in a decline in female representation from 6.2 percent in 1994 to 5.7 percent in the 1998 elections. It was not until the enactment of Law No. 12034 in 2009 that gender quotas became mandatory, transitioning from a party quota to a legislative quota. Generally, gender quotas are classified into three main types: party quotas, legislative quotas, and reserved seat quotas. Party quotas, adopted voluntarily by political parties, require a certain percentage of female candidates. Legislative quotas are embedded within electoral or constitutional laws, compelling all parties to nominate a fixed proportion of women. Reserved seat quotas, the most direct approach, ensure that a specified minimum of women not only contest elections but also secure seats in government (Krook 2009).

Costa Rica, like Brazil, exemplifies how inadequately designed gender quotas can produce unintended setbacks in female representation. In 1990, the country enacted the *Law for the Promotion of Women's Social Equality* (Law No. 7142) and later intensified its commitment to gender parity by revising its electoral code to mandate that 50 percent of candidates be women. This reform also introduced the "rule of alternation," which prevents successive listings of candidates from the same gender, ensuring balanced representation on ballots. Furthermore, Costa Rica allocated resources to capacity-building initiatives designed to equip both women and men in public office with the skills essential for effective governance, ensuring that women in government could actively wield political influence (COHA 2013; Muñoz-Pogossian et al. 2017; IPU 2018).

In the 2014 elections, Costa Rica witnessed a notable decline in female parliamentary representation, dropping by over 5 percent. This setback occurred as political parties found ways to sidestep parity measures by placing male candidates at the top of their lists, thus undermining the law's original intent. In response, Costa Rica's Superior Electoral Tribunal revised the definition of parity in 2016, mandating equal representation both vertically (within party lists) and horizontally (across districts). This reform led to substantial transformation in the 2018 elections, with women's parliamentary representation rising by 12.3 percent, from 33.3 percent to 45.6 percent. This case highlights the importance of meticulously designed and enforced implementation strategies in realizing the intended impact of legal reforms (Schwindt-Bayer 2009; IPU 2018; Marques 2018). Thus, the potential of gender quotas depends not only on their adoption but also on well-designed application and oversight.

In the Brazilian context, several entrenched structural factors perpetuate gendered political violence within institutional frameworks. Among these are the predominance of men in leadership across political parties; the colonial racial-patriarchal order that relegates women to domestic roles while fostering hostile environments within political institutions; the concentrated ownership of resources and property among White male elites; and pervasive financial inequalities, with women consistently receiving significantly less campaign funding than their male counterparts. These interlocking barriers do more than merely discourage women from pursuing institutional political roles; they often compel them to exit the political arena entirely, sustaining cycles of exclusion and limiting possibilities for transformative representation.

Women who persevere in the formal political arena, refusing to be silenced or sidelined, continue to confront both micro and macro forms of institutional misogyny. This reality was starkly demonstrated by the 2016 impeachment of Dilma Rousseff, Brazil's first female president, followed by the assassination of Marielle Franco just a year later – each event underscoring the pervasive and interconnected nature of political femicide. Elected in 2010 and reelected in 2014, Rousseff was ultimately removed from office in 2016 under intensely controversial and highly politicized circumstances. These pivotal moments unveil the layered, and at times lethal, dimensions of gendered violence deeply embedded within the Whiteness fabric of political structures.

Predictably, enthusiasm for political representation was limited even among the Brazilian women campaigning in 2018. Through my conversations with women active in grassroots movements and political parties, it became evident that formal political spaces are, from their perspective, acutely masculinized and rife with structural violence. Florismar da Silva (2018) and Luzarina da Silva (2018), seasoned activists and unionists involved in their political party since its inception in the 1980s in Manaus, described the deeply entrenched patriarchy within these structures. They spoke of the ongoing struggle to "confront the macho men" (*peitar a macharada*) within their own party ranks and noted that parties often sought female leaders, not out of a genuine commitment to inclusion, but rather to attract votes for male candidates. Similarly, Perpétua Cerqueira, a Kukama activist and a 2018 candidate for state deputy, articulated the challenges of having her voice truly recognized within any political forum: "Today, we finally have the Indigenous section inside the party, and we write. Now, I want to have a voice. I, an Indigenous woman, need to have a voice inside the party" (2018). These voices and perspectives lay bare the pervasive colonial racial-patriarchal order underpinning the representational democracy of today.

Women's accounts from within political spheres consistently depict parties as deeply inhospitable environments – saturated with sexism, hypermasculinity, racism, transphobia, and a pervasive interplay of structural and interpersonal violence. Within these institutions, aggressiveness, dispossession, abuse, and entrenched discrimination are pervasive. Marklize Siqueira observed this dynamic, reflecting on the Amazon region but capturing a broader national reality: "We have a completely male-oriented society in all political realms" (2018).

It is essential to acknowledge an evident, if frequently unspoken, reality: gendered violence within formal political institutions is not confined to Brazil or to formerly colonized nations; it transcends regional and historical boundaries, permeating political spheres across the globe. The Inter-Parliamentary Union's 2018 report, *Sexism, Harassment, and Violence Against Women in Parliaments in Europe*, underscores the pervasive nature of these abuses globally. Based on interviews with 123 women parliamentarians and staff across 45 European countries, the report reveals that an alarming 85.2 percent of respondents experienced psychological violence during their terms, 67.9 percent endured remarks targeting their physical appearance or reinforcing gender stereotypes, and 46.9 percent received death threats or threats of rape or physical assault. Significantly, these abuses came not only from political adversaries but also from colleagues within their own parties (IPU and PACE 2018).

In 2018, a series of judicial decisions aimed to advance gender equity within political representation in Brazil. The Supreme Court (STF) mandated that 30 percent of party funds be allocated to support women's candidacies, and the Electoral Court (TSE) required that a corresponding share of campaign airtime be dedicated to female candidates. Yet Brazil's progress remains impeded by a critical gap in racialized political representation: there is a glaring lack of quantitative studies and statistical data on Black and Indigenous women in politics. This absence is partly due to the delayed inclusion of race in electoral data, which only began in 2010. It was not until 2014 that Brazil produced its first comprehensive dataset disaggregated by both gender and racial categories (SEPPIR 2014; Rios 2017). This structural omission continues to obliterate the full scope of racialized gender disparities in political participation and representation.

Amid the rise of a far-right authoritarian populist in Brazil's 2018 elections, a profound countermovement was simultaneously taking root, inspired by the enduring legacy of Marielle Franco. Like seeds breaking through hardened soil, Black and Indigenous women surged forward as a powerful collective force, with an unprecedented number running for office. Franco (2018a) underscored the importance of Black activist women not as isolated, exceptional figures, but as part of a collective movement to *ocupar* – to occupy – spaces of institutional politics. Drawing back to Galindo's critique, Franco's call to occupy transcended the colonial logic of invasion or mere inclusion within existing power structures. It went beyond symbolic representation or superficial integration into what Frantz Fanon (1952) termed the "zone of being." Instead, Franco envisioned a radical disruption of the racialized spatial divisions that separate "zones of being" from "zones of non-being" – a transformative force emerging from below, rooted in the lived experiences of historically marginalized communities, aimed at dismantling the structures of "juridical colonialism" (Pires 2020) and its attendant political hierarchies.

The urgency of this radical contestation was brought into sharp relief during my conversation with Marklize Siqueira, an Afro-Indigenous activist, educator, and member of the Rosa Zumbi collective in Manaus. Marklize acknowledged how political parties have historically co-opted and instrumentalized social movements, but she firmly asserted that "the political party should serve as an instrument for social struggles; it is not the party that should exploit the movements, but the movements that must make use of the party" (2018). She further highlighted how, in Brazil, party affiliation often stigmatizes individuals, branding them as corrupt or untrustworthy – an ideological construct, she argues, designed to perpetuate the status quo.

> When you alienate people from politics, especially party politics, you help maintain the very conditions of exclusion. People hesitate to engage because they feel they don't belong in these spaces, but the truth is the opposite – these spaces are ours! When will those of us from the periphery finally claim them?
>
> (2018)

Marielle Franco's call to occupy institutional politics resonated deeply throughout my conversations with Black and Indigenous activists. In my encounter with Gabriele Roza, a Black ciswoman activist and journalism student affiliated with *Rede Umunna: Mulheres Negras Decidem* and the collective *Nuvem Negra* in Rio de Janeiro, I gleaned invaluable insights into how Umunna began its work in the context of Franco's femicide. This network strives to connect Black women and, through data analysis, to forge a platform for public policies. Roza emphasized that Black women, comprising 27 percent of Brazil's population, constitute the largest demographic group in the country, and yet, remain politically marginalized. As she remarked, "we know that our political agendas are not there" (2018), underscoring the significant disconnect between the lived realities of Black women and the priorities of institutional politics. Toward the conclusion of our conversation, Roza articulated her radical aspiration to strengthen the existing bonds among Black women, believing that this kinship must be translated into the political arena. Taking a stand, she asserted: "I'm only voting for Black women" (2018).

The 2018 election marked a historic milestone in Brazilian politics, with the unprecedented rise of Black and Indigenous women to political office. Among the 513 federal deputies elected that year, 77 were women – a remarkable 50 percent increase from 2014. This cohort included 13 Black women and 63 White women. Notably, Joenia Wapichana (*Rede Sustentabilidade*) made history as the first Indigenous woman elected to Congress, while Olívia Santana (Communist Party of Brazil, PCdoB) became the first Black deputy in Salvador, the Blackest city in the country. Another groundbreaking achievement was the election of Erica Malunguinho (Socialism and Liberty Party, PSOL), who became the first transgender individual to hold a seat as a state deputy in the Legislative Assembly of São Paulo. Her political platform, *Mandata Quilombo*, embodies a radical vision rooted in the countercolonial legacy of the quilombo, committed to occupying while transforming political institutions from within.

Aquilombar *the Institutional Politics*

In the concluding section of this chapter, we learn of Malunguinho's countercolonial feminist praxis, delving into her politics of redress and radical redefinition of justice. I had the opportunity to interview Erica Malunguinho in both 2020 and 2022, and the following analysis draws inspiration from those enlightening conversations and her profound onto-epistemological contributions to political discourse and practice.

Erica Malunguinho da Silva is an educator, artist, and activist born in Recife on November 20, 1981, a day that significantly coincides with both Brazil's Black Consciousness Day and the International Transgender Day of Remembrance. Her last name "Malunguinho" carries rich historical connotations. It references the Quilombo Malunguinho, or Catucá, which thrived in Recife from 1828 to 1836 (Carneiro 2001), encompassing a vital ancestral lineage from Pernambuco intertwined with the Sacred Jurema, an Afro-Indigenous spiritual entity from the region (Malunguinho 2019a, 2020a). Additionally, the term "malungo," derived from Bantu words for "boat," evokes the harrowing legacy of the Middle Passage. As noted in the "New Bantu Dictionary of Brazil" (Lopes 2012), it signifies comrade or companionship, a term employed by enslaved Africans to describe their shared traumatic experiences aboard the slave ships.

By enacting ancestral knowledges within contemporary contexts, Erica Malunguinho established Aparelha Luzia in 2016, which stands as a prominent example of an urban quilombo in Brazil. Situated in the Barra Funda neighborhood of São Paulo, Aparelha Luzia serves as a dynamic space of transatlanticity, where political, cultural, and artistic practices converge and flourish. Malunguinho (2017) envisions Aparelha as the culmination of a rich history of Black resistance, establishing a lineage that connects it to significant movements such as the Black Experimental Theater (*Teatro Experimental do Negro*), founded by Abdias do Nascimento in 1944, as well as the Brazilian Black Unified Movement (*Movimento Negro Unificado*), which emerged during the 1970s. This nexus of historical consciousness and contemporary activism illustrates how Aparelha Luzia not only honors past struggles but also catalyzes redressive forms of resistance, re-membering, and community engagement.

Building on Marielle Franco's call to occupy institutional politics, Malunguinho invokes the concept of *aquilombar* institutional politics, envisioning quilombo as a dynamic and ongoing practice in the present day. As noted in Part 0, traditional historiography, which largely relies on legal sources and colonial archives, has typically characterized the quilombo as a collective of enslaved individuals who escaped captivity in Brazil. The earliest documented reference to the term appears in a Portuguese colonial document from 1559. However, it was only until 1740 that the Overseas Council formally defined quilombo, designating it as a criminal act of insurgency, punishable by death (B. Nascimento 1975, 1985).[18] This criminalization remained in effect until 1888, when Brazil became the last country in the Western world to formally abolish slavery.

As I have argued elsewhere (Streva 2021a; Streva, Tosold, and Gutiérrez Rodríguez 2021; Streva 2021b; Streva and Nafafé 2023), quilombo, also known as *mocambo*, refers to countercolonial movements that transcend both the colonial definition of "runaway slaves" and the contemporary legal framework of "remnant communities of quilombo," as recognized by Brazil's 1988 Constitution. Quilombo entails tactics, technologies, strategies, and choreographies of survival performed by Afro-diasporic peoples in Brazil during the colonial slavery regime. It encompasses the formation of communities that resisted and subverted the colonial order, constituting a radical form of contestation, resurgence, and refusal of White supremacy. The enduring presence of quilombo, not only in rural areas but also within urban landscapes, is a key assertion made by Beatriz Nascimento and upheld by the Black Movement political platform, which continues to activate and perpetuate the grammar and legacy of quilombo today. In this context, quilombo and the practice of *aquilombar* have become the closest form of racial reparations experienced in Brazil.

I draw upon the insights of Beatriz Nascimento and Erica Malunguinho to conceptualize the quilombo as a radical and ongoing countercolonial struggle for liberation, perpetually activated through its epistemologies and ontologies in the contemporary context. Nascimento (1985) refers to quilombo practices as "tactics," while Malunguinho (2022) describes them as "social technologies." Rather than adhering to hegemonic definitions – where "tactics" are often linked to wartime strategies and "technology" to social engineering or digital media – I propose interpreting these notions as constellations of gestures, actions, choreographies, movements, and knowledge,

18 There were various definitions of quilombos at the municipal level (Gomes 2015), but in general, colonial legislation officially classified and persecuted them as acts of insurgency.

each contextualized in time and space. These elements make it possible to access and materialize the ongoing process of decolonization, which, in the Fanonian sense, is a historical process of radical disordering of the colonial system (Fanon 1961).

At the inauguration of the *Mandata Quilombo* in São Paulo's Legislative Assembly in 2018, Malunguinho declared: "Welcome to the reintegration of possession (*reintegração de posse*). Our project does not seek conflict with anyone; we wish to live well. Black people demand alternation of power (*alternância de poder*), and we are here to enter the Assembly through the front door" (Malunguinho 2019b; my translation). Passing through "the front door," I aim to analyze two pivotal technologies and tactics employed by *Mandata Quilombo* to *aquilombar* institutional politics: the interplay between alternation of power and reintegration of possession.

To address the concept of alternation of power, we must first engage with the debate on "identity politics," which exposes the limitations of representative democracy and interrogates the conservative instrumentalization of difference. "Identity politics" has often been misconceived as a framework limited to isolated struggles for individual rights led by so-called minorities. As Beatriz Nascimento (1992) critiques, the essentialized notion of minority associated with identity politics portrays the group as a "monolithic block," flattening internal nuances, differences, and complexities. This repetitive reinforcement of stereotypes ultimately perpetuates domination and the subordination of bodies and territories.

Drawing upon Nascimento's foundational work, I interpret the countercolonial feminist praxis manifested and contemporized through Malunguinho's mandate as a transformative approach to reframing the entrenched dichotomy between "identity politics" and "traditional politics." Traditional politics has been characterized as a non-identity-based form of political mobilization; however, it has historically been designed and dominated by White, cisheteronormative men, who present it as neutral and universal. As if it were possible to detach political action from one's subject-position, Malunguinho (2020b) observes that, "those who have wielded power for centuries are astonishingly also people with identities." This dynamic perpetuates what Malunguinho identifies as the "vicious circle of representation" and "institutional dysphoria" (2020b, 2020a), which denotes a repetitive and unsustainable monopoly of institutional politics that is intolerable in its implications. Conversely, political movements organized by historically marginalized groups are often relegated to the realm of "identity politics," narrowly perceived as segmented struggles for self-interest that prioritize recognition and inclusion. Such mischaracterization implies that, for instance, Afro-Brazilian feminist political projects are exclusively focused on Black women issues and necessarily disengaged from broader socioeconomic, juridical, cultural, and political justice for society at large.

In challenging dominant political narratives, I turn to the anticolonial, antiracist, and feminist legacies that inform and reaffirm the concept of "identity politics" as initially envisioned by the Combahee River Collective (1983). Founded in Boston in 1974, this Black lesbian feminist and socialist organization articulated a vision of racial, sexual, heterosexual, and class-based struggles as inherently intertwined and inseparable. "The major difficulty in our political work," they argued, "is that we are not merely fighting oppression on one front or even two, but addressing a whole range of oppressions" (1983, 7). Deeply resonant with the concept of quilombo, the collective's name honors the 1863 Combahee River raid, where Harriet Tubman led a strategic military operation that freed over 750 enslaved subjects (Harris 2008). In this sense, the interwoven nature of these struggles gives rise to a fugitive political epistemology, attentive to the profound historicity and entanglement of oppressive structures.

The foundational idea of identity politics emerges as a resilient network of solidarity, shaped through coalition-building and articulation, that honors positionality while upholding the interconnectedness of diverse struggles. Malunguinho encapsulates this ethos, stating, "Since we [Black women] have been subjected to every form of structural violence, we have cultivated the ability to see the whole and understand that if there is no peace for us, there will be no peace for anyone" (2018; my translation). This profound interdependence nurtures the transformative potential to dissolve rigid binaries – public and private, universal and particular, production and reproduction, political and domestic – and envisions a democracy reimagined beyond the limits of liberal frameworks.

Turning to the second praxis outlined, the juridical concept of "reintegration of possession" (*reintegração de posse*) is a provision in Brazilian law that allows for reclaiming possession of property unjustly appropriated by another (Law 13.105/2015; Law 10.406/2002). Historically, this legal mechanism has served those who hold wealth and power – the so-called Human, masters, property owners (Part 0), subject of rights, and citizens (Part 1) – while neglecting the claims of those rendered dispossessed, displaced, and exploited under the regimes of colonial slavery and racial capitalism.

Rather than merely reinscribing the discourse of individual rights, Erica Malunguinho reinterprets reintegration of possession in *pretuguês* (concept introduced in Part 0), transcending the conventional territorial confines of private property and ownership. Through Mandata Quilombo, she subverts the traditional concept of reintegration of possession, employing both legal and extra-legal frameworks to redress and re-membering the historical attempt to dispossess Indigenous and Black communities from their lands, knowledge, and bodies (2019a, 2020a). Malunguinho's praxis challenges the role of legal reason in constructing liberal scripts of property, identity, and representation. The politics of reintegration of possession serves as both a legal and extra-legal redressive and reparative claim. This praxis asserts not only symbolic but also material claims, advocating for the right to housing and the demarcation of traditional lands within the Legislative Assembly (Malunguinho 2019b, 2021a).

By activating quilombo tactics within institutional frameworks, Malunguinho conceives her mandate as a "Black trans paranauê counter-coup" (*contra golpe Black trans paranauê*) cultivating and renewing the ancestral legacies of resistance embedded in quilombos, candomblé, and other resilient forms of cultural defiance (Malunguinho 2020a). She describes this approach as a "politics of radical revolt" (2019c), a praxis profoundly grounded in the preservation and affirmation of life – a politics of vitality. Within this reimagined framework, Malunguinho transforms institutional politics into a site of insurgent care and transformative lawmaking, where the legacies of survival and defiance become potent instruments against systemic violence, nurturing pathways toward collective reparation and healing.

From a generative abolitionist perspective, I interpret Malunguinho's "politics of radical revolt" alongside Beatriz Nascimento's concept of "quilombola peace" (1975, 75–76). In this spirit, when Erica Malunguinho assumed office, she articulated the Mandata Quilombo's political vision: "Our project doesn't seek war with anyone; we want to live well" (2019c). Rooted in the *ntu* principle of vitality, the institutional transformations ignited by Black and Indigenous liberation's countercolonial legacies invigorate the life force, catalyzing a process of re/de/composition that, as Malunguinho asserts, is "a gain for society as a whole" (2020c).

Traditional historiography has largely emphasized the war-like dimension of quilombos, a focus influenced by colonial archives – such as police records and legal documents – that criminalized and rationalized the extermination of quilombos and their inhabitants. This approach sustains colonial narratives that cast quilombos as mere violent reactions to colonial authority. Problematizing the violence inscribed in these legal frameworks and national archives, Beatriz Nascimento argues that quilombo history cannot be reduced to these colonial sources. Instead, she proposes the notion of "quilombola peace," a framework for reconfiguring the sensible.

In a similar vein to Saidiya Hartman's practice of critical fabulation (2008), where the archive is reimagined as a site of transformability through the fabulation of counternarratives, Nascimento envisioned a speculative approach to quilombo's historiography. Although discussions of peace are scarce in quilombo literature, Nascimento suggests that if enslaved persons had left their own records, "we would have more sources on quilombola 'peace' than on war" (1975, 76).

Emerging from the radical praxis of liberation embodied by quilombo communities, "quilombola peace" diverges from depoliticized pacifism or any idealized utopic future projection. As the historian explains, "Quilombo is a warrior when it needs to be. And it is also a retreat when struggle is unnecessary" (B. Nascimento 1977, 190). Rather than disregarding the violence entailed in decolonization, as Frantz Fanon underscores (1961), this concept reveals the quilombo's abolitionist struggle as both a force of dismantling and a profoundly generative capacity. These creative practices enact redressive justice, and multispecies interrelationships among living beings and nonliving entities. Nascimento's evocative words frame the quilombo as "the continuity of life, the act of creating a happy moment" (1977, 190). Here, "peace" is reconceptualized not as an absence of conflict, but as an enduring mode of livability, interdependence, and joy – a kind of ecopolitical coalition-building among humans and more-than-humans embedded in countercolonial acts of un-worlding and world-making.

Fred Moten and Stefano Harney's concept of coalition resonates strongly here. In *The Undercommons* (2013), they envision coalition as a collective force born from the understanding that transformation is imperative for survival not of a specific group but of all of us. This perspective aligns with Malunguinho's vision of Mandata Quilombo as a movement rooted in quilombo coalitional practices that intentionally include rather than exclude. It aims to "rebalance forces, producing new horizons that are genuinely humane, for this is a struggle for life" (2018; my translation). The call to *aquilombar* embodies coalition as a foundation for political choreographies of contestation and refusal, embracing not separability (Ferreira da Silva 2016) but relationality and difference. Moving from the "bottom geologies" where colonial structures took shape, this radical, grassroots movement destabilizes and unsettles the system, potentially fracturing and eroding the very foundations of structural violence – an implosive collapse of the front door of violence.

In this framework, the modern nation-state and constitutional representative democracy are understood not as monolithic, essentialized entities but as dynamic arenas of contestation, continuously reconstituted through historical struggles. Here, power operates as a fluid force, as conceived in a Foucauldian sense, shaping the ontological, political, and legal connections among humans and more-than-human entities. As Beatriz Nascimento reminds us, "No matter how dominant a social system is, it is possible to create another system" (1989, 334; my translation). This perspective does not overlook the violence encoded in constructions of national identity nor the power dynamics inherent in (and inherited by) institutional politics (as discussed in Part 1). Rather, it positions institutional politics as a living territory where the colonial racial-patriarchal order – underpinning political femicide and racial capitalist dispossession – can be contested, refused, re/de/composed, and radically redressed.

In my conversations with Erica Malunguinho, she articulated a vision of the state not merely as an apparatus of expropriation and dispossession but as a "living organism" capable of transformative change through structural re/de/compositions. Her Black queer feminist praxis draws upon radical ecologies of livability, grounded in the understanding that "we are a biome" – a collective ecosystem in constant interrelation (Malunguinho 2021b). The word "biome" derives from Greek *bios* meaning "life" and the suffix *-oma* referring to "group and community" – that is, a kinship forged through the politics of vitality.

Malunguinho's conception of formal politics resonates profoundly with the involving ideas of Antônio Bispo dos Santos, whose work fosters organic knowledge repertoires that disrupt and exceed the colonial monocultural framework. Bispo dos Santos's approach introduces the notion of biointeraction (*biointeração*), which posits an interdependent relationship across all forms of life, encompassing both humans and more-than-human entities (2015). This perspective challenges the synthetic linear narratives of colonial monoculture, reconfiguring them as spiral, grounded, and organic ways of knowing. In this re/de/composition, the Western divide between nature and culture becomes unsettled and reconfigured, yielding a richly entangled praxis of cultivation where the germination of plants, seeds, relationships, words, and worlds converges in an intricate confluence with a politics of vitality. Biointeraction, then, generates a dialogic space that enables coalition across diverse peoples and beings, cultivating a fertile ground for multispecies justice, coexistence, and resonance (Bispo dos Santos 2023).

The multispecies kinship embodied by the biome and the generative confluence of biointeraction compel a reimagining of the legal lexicon itself – justice, subjectivity, personhood, the Human, reparation, crime, and the very processes of lawmaking. Malunguinho, drawing on Sueli Carneiro, asserts, "our existence is not negotiable" (2022, 2020d). This assertion underscores that cultivating countercolonial legal imaginaries and enacting radical practices of redress is not a theoretical ideal deferred to a promised future but an active, lived praxis, one that continually reshapes the terrain of possibility.

Bibliography

Acker, J., K. Barry, and J. Esseveld. 1982. "Objectivity and Truth: Problems in Doing Feminist Research." *Women's Studies International Forum* 6 (4): 423–435.

Agozino, Biko. 2021. "Reparative Justice: The Final Stage of Decolonization." *Punishment & Society* 23 (5. Special Issue: Legacies of Empire): 613–630.

Ahmed, Sara. 2017. *Living a Feminist Life*. Durham and London: Duke University Press.

Alvarez, Sonia E. 1990. *Engendering Democracy in Brazil: Women's Movements in Transition Politics*. Princeton: Princeton University Press.

AMAERJ (Associação de Magistrados do Estado do Rio de Janeiro). 2018. "Projetos de Lei da vereadora Marielle Franco serão votados em Sessão Extraordinária na Câmara do Rio." *AMAERJ* (blog), May. https://www2.amaerj.org.br/premio/noticias/projetos-de-lei-da-vereadora-marielle-franco-serao-votados-em-sessao-extraordinaria-na-camara-do-rio/.

Artigo19. 2018. *Dados sobre Feminicídio no Brasil #InvisibilidadeMata*. São Paulo: Artigo19.

Augusto, Geri. 2020. "For Marielle: Mulhere(s) da Maré – Danger, Seeds and Tides." *Transition* 129: 246–264.
Bairros, Luiza. 1999. "Lembrando Lélia Gonzalez, 1935–1994." *Afro-Ásia* 23.
Benites, Sandra. 2018. Conversation. Interview by Juliana Streva. June, Rio de Janeiro.
Bispo dos Santos, Antônio Nego. 2015. *Colonização, Quilombos: Modos e Significados*. Brasília: Universidade de Brasília, Coordenação CNPq.
Bispo dos Santos, Antônio Nego. 2020. A difícil arte da confluência. Entrevista com Antônio Bispo dos Santos. Interview by Liliana Coutinho. https://www.youtube.com/watch?v=XZhhs98SVxc.
Bispo dos Santos, Antônio Nego. 2023. "'Estamos no começo do replantio das palavras': uma conversa com Antônio Bispo dos Santos (Nego Bispo). Interview by Edgar Rodrigues Barbosa Neto, Natalino Neves da Silva, and Walter Francisco Figueiredo Lowande." *PerCursos, Florianópolis*, 24 (601): 1–26.
Bispo dos Santos, Antônio Nego, Natacha Simei Leal, Greice Martins, Henrique Junio Felipe, and SuzEvany Lima da Silva. 2020. "Das Confluências, Cosmologias e Contra-Colonizações. Uma conversa com Nego Bispo." *Revista Entrerios, Programa de Pós-Graduação em Antropologia* 2 (1): 73–84.
Borges, Charlene da Silva. 2018. Conversation. Interview by Juliana Streva. June, Salvador.
BRASIL. 2018. "Violência LGBTFóbicas no Brasil: Dados da Violência. Ano 2016." Brasília: Ministério dos Direitos Humanos and Secretaria Nacional de Cidadania.
BRASIL. Comissão Nacional da Verdade. 2014a. "Capítulo 10: Violência Sexual, Violência de Gênero e Violência contra Crianças e Adolescentes." Relatório da Comissão Nacional da Verdade. Brasília: CNV.
BRASIL. Comissão Nacional da Verdade. 2014b. "Texto 7: Ditadura e Homossexualidades." Relatório da Comissão Nacional da Verdade. Brasília: CNV.
Brown, Wendy. 2006. *Regulating Aversion. Tolerance in the Age of Identity and Empire*. Princeton and Oxford: Princeton University Press.
Butler, Judith. 2009. *Frames of War: When is Life Grievable*? London and New York: Verso.
Campello, André Barreto. 2018. *Manual Jurídico da Escravidão: Império do Brasil*. Jundiaí and São Paulo: Paco.
Campos, Carmen Hein de. 2017. "Lei Maria da Penha: Fundamentos e Perspectivas." In *Uma Década de Lei Maria da Penha: Percursos, Práticas e Desafios*, edited by Isadora Vier Machado. Curitiba: Editora CRV.
Campt, Tina M. 2019. "Black Visuality and the Practice of Refusal." *Women & Performance: A Journal of Feminist Theory* 29 (1): 79–87.
Carneiro, Edison. 2001. "Singularidades dos Quilombos." In *Os Quilombos na Dinâmica Social do Brasil*, edited by Clóvis Moura. Maceió: EDUFAL.
Carvalho, Igor. 2024. "Júri Popular: 'Mandato de Marielle foi uma pedra no sapato nos interesses milicianos', disse Delegado da PF." *Brasil de Fato*, October 30. https://www.brasildefato.com.br/2024/10/30/juri-popular-mandato-de-marielle-foi-uma-pedra-no-sapato-nos-interesses-milicianos-disse-delegado-da-pf.
Cerqueira, Perpétua Pereira. 2018. Conversation. Interview by Juliana Streva. June, Manaus.
Césaire, Aimé. 1950. *Discours sur le Colonialisme*. Paris: Reclame.
Chao, Sophie. 2023. Palm Oil Worlds. An Interview with Dr. Sophie Chao. Interview by Kymberley Chu. American Ethnologist website. https://americanethnologist.org/online-content/interviews/an-interview-with-dr-sophie-chao-on-palm-oil-worlds/.
Chigumadzi, Panashe. 2021. "Can White South Africa Live up to Ubuntu, the African Philosophy Tutu Globalised?" *The Guardian*, December 31, 2021, sec.

Opinion – South Africa. https://www.theguardian.com/commentisfree/2021/dec/31/white-south-africa-ubuntu-african-tutu.
Clastres, Pierre. 1974. *Society Against the State*. Translated by Robert Hurley. 6th ed. New York: Zone Books.
CMRJ (Câmara Municipal do Rio de Janeiro). 2017. "Vereadora Marielle Franco." *Official Page* (blog), 2020. https://www.camara.rio/vereadores/marielle-franco/.
COHA. 2013. *Overcoming Entrenched Perceptions: Women and Leadership in Costa Rica*. Washington, DC: Council on Hemispheric Affairs (COHA).
Collins, Patricia Hill. 1986. "Learning from the Outsider Within: The Sociological Significal Significance of Black Feminist Thought." *Social Problems, Special Theory Issue* 33 (6): 14–32.
Combahee River Collective. 1983. "The Combahee River Collective's Statement." In *Home Girls: A Black Feminist Anthology*, edited by Barbara Smith. New York: Kitchen Table.
Cornell, Drucilla. 2014. "Ubuntu and Subaltern Legality." In *Ubuntu. Curating the Archive*, edited by Leonhard Praeg and Siphokazi Magadla, 121–136. South Africa: University of KwaZulu-Natal Press.
Cornell, Drucilla, and Karin van Marle. 2015. "Ubuntu Feminism: Tentative Reflections." *Verbum et Ecclesia* 36 (2): 8.
Crisóstomo, Laina. 2018. Conversation. Interview by Juliana Streva. June, Salvador.
Cusicanqui, Silvia Rivera. 2010. "Ch'ixinakax Utxiwa: A Reflection on the Practices and Discourses of Decolonization." In *Ch'ixinakax Utxiwa. On Practices and Discourses of Decolonization*, translated by Molly Geidel, 46–70. Cambridge: Polity Press.
Damazio, Natália. 2018. Conversation. Interview by Juliana Streva. June, Rio de Janeiro.
Davis, Angela. 2003. *Are Prisons Obsolete?* New York: Seven Stories Press.
Davis, Angela, Gina Dent, Erica R. Meiners, and Beth E. Richie. 2022. *Abolition. Feminism. Now*. Dublin: Penguin Books.
ECLAC (Economic Commission for Latin America and the Caribbean). 2015. *Latin America and the Caribbean: Looking Ahead after the Millennium Development Goals: Regional Monitoring Report on the Millennium Development Goals in Latin America and the Caribbean*. Santiago de Chile: ECLAC.
Eze, Michael Onyebuchi. 2017. "I Am Because You Are: Cosmopolitanism in the Age of Xenophobia." *Philosophical Papers* 46 (1): 85–109.
Fanon, Frantz. 1952. *Black Skin, White Masks*. Translated by Richard Philcox. New York: Grove Press.
Fanon, Frantz. 1961. *The Wretched of the Earth*. Translated by Richard Philcox. New York: Grove Press.
Ferreira da Silva, Denise. 2007. *Toward a Global Idea of Race*. Borderlines, Vol. 27. Minneapolis: University of Minnesota Press.
Ferreira da Silva, Denise. 2009. "No-Bodies: Law, Raciality and Violence." *Griffith Law Review* 18 (2): 212–236.
Ferreira da Silva, Denise. 2013. "To Be Announced – Radical Praxis or Knowing (at) the Limits of Justice." *Social Text, Duke University Press* 31 (1): 43–62.
Ferreira da Silva, Denise. 2014. "Toward a Black Feminist Poethics: The Quest(ion) of Blackness Toward the End of the World." *The Black Scholar* 44 (2): 81–97. https://doi.org/10.1080/00064246.2014.11413690.
Ferreira da Silva, Denise. 2016. "Sobre Diferença sem Separabilidade." *Catálogo 32a Bienal de São Paulo. Incerteza Viva* 7: 57–65.
Ferreira da Silva, Denise. 2017. "Speculations on a Transformative Theory of Justice." *Hearings: An Online Journal of Contour Biennale* 8. Polyphonic Worlds: Justice as Medium (April 11).

Ferreira da Silva, Denise. 2018. "Hacking the Subject: Black Feminism and Refusal beyond the Limits of Critique." *philoSOPHIA* 8 (1): 19–41.
Ferreira da Silva, Denise. 2022. *Unpayable Debt*. On the Antipolitical, Vol. 1. London: Sternberg Press.
Florentino, Manolo, Alexandre Vieira Ribeiro, and Daniel Domingues da Silva. 2004. "Aspectos Comparativos do Tráfico de Africanos para o Brasil (Séculos XVIII e XIX)." *Afro-Ásia* 31: 83–126.
Foucault, Michel. 1975. *Em Defesa da Sociedade. Curso no Collège de France (1975–1976)*. Translated by Maria Ermantina de Almeida Prado Galvão. 2nd ed. São Paulo: Martins Fontes.
Foucault, Michel. 2008. *The Birth of Biopolitics. Lectures at the Collège de France, 1978–79*. Translated by Graham Burchell. New York: Palgrave Macmillan.
Franco, Marielle. 2018a. "Mulher, Negra, Favelada e Parlamentar: Resistir é Pleonasmo." In *O Golpe na Perspectiva de Gênero*, edited by Linda Rubim and Fernanda Argolo. Salvador: Edufba.
Franco, Marielle. 2018b. "Tweet Marielle Franco." *Twitter* (blog), March 13. https://twitter.com/mariellefranco/status/973568966403731456.
Franco, Marielle, and Luisa Fenizola. 2020. "The Words of Marielle Franco: Love and Dedication to Justice and the Favela #2YearsWithoutMarielle." Translated by Edmund Ruge. *RioOnWatch*, March 14, #MarielleLegacy ed. https://rioonwatch.org/?p=58297.
G1. 2024. "'Justiça é lenta, é cega, é burra, é injusta, é errada, é torta, mas chega', diz Juíza ao ler sentença para assassinos de Marielle." *Globo*, Rio de Janeiro, October 31. https://g1.globo.com/rj/rio-de-janeiro/noticia/2024/10/31/justica-e-lenta-e-cega-e-burra-e-injusta-e-errada-e-torta-mas-chega-diz-juiza-ao-ler-sentenca-para-assassinos-de-marielle.ghtml.
Galindo, Maria. 2013. *No Se Puede Descolonizar Sin Despatriarcalizar. Teoría y Propuesta de la Despatriarcalización*. La Paz, Bolívia: Mujeres Creando.
Galvão, Joana Montanha. 2018. Conversation. Interview by Juliana Streva. June, Manaus.
Gatto, Malu. 2017. "The Variation of Quota Designs and Their Origins in Latin America (1991–2015)." In *Women, Politics, and Democracy in Latin America. Crossing Boundaries of Gender and Politics in the Global South*, edited by Tomáš Došek, Flavia Freidenberg, Mariana Caminotti, and Betilde Muñoz-Pogossian. New York: Palgrave Macmillan.
Gerald, Samuel, Matthew Durington Collins, and Harjant Gill. 2017. "Multimodality: An Invitation." *Multimodal Anthropologies – American Anthropologist* 119 (1): 142–153.
Glissant, Édouard. 1990. *Poetics of Relation*. Ann Arbor: The University of Michigan Press.
Gobineau, Arthur de. 1967. *Essai sur l'inégalité des Races Humaines (1853–1855)*. Paris: Éditions Pierre Belfond.
Gobineau, Arthur de. 1990. *Arthur de Gobineau et Le Bresil: Correspondance Diplomatique du Ministre de France à Rio de Janeiro 1869–1870*. Grenoble: Presses Universitaires de Grenoble.
Gomes, Joyce Alves. 2018. Conversation. Interview by Juliana Streva. June, Manaus.
Gonzalez, Lélia. 1983. "Racismo e Sexismo na Cultura Brasileira." *Revista Ciências Sociais Hoje, ANPOCS*: 223–244.
Gordon, Lewis R. 2014. "Justice Otherwise: Thoughts on Ubuntu." In *Ubuntu. Curating the Archive*, edited by Leonhard Praeg and Siphokazi Magadla, 10–26. South Africa, Pietermaritzburg: University of KwaZulu-Natal Press.

Grosfoguel, Ramón. 2016. "Del 'Extractivismo Económico' al 'Extractivismo Epistémico' y al 'Extractivismo Ontológico': Una Forma Destructiva de Conocer, Ser y Estar en el Mundo." *Tabula Rasa, Bogotá* 24 (June): 123–143.
Halberstam, Jack. 2013. "The Wild Beyond: With and for the Undercommons." In *The Undercommons: Fugitive Planning & Black Study*, 2–13. New York: Minor Compositions.
Haraway, Donna. 1988. "Situated Knowledges: The Science Question in Feminism and the Privilege of Partial Perspectives." *Feminist Studies* 14 (3): 575–599.
Harding, Sandra. 1993. "Rethinking Standpoint Epistemology: What is 'Strong Objectivity'?" In *Feminist Epistemologies*, edited by Linda Alcoff and Elizabeth Potter. London: Routledge.
Harris, Duchess. 2008. "'All of Who I Am in the Same Place': The Combahee River Collective." *Internet Archive* 2 (1): 1–26. Originally published at *Womanist Theory and Research*. https://web.archive.org/web/20080315192601/http://www.uga.edu/~womanist/harris3.1.htm.
Hartman, Saidiya. 1997. *Scenes of Subjection: Terror, Slavery, and Self-Making in Nineteenth-Century America*. 2nd ed. New York and London: Oxford University Press.
Hartman, Saidiya. 2008. "Venus in Two Acts." *Small Axe (SX26). A Caribbean Journal of Criticism* 12 (2): 1–14.
Hartman, Saidiya. 2019. *Wayward Lives, Beautiful Experiments. Intimate Histories of Social Upheaval*. New York and London: W.W. Norton & Company.
Hersey, Tricia. 2022. *Rest is Resistance. A Manifesto*. New York: Hachette Book Group.
IBGE (Instituto Brasileiro de Geografia e Estatística). 2018. "Informação Demográfica e Socioeconômica." *Estudos e Pesquisas*. Brazil: IBGE.
Instituto Patrícia Galvão. 2017. *Femicídio #InvisibilidadeMata*. São Paulo: Fundação Rosa Luxemburgo.
Inter-American Court of Human Rights (IACourtHR). 2010. "Caso Gomes Lund and Others ('Guerrilha do Araguaia') v. Brazil." OAS, Inter-American Court of Human Rights.
IPEA (Instituto de Pesquisa Econômica Aplicada). 2015. "Avaliando a Efetividade da Lei Maria da Penha." 2048 Texto para Discussão. Brasília: IPEA.
IPEA, and FBSP. 2019. "Atlas da Violência 2019." Brasil: Instituto de Pesquisa Economica Aplicada (IPEA) and Forum Brasileiro de Segurança Pública (FBSP).
IPU (Inter-Parliamentary Union). 2015. "Parline Database on National Parliaments." IPU.
IPU. 2018. "Women in Parliament in 2018." The Year in Review. Geneva: Inter-Parliamentary Union.
IPU, and PACE. 2018. "Sexism, Harassment and Violence against Women in Parliaments in Europe." Issues Brief. Geneva: Inter-Parliamentary Union (IPU); Parliamentary Assembly of the Council of Europe (PACE).
IPU, and UNWomen. 2017. "Women in Politics: 2017." UN Women, Inter-Parliamentary Union.
Kilomba, Grada. 2008. *Plantation Memories. Episodes of Everyday Racism*. 5th ed. Münster: Unrast.
Kilomba, Grada. 2015. "Decolonising Knowledge." In *The Struggle Is Not Over Yet. An Archive in Relation*, 191–208. Berlin: Archive Books.
Kopenawa, Davi, and Bruce Albert. 2010. *A Queda do Céu. Palavras de um Xamã Yanomami*. Translated by Beatriz Perrone-Moisés. São Paulo: Companhia das Letras.
Krenak, Ailton. 2019. *Ideias para Adiar o Fim do Mundo*. São Paulo: Companhia das Letras.

Krook, Mona Lena. 2009. *Quotas for Women in Politics: Gender and Candidate Selection Reform Worldwide.* Oxford and New York: Oxford University Press.

Laurent, Claire, Michael Platzer, and Maria Idomir. 2013. "Femicide: A Global Issue that Demands Action." Vienna Liaison Office: Academic Council on the United Nations System (ACUNS).

Leal, Maria do Carmo, Silvana Granado Nogueira da Gama, Ana Paula Esteves Pereira, Vanessa Eufrauzino Pacheco, Cleber Nascimento do Carmo, and Ricardo Ventura Santos. 2017. "A Cor da Dor: Iniquidades Raciais na Atenção Pré-Natal e ao Parto no Brasil." *Caderno Saúde Pública* 33 (1): 1–17. https://doi.org/10.1590/0102-311X00078816.

Lopes, Nei. 2012. *Novo Dicionário Banto do Brasil.* 2nd ed. Rio de Janeiro: Pallas.

Lorde, Audre. 1981 [2017]. "Uses of Anger: Women Responding to Racism." In *The Master's Tools Will Never Dismantle the Master's House.* Penguin Modern: 23. UK: Penguin.

Macdowell Santos, Cecília, and Wânia Pasinato. 2005. "Violência contra as Mulheres e Violência de Gênero: Notas sobre Estudos Feministas no Brasil." *Estudios Interdisciplinarios de América Latina y El Caribe* 16 (1): 147–164.

Machado, Manuelita Carolina. 2018. Conversation. Interview by Juliana Streva. June, Salvador.

Malunguinho, Erica. 2017. "Erica Malunguinho: A Mulher que Pariu um Quilombo Urbano." *Revista Trip – TPM*, June 3. https://revistatrip.uol.com.br/tpm/erica-malunguinho-mulher-negra-trans-aparelha-luzia-resistencia-negra-sao-paulo-quilombo-urbano.

Malunguinho, Erica. 2018. "Enquanto não houver paz para o nosso povo, não haverá para ninguém", afirma Erica Malunguinho. Interview by Aline Bernardes and Pedro Borges. https://almapreta.com/sessao/cotidiano/enquanto-nao-houver-paz-para-o-nosso-povo-nao-havera-para-ninguem-afirma-erica-malunguinho.

Malunguinho, Erica. 2019a. A mandata quilombo de resistência. Interview by Natalia Souza. https://livro-reportagem.com.br/a-mandata-quilombo-de-resistencia/.

Malunguinho, Erica. 2019b. "Lançamento da Frente Parlamentar em Defesa dos Direitos das Pessoas LGBTQIA+." *Diário Oficial* 129 (135). 10a Sessão Solene. São Paulo: Poder Legislativo de São Paulo.

Malunguinho, Erica. 2019c. Malunguinho: População trans ainda luta "pelo direito à vida." Interview by Anna Beatriz Anjos. https://apublica.org/2019/08/malunguinho-populacao-trans-ainda-luta-pelo-direito-a-vida/.

Malunguinho, Erica. 2019d. "Projeto de afeto e vitória coletiva do povo negro", diz Erica Malunguinho. Interview by Caê Vasconcelos. https://ponte.org/e-um-projeto-de-afeto-e-uma-vitoria-coletiva-do-povo-negro-diz-erica-malunguinho/ (27.10.2020).

Malunguinho, Erica. 2020a. Conversa com Erica Malunguinho. Encontro com Estudantes, Professorxs e Pesquisadorxs. Interview by Juliana Streva. Video-Zoom.

Malunguinho, Erica. 2020b. Erica Malunguinho: alternar o poder é ter raça e gênero como fundamento. Interview by Débora Britto. https://marcozero.org/erica-malunguinho-alternar-o-poder-e-ter-raca-e-genero-como-fundamento/.

Malunguinho, Erica. 2020c. Erica Malunguinho: mulher trans, deputada, educadora e artista plástica. Interview by Caê Vasconcelos. https://ponte.org/erica-malunguinho-mulher-trans-deputada-educadora-e-artista-plastica/ (27.10.2020).

Malunguinho, Erica. 2020d. "Janaina, Jair, Impeachments e a Seleção Artificial." *Portal Geledés*, March 26. https://www.geledes.org.br/janaina-jair-impeachments-e-a-selecao-artificial/ (27/10/2020).

Malunguinho, Erica. 2021a. "Histórico Proposições." *Assembleia Legislativa do Estado de São Paulo.* São Paulo: ALESP. https://www.al.sp.gov.br/deputado/?matricula=300625.

Malunguinho, Erica. 2021b. Why Brazil's First Trans State Legislator Built a Refuge for Black Queer and Trans People. Interview by Thomas Jean Lax. *The Nation*. https://www.thenation.com/article/world/erica-malunguinho-interview/.

Malunguinho, Erica. 2022. Entrevista com Erica Malunguinho. Interview by Juliana Streva. Video-Zoom.

Marques, Danusa. 2018. "O que são as cotas para mulheres na política e qual é sua importância?" *Gênero e Número*, September 13. https://www.generonumero.media/reportagens/o-que-sao-as-cotas-para-mulheres-na-politica-e-qual-e-sua-importancia/

Martins, Leda Maria. 1997. *Afrografias da Memória*. 2 ed. São Paulo and Belo Horizonte: Perspectiva and Mazza Edições.

Martins, Leda Maria. 2003. "'Performances da Oralitura: Corpo, Lugar da Memória.' Letras, Revista do Programa de Pós-Graduação em Letras da Universidade Federal de Santa Maria." *Língua e Literatura: Limites e Fronteiras*, no. 26, 63–81.

McGranahan, Carole. 2022. "Theory as Ethics." *American Ethnologist* 49 (3): 289–301.

McKittrick, Katherine. 2021. *Dear Science and Other Stories (Errantries)*. Durham: Duke University Press.

McMillan, Lesley. 2007. *Feminists Organising Against Gendered Violence*. New York: Palgrave MacMillan.

Menezes, Larissa Guedes. 2018. Conversation. Interview by Juliana Streva. June, Salvador.

Miskolci, Richard. 2013. *O Desejo da Nação: Masculinidade e Branquitude no Brasil de Fins do XIX*. São Paulo: Annablume.

Mohanty, Chandra Talpade. 1984. "Under Western Eyes: Feminist Scholarship and Colonial Discourses." *Boundary 2, On Humanism and the University I: The Discourse of Humanism* 12 (3): 333–358.

Mombaça, Jota. 2021a. "A coisa tá branca." In *Não Vão Nos Matar Agora*, 35–47. Rio de Janeiro: Cobogó.

Mombaça, Jota. 2021b. "Carta às que vivem e vibram apesar do Brasil." In *Não Vão Nos Matar Agora*, 13–19. Rio de Janeiro: Cobogó.

Mombaça, Jota. 2021c. "Notas estratégicas quanto aos usos políticos do conceito de lugar de fala." In *Não Vão Nos Matar Agora*, 85–90. Rio de Janeiro: Cobogó.

Mombaça, Jota. 2021d. "Rumo a uma redistribuição desobediente de gênero e anticolonial da violência." In *Não Vão Nos Matar Agora*, 63–83. Rio de Janeiro: Cobogó.

Mombaça, Jota. 2021e. "Na quebra. Juntas." In *Não Vão Nos Matar Agora*, 21–26. Rio de Janeiro: Cobogó.

Mombaça, Jota. 2021f. "O mundo é meu trauma." In *Não Vão Nos Matar Agora*, 27–34. Rio de Janeiro: Cobogó.

Moten, Fred. 2003. *In the Break. The Aesthetics of the Black Radical Tradition*. Minneapolis and London: University of Minnesota Press.

Moten, Fred, and Stefano Harney. 2013. *The Undercommons: Fugitive Planning & Black Study*. New York: Minor Compositions.

Muñoz-Pogossian, Betilde, Flavia Freidenberg, Mariana Caminotti, and Tomáš Došek. 2017. "Women, Politics, and Democracy in Latin America: An Introduction." In *Women, Politics, and Democracy in Latin America. Crossing Boundaries of Gender and Politics in the Global South*, edited by Tomáš Došek, Flavia Freidenberg, Mariana Caminotti, and Betilde Muñoz-Pogossian. New York: Palgrave Macmillan.

Muñoz, Sandra. 2018. Conversation. Interview by Juliana Streva. June, Salvador.

Nascimento, Beatriz. 1975 [2018]. "'Quilombos': Mudança Social ou Conservantismo? [1975]." In *Beatriz Nascimento. Quilombola e Intelectual. Possibilidade nos Dias da Destruição*, edited by União dos Coletivos Pan-Africanistas, 66–79. Diáspora Africana: Editora Filhos da África.

Nascimento, Beatriz. 1977 [2018]. "Historiografia do Quilombo [1977]." In *Beatriz Nascimento. Quilombola e Intelectual. Possibilidade nos Dias da Destruição*, edited by União dos Coletivos Pan-Africanistas, 125–165. São Paulo: Editora Filhos da África.

Nascimento, Beatriz. 1985 [2018]. "O Conceito de Quilombo e a Resistência Cultural Negra [1985]." In *Beatriz Nascimento. Quilombola e Intelectual. Possibilidade nos Dias da Destruição*, edited by União dos Coletivos Pan-Africanistas, 273–294. São Paulo: Editora Filhos da África.

Nascimento, Beatriz. 1989 [2018]. "Transcrição do Documentário Orí [1989]." In *Beatriz Nascimento. Quilombola e Intelectual. Possibilidade nos Dias da Destruição*, edited by União dos Coletivos Pan-Africanistas, 326–340. São Paulo: Editora Filhos da África.

Nascimento, Beatriz. 1992 [2018]. "Por Um Território (Novo) Existencial e Físico [1992]." In *Beatriz Nascimento. Quilombola e Intelectual. Possibilidade nos Dias da Destruição*, edited by União dos Coletivos Pan-Africanistas, 413–430. São Paulo: Editora Filhos da África.

Núñez, Geni, João Manuel de Oliveira, and Mara Coelho de Souza Lago. 2021. "Monogamia e (Anti)Colonialidades: Uma Artesania Narrativa Indígena." *Teoria e Cultura* 16 (3): 76–88.

Oakley, Ann. 1981. "Interviewing Women: A Contradiction in Terms." In *Doing Feminist Research*, edited by H. Roberts. London: Routledge and Kegan Paul.

Observatório da Mulher Contra a Violência. 2018. *Panorama de Violência contra as Mulheres no Brasil. Indicadores Nacionais e Estaduais*. Brasília: Senado Federal.

Oliveira, Edna da Silva Pinho de. 2018. Conversation. Interview by Juliana Streva. June, Salvador.

Oliveros, Pauline. 2005. *Deep Listening: A Composer's Sound Practice*. Bloomington: iUniverse, Inc.

Oliveros, Pauline. 2022. *Quantum Listening*. London: Ignota Press.

Padro, Monique Rodrigues do. 2021. "Mulheres Negras: Nem 'Super Mulheres' e Nem 'Raivosas', Somos Humanas." *Alma Preta*, de abril de, sec. Quilombo. https://almapreta.com.br/sessao/quilombo/mulheres-negras-nem-super-mulheres-e-nem-raivosas-somos-humanas/.

Pádua, Roberta de. 2018. Conversation. Interview by Juliana Streva. June, Rio de Janeiro.

Paine, Robert. 1989. "Our Authorial Authority." *Culture* 9 (2): 35–47. https://doi.org/10.7202/1079364ar.

Pasinato, Wânia. 2017. "Dez Anos Mais Um: A Implementação da Lei Maria da Penha no Passar dos Anos." In *Uma Década de Lei Maria da Penha: Percursos, Práticas e Desafios*, edited by Isadora Vier Machado. Curitiba: Editora CRV.

Pasinato, Wânia, and Cecília MacDowell Santos. 2008. "Mapeamento das Delegacias da Mulher no Brasil." *Projeto Acesso à Justiça para Mulheres Em Situação de Violência: Estudo Comparativo das Delegacias da Mulher na América Latina (Brasil, Equador, Nicarágua, Peru)*. Campinas: Núcleo de Estudos de Gênero Pagu (PAGU), Universidade Estadual de Campinas (UNICAMP).

Paulino, Maria Alice da Silva. 2018. Conversation. Interview by Juliana Streva. June, Manaus.

Petersmann, Marie. 2024. "'Re/de/Composing' International Law." *Völkerrechtsblog* (blog), July 31. https://voelkerrechtsblog.org/re-de-composing-international-law/.

Pires, Thula. 2020. "Direitos Humanos e Améfrica Ladina: Por Uma Crítica Amefricana ao Colonialismo Jurídico." *LASA Forum 2019. Améfrica Ladina: Vinculando Mundos y Saberes, Tejiendo Esperanzas, Dossier: El pensamiento de Lélia Gonzalez, un legado y un horizonte* 50 (3): 69–74.

Pires, Thula, and Luanna Tomaz Souza. 2020. "É Possível Compatibiliizar Abolicionismos e Feminismos no Enfrentamento às Violências Cometidas contra Mulheres?" *Revista Direitos Culturais, Santo Ângelo* 15 (35): 129–157.
Ramos, Guerreiro. 1957. "Patologia Social do 'Branco' Brasileiro." In *Introdução Crítica à Sociologia Brasileira*. Rio de Janeiro: Editorial Andes Limitada.
Ramose, Mogobe B. 2014. "Ubuntu. Affirming a Right and Seeking Remedies in South Africa." In *Ubuntu. Curating the Archive*, edited by Leonhard Praeg and Siphokazi Magadla, 121–136. South Africa: University of KwaZulu-Natal Press.
Ribeiro, Flávia. 2020. "Estereótipo sobre 'Ser Forte' Afeta Saúde Mental das Mulheres Negras." *Alma Preta*, Setembro, sec. Cotidiano. https://almapreta.com.br/sessao/cotidiano/estereotipo-sobre-ser-forte-afeta-saude-mental-das-mulheres-negras/.
Rios, Flavia. 2017. "A Cidadania Imaginada pelas Mulheres Afro-Brasileiras: Da Ditadura Militar à Democracia." In *50 Anos de Feminismo: Argentina, Brasil e Chile. A Construção das Mulheres como Atores Políticos e Democráticos*, edited by Eva Alterman Blay and Lúcia Avelar. São Paulo: Editora da Universidade de São Paulo.
Rodrigues, Cleber, Bruno Laforé, and Yasmin Oliveira. 2024. "Caso Marielle: Júri de homens brancos de meia-idade não deve interferir em sentença, segundo MP." *CNN Brasil*, October 31. https://www.cnnbrasil.com.br/nacional/caso-marielle-juri-de-homens-brancos-de-meia-idade-nao-deve-interferir-em-sentenca-segundo-mp/.
Roza, Gabriele da Silva. 2018. Conversation. Interview by Juliana Streva. May, Rio de Janeiro.
Said, Edward. 1989. "Representing the Colonized: Anthropology's Interlocutors." *Critical Inquiry* 15 (2): 205–225.
Schwarcz, Lilia Moritz. 2007. *O Espetáculo das Raças: Cientistas, Instituições e Questão Racial no Brasil (1870–1930)*. São Paulo: Companhia das Letras.
Schwarcz, Lilia Moritz. 2012. *Nem Preto Nem Branco, Muito pelo Contrário: Cor e Raça na Sociabilidade Brasileira*. São Paulo: Claroenigma.
Schwindt-Bayer, Leslie A. 2009. "Making Quotas Work: The Effect of Gender Quota Laws on the Election of Women." *Legislative Studies Quarterly* XXXIV (1): 5–28.
Senado. 2013. *Relatório Final: Situação da Violência contra a Mulher no Brasil*. Brasília: Comissão Parlamentar Mista de Inquério (CPMI).
SEPPIR, Secretaria Nacional de Políticas de Promoção da Igualdade Racial. 2014. *A Participação das Mulheres Negras nos Espaços de Poder*. Brazil: Secretaria de Políticas de Promoção da Igualdade Racial; Programa Interagencial para a Promoção da Igualdade de Gênero, Raça e Etnia do Sistema Nações Unidas no Brasil.
Silva, Florismar Ferreira da. 2018. Conversation. Interview by Juliana Streva. June, Manaus.
Silva, Lívia Ferreira da. 2018. Conversation. Interview by Juliana Streva. June, Salvador.
Silva, Luzanira Varela da. 2018. Conversation. Interview by Juliana Streva. June, Manaus.
Simpson, Audra. 2014. *Mohawk Interruptus. Political Life Across the Borders of Settler States*. Durham and London: Duke University Press.
Simpson, Audra. 2017. "The Ruse of Consent and the Anatomy of 'Refusal': Cases from Indigenous North America and Australia." *Postcolonial Studies* 20 (1): 18–33. https://doi.org/10.1080/13688790.2017.1334283.
Simpson, Leanne Betasamosake. 2014. "Land as Pedagogy: Nishnaabeg Intelligence and Rebellious Transformation." *Decolonization: Indigeneity, Education & Society* 3 (3): 1–25.

Simpson, Leanne Betasamosake. 2016. "Indigenous Resurgence and Co-resistance." *Critical Ethnic Studies* 2 (2): 19–34.
Siqueira, Marklize dos Santos. 2018. Conversation. Interview by Juliana M. Streva. June, Manaus.
Skidmore, Thomas E. 1976 [2012]. *Preto no Branco: Raça e Nacionalidade no Pensamento Brasileiro, 1870–1930.* Translated by Donaldson M. Garschagen. São Paulo: Companhia das Letras.
Smith, Linda Tuhiwai. 1999. *Decolonizing Methodologies. Research and Indigenous Peoples.* London and New York: Zed Books and University of Otago Press.
Spillers, Hortense J. 1987. "Mama's Baby, Papa's Maybe: An American Grammar Book." *Diacritics, Culture and Countermemory: The "American" Connection. The Johns Hopkins University Press* 17 (2): 64–81.
Spivak, Gayatri Chakravorty. 1988. *Can the Subaltern Speak?* Basingstoke: Macmillan.
Streva, Juliana. 2016. "O Poder de Matar do Estado em Michel Foucault: Uma Investigação sobre o Racismo." In *Reinvenções de Foucault*, edited by Ana Kiffer, Antonio Pele, Mauricio Rocha, Francisco Guimaraens, and Rafael Becker, 59–68. Rio de Janeiro: Lamparina.
Streva, Juliana. 2017. "Auto de Resistência, Biopolítica e Colonialidade: Racismo como Mecanismo de Poder." *Revista Brasileira de Ciências Criminais* 138 (25): 237–267.
Streva, Juliana. 2018. *Corpo, Raça, Poder: Extermínio Negro no Brasil.* Rio de Janeiro: Editora Multifoco.
Streva, Juliana. 2021a. "Aquilombar Democracy: Fugitive Routes from the End of the World." *São Paulo: The Maria Sibylla Merian International Centre for Advanced Studies in the Humanities and Social Sciences Conviviality- Inequality in Latin America* 37: 1–30. http://doi.org/10.46877/streva.2021.37.
Streva, Juliana. 2021b. "Decolonial Coalitions: Afro-Brazilian Feminisms and the Poetic-Politics of Quilombo." *Femina Politica – Zeitschrift Für Feministische Politikwissenschaft, Schwarze Feminismen – Black Feminisms* 1: 93–105.
Streva, Juliana, and Iracema Dulley. 2023. "Invitation, To Exi(s)t." In *Displacing Theory Through the Global South*, edited by Özgün Eylül Iscen and Iracema Dulley. Berlin: ICI Berlin Press.
Streva, Juliana, and José Nafafé. 2023. "Transcending Lusotropicalism: From Macamba to Quilombo." In *O Quilombismo. Reader*, edited by Eric Sumba and Cosima Costinas. Berlin: HKW Press and Archive Books. https://www.hkw.de/en/programme/o-quilombismo/o-quilombismo-reader.
Streva, Juliana, Léa Tosold, and Encarnación Gutiérrez Rodríguez. n.d. "Aquilombar com o Oceano: Diálogos Poético-Políticos sobre Violências, Conhecimentos e (R) Existências." *Diálogos Mecila* (2021). https://open.spotify.com/episode/1aAyilDlihRvcJjLX8PICM?si=eDLPxm4pQr2AuaqOXwusrA (15.6.2021).
Streva, Juliana, Sarah R. Case, and Marie Petersmann. 2024. "The Inhuman as Refusal." *Critical Legal Thinking: Law and the Political* (blog). https://criticallegalthinking.com/.
Tamale, Sylvia. 2020. *Decolonization and Afro-Feminism.* Ottawa: Daraja Press.
Teles, Maria Amélia de Almeida. 2015. "A Construção da Memória e da Verdade numa Perspectiva de Gênero." *Revista Direito GV, São Paulo* 11 (2): 505–522.
TGEU. 2016. "Transrespect versus Transphobia Worldwide. Annual Report 2016. An Introduction to the Trans Murder Monitoring." In TvT Publication Series Vol. 14, edited by Carsten Balzer, Carla LaGata, and Lukas Berredo. Transgender Europe (TGEU). https://transrespect.org/wp-content/uploads/2016/11/TvT-PS-Vol14-2016.pdf.

Torres, Sergio. 1995. "Acusado de Matar Professora é Preso no Rio." *Folha de S. Paulo*, September 2, sec. Cotidiano. https://www1.folha.uol.com.br/fsp/1995/2/09/cotidiano/13.html.
Trinh, Minh-Ha T. 1989. *Woman, Native, Other. Writing Postcoloniality and Feminism*. Bloomington and Indianapolis: Indiana University Press.
Trinh, Minh-Ha T. 1991. *When the Moon Waxes Red. Representation, Gender and Cultural Politics*. New York and London: Routledge.
Tuck, Eve, and K. Wayne Yang. 2016. "What Justice Wants." *Critical Ethnic Studies* 2 (2): 1–15.
Tupinambá, Glicélia (Célia). 2022. "An Indigenous Woman Troubling the Museum's Colonialist Legacy: Conversation with Glicéria Tupinambá." Translated by Pedro Marco Gonçalves. *Museum International. Towards Decolonisation* 74 (3–4): 10–23.
UNDP. 2015. *Más Allá de los Números: Las Mujeres Transforman el Poder Legislativo en América Latina y el Caribe*. Translated by Regional Center. Panama: United Nations Development Fund (UNDP).
Wallace, Michele. 1978 [2015]. *Black Macho and the Myth of the Superwoman*. London: Verso.
Weiss, Erica. 2021. "Pseudonyms as Anti-Citation." *American Ethnologist – Rethinking Pseudonyms in Ethnography* (blog), December 13. https://americanethnologist.org/features/collections/rethinking-pseudonyms-in-ethnography/pseudonyms-as-anti-citation.
Werneck, Jurema. 2005. "De Ialodês e Feministas – Reflexões sobre a Ação Política das Mulheres Negras na América Latina e Caribe." *Nouvelles Questions Féministes – Revue Internationale Francophone* 24 (2).
Werneck, Jurema. 2010. "Nossos Passos Vêm de Longe – Movimentos de Mulheres Negras e Estratégias Políticas contra o Sexismo e o Racismo." *Revista da Associação Brasileira de Pesquisadores(as) Negros(As)* 1 (1).
Westmoreland, Mark R. 2022. "Multimodality: Reshaping Anthropology." *Annual Review of Anthropology* 51: 173–194. https://doi.org/10.1146/annurev-anthro-121319-071409.
Williams, Patricia J. 1987. "Alchemical Notes: Reconstructing Ideals from Deconstructed Rights." *Harvard Civil Rights – Civil Liberties Law Review* 22 (2): 401–433.
Wynter, Sylvia. 1970s. "Black Metamorphosis: New Natives in a New World." Unpublished Manuscript, Institute of the Black World Records. Schomburg Center for Research in Black Culture, New York.
Wynter, Sylvia. 2015. *Sylvia Wynter. On Being Human as Praxis*. Durham and London: Duke University Press.

Stills from the film *Women in Movement* (2020), by Juliana Streva

After-words/After-worlds

It feels

as though

the ground is

trembling

again

while

the sky

falls[1]

The somatic weight of political violence and environmental collapse, unequally distributed, presses deeply into bodies, into the body of this book, and into countless other bodies tethered to the Earth. And yet, *we* stand.

This *we* is not the homogeneous, national *we*: a flattening category that erases positions, trajectories, conditions of speakability, or inherited legacies. Instead, the *we* invoked here emerges in the intersections, the *encruzilhadas*, as a meeting point where struggles intertwine and seeds of possibility are sown; where we can find each other (Moten and Harney 2013; Halberstam 2013). These crossroads cultivate the potential for confluences in what may seem like an impossible world.

This collapsing world, a relentless reiteration of the colonial order, recomposes itself daily in its porosity, in its politics, in its laws. Once again, *we* face

1 The "sky falls" is inspired by the book *The Falling Sky* (2010) by Yanomami shaman Davi Kopenawa and French anthropologist Bruce Albert.

the enactments of colonialism in the ongoing genocide; the rise of neoliberal populism fortified by White supremacist, misogynist, and neoliberal ideologies; the ecological disasters: from floods to fires, from desolation to bombs. And yet, *we* stand.

These are events that, each in their own way, could leave *us* speechless, silenced, stripped bare of language, or brought to the ground – *tombar*. And yet, this book insists on the attempt to find words, pathways, everyday choreographies of the otherwise. It persists on un/re/writing beyond and despite the architectures of violence; beyond and despite Brazil; beyond and despite the afterlives of colonialism; beyond and despite the extractivist logics of academia; beyond and despite exhaustion.

This book does not presume to offer a recipe or solution for dismantling these entrenched architectures of violence. Such a claim would fall into the illusion of a totalizing answer – a false promise I refuse to make. There is no single formula, or definitive path to undoing the monumental legacies of colonialism. This is a task that necessarily exceeds these pages, and any page that could ever be written.

Writing, for me, is both a necessity and a reckoning: an act of excavation, a means to unearth, displace, unsettle, disrupt, sabotage, and disturb the sedimented legacies of colonialism – its epistemologies, its methodologies, its inherited debt, its irreparable fracture. It is an act of learning with each other, spreading these persistent and ongoing strategies, tactics, and technologies across spaces and generations.

In this shifting landscape, the ground itself resists fixity, embodying the refusal to remain static. Erosion teaches us that the Earth is not fixed but a living, mutable force: constantly reshaping and being reshaped (Boon, Butler, and Jefferies 2018). This ever-changing geography unsettles the colonial imaginary that seeks to render land and bodies into static, commodifiable forms. Instead, an insurgent, moving Earth disrupts the logic of containment, dissolving boundaries that reduce life to countable, exploitable metrics. Against the colonial mathematics of violence, the incommensurable fullness of our lives asserts itself: unquantifiable, irreducible, and nonnegotiable.

Unlike the monoculture, monologue, and monolingual fixations of colonialism, countercolonial practices thrive on multiplicity, on generative tensions that refuse closure and invite improvisations. This dynamism finds resonance in the Afro-Brazilian notion of the *encruzilhada* (the crossroads). The *encruzilhada* offers a framework of relationality, where intersecting practices, theories, and worldviews dissolve fixed centers and give way to constellations of movement and possibility. It is a space where groundedness is not stagnation but movement, where the soil holds the potential for transformation.

Grounded in these earthy displacements, this book refuses the disciplinary divides that separate legal studies from their historical, political, epistemological, social, and ontological entanglements. It refuses to reduce situated knowledge to a mere case study. It refuses the framing of activists' experiences and embodied knowledge as objects of research or sources of "qualitative data." Here, our conversations are cited alongside written texts, acknowledged as scholarship, as acts of theory-making.

In this fertile ground, resistance and radical transformations take root – not as final answers but as enduring practices. To write, then, is to till the soil of possibility, scattering seeds of refusal, of real abolition, and of reparation that reimagine justice beyond the boundaries set by the colonial and liberal order. Writing becomes a collective and ongoing rehearsal of redress, one that engages with the limits and reconfigurations of law.

Legal discourse has long served as a key instrument in the consolidation of social hierarchies, delineating who counts as citizen and Human, and who is rendered noncitizen and property. At the core of this juridico-political architecture lies the right to ownership and private property – a foundational mechanism for the dehumanization, commodification, and extermination of the Other (humans and more-than-humans). Private property functioned as the terrain upon which the entitlement of White conquest-driven masculinity was institutionalized, granting White cismen the exclusive rights to own, accumulate, and thereby consolidate economic and political power: *a femicidal juridico-political order*. In stark contrast, racialized women have historically borne, and continue to bear, the legacies of dispossession, both in relation to their bodies and territories.

The shift from colonial modernity to neocolonial contemporary times has not abolished these hierarchies but rather reconfigured them. The dialectics of master and slave, human and nonhuman, have morphed into those of citizen and noncitizen. Colonial legacies persist, rearticulated through the language of inequality, difference, inclusion, independence, and meritocracy, all embedded within the ostensibly egalitarian discourse of constitutional democracy. Emancipation, once imbued with the promise of liberation, has been hollowed out, reduced to the narrow metric of individual economic success. Within this framework, the politics of rights, while symbolically significant, reveal their limitations as tools for grounded transformation. The dialectic of equality and difference has been reframed into the binary of inclusion and exclusion, continuing to fuel cycles of marginalization.

At the level of language, this book revisits, displaces, and reimagines foundational legal and political concepts such as justice, identity, nation, independence, emancipation, repair, and representation. These terms, contested from their conventional usages, have been excavated to uncover the sedimented histories they carry and expanded to reveal new terrains of meaning. Language, in this context, is not a mere vehicle for representation but a site of intervention, a fertile ground for rethinking and replanting ideas.

Drawing on decolonial calls for a new grammar (Fanon 1952; Glissant 1990; B. Nascimento 1992; Wynter and McKittrick 2015; Bispo dos Santos 2023), this work positions language as a living and transformative soil. To revisit, rethink, and seed new terms is not simply an intellectual exercise but

Stills from the film *Women in Movement* (2020), by Juliana Streva

a practice of resistance and renewal. Language becomes a site where the colonial residues embedded in words and frameworks are dislodged, allowing for the cultivation of meanings that nourish alternate ways of being, relating, and imagining justice. In this act of linguistic replanting, the book joins a broader movement to unearth the generative possibilities buried beneath the weight of history, preparing the ground for futures not yet written but already germinating.

These reframings draw nourishment from the enduring strategies and tactics enacted by Indigenous, Black, and queer confluence – kinships that defy colonial architectures of domination and persist as vital forms of world-making. Within these practices lies a *politics of vitality*, where erosion and germination coexist, cultivating new grounds for being and becoming. These *choreographies of survival* form the rhizomatic soil from which this book emerges, rooting its inquiry in collective and persistent efforts to rehearse worlds otherwise.

As Michel-Rolph Trouillot reminds us, "The unthinkable is that which one cannot conceive within the range of possible alternatives, that which perverts all answers because it defies the terms under which the questions were phrased" (1995, 82). To confront the unthinkable is to face the limits of imagination imposed by colonial and liberal frameworks. This book embraces that challenge, seeking to refigure the contours of justice – not through abstract theorizing but through the grounded, embodied choreographies enacted by women in grassroots movements. These practices unearth the unthinkable, cultivating new terrains where justice and subject-positions can be reimagined and re/de/composed.

Despite all the despites, *we* stand on ground tilled by those who came before us, whose trajectories and memories have carved space for new seeds to be sown. Here, survival is not merely endurance but an insistence on life: an improvised rehearsal of choreographies of survival through which other worlds can, and must, grow.

Bibliography

Bispo dos Santos, Antônio Nego. 2023. "'Estamos no começo do replantio das palavras': uma conversa com Antônio Bispo dos Santos (Nego Bispo)." Interview by Edgar Rodrigues Barbosa Neto, Natalino Neves da Silva, and Walter Francisco Figueiredo Lowande. *PerCursos, Florianópolis*, 24 (601): 1–26.

Bispo dos Santos, Antônio Nego, and Joviano Maia. 2020. "Início, Meio, Início: Conversa com Antônio Bispo dos Santos." *Indisciplinar* 6 (1): 52–69. https://doi.org/10.35699/2525-3263.2020.26241.

Boon, Sonja, Lesley Butler, and Daze Jefferies. 2018. "Erosion: Fugitivity." In *Autoethnography and Feminist Theory at the Water's Edge. Unsettled Islands*, 69–74. Switzerland: Palgrave Macmilllan.

Fanon, Frantz. 1952. *Black Skin, White Masks*. Translated by Richard Philcox. New York: Grove Press.

Glissant, Édouard. 1990. *Poetics of Relation*. Ann Arbor: The University of Michigan Press.

Halberstam, Jack. 2013. "The Wild Beyond: With and for the Undercommons." In *The Undercommons: Fugitive Planning & Black Study*, edited by Fred Moten and Stefano Harney, 2–13. New York: Minor Compositions.

Kopenawa, Davi, and Bruce Albert. 2010. *A Queda do Céu. Palavras de um Xamã Yanomami*. Translated by Beatriz Perrone-Moisés. São Paulo: Companhia das Letras.

Moten, Fred, and Stefano Harney. 2013. *The Undercommons: Fugitive Planning & Black Study*. New York: Minor Compositions.

Nascimento, Beatriz. 1992 [2018]. "Por um Território (Novo) Existencial e Físico [1992]." In *Beatriz Nascimento. Quilombola e Intelectual. Possibilidade nos Dias da Destruição*, edited by União dos Coletivos Pan-Africanistas, 413–430. São Paulo: Editora Filhos da África.

Trouillot, Michel-Rolph. 1995. *Silencing the Past. Power and the Production of History*. Boston: Beacon Press.

Wynter, Sylvia, and Katherine McKittrick. 2015. "Unparalleled Catastrophe for Our Species? Or, to Give Humanness a Different Future: Conversations." In *Sylvia Wynter. On Being Human as Praxis*, 9–89. Durham and London: Duke University Press.

Appendix 1

Film *Mulheres em Movimento* (2020)

Women in Movement, 68'
Rio de Janeiro, Salvador, and Manaus, Brazil (2018–2020)

Listening to and learning with

Movements

Articulação Brasileira de Mulheres
Associação de Travestis, Transexuais e Transgeneros do Amazonas – ASSOTRAM (Manaus)
Associação Nacional das Baianas de Acarajé – ABAM (Salvador)
Associação Nacional de Ação Indigenista – NAI (Salvador)
Associação de Mulheres Indígenas do Alto Rio Negro – AMARN (Manaus)
Associação de Prostitutas do Amazonas – APAM (Manaus)
Casa de Mulheres da Maré (Rio de Janeiro)
Coletivo Difusão (Manaus)
Coletivo Feminista Classista Ana Montenegro (Salvador)
Coletivo Lesbibahia (Salvador)
Coletivo Madame Satã (Rio de Janeiro)
Coletivo Nuvem Negra (Rio de Janeiro)
Coletivo Yukaka (Manaus)
Coletivo Rosa Zumbi (Manaus)
Comunidade Indígena Karapãna (Manaus)
Forum Permanente das Mulheres (Manaus)
Grupo de Apoio à Prevenção da AIDS – GAPA (Salvador)
Instituto Mana (Manaus)
Marcha das Vadias (Salvador)
Movimento Feminino Novas Felipas (Vera Cruz de Itaparica)
Movimento de Mulheres do Subúrbio Ginga (Salvador)
Movimento de Mulheres Indígenas Guarani Nhandewa
Movimento de Mulheres Solidárias do Amazonas – MUSA (Manaus)

Oitava Feminista (Niterói)
Rede Nacional de Feministas Antiproibicionistas – RENFA
Rede Jurídica por uma Nova Política de Drogas – REFORMA
Rede Umunna (Rio de Janeiro)
Rede Sapata (Salvador)
Tamojuntas (Salvador)
União Nacional LGBT

Direction, Montage, Editing, Production: Juliana Streva

Appendix 2

This appendix traces the main mechanisms, declarations, conventions, comments, and decisions pertaining to femicide and gender-based violence within the international human rights system, with a specific emphasis on the Latin American context.

1928: The **Inter-American Commission of Women** (CIM) was established as the first intergovernmental agency dedicated to promoting full citizenship for women. Later, it became part of the Organization of American States (OAS), founded in 1948.

1946: A year after the establishment of the United Nations (UN), the **Commission on the Status of Women** (CSW) was founded. Based on the Economic and Social Council's resolution 11(II), the CSW functions as a global entity committed to advancing "gender equality and the empowerment of women." The CSW has taken the responsibility of monitoring and assessing the implementation of the Beijing Declaration and the Platform for Action (1995), while also advocating for the integration of a gender perspective in UN activities.

1967: The United Nations issued the **Declaration on the Elimination of Discrimination Against Women.** Within this declaration, discrimination against women is recognized as an offense against human dignity. In a non-binding way, the UN outlines the responsibility of states to "abolish existing laws, customs, regulations and practices which are discriminatory against women, and to establish adequate legal protection for equal rights of men and women." However, the declaration falls short of addressing the issue of violence against women.

1979: Still focusing on the matter of discrimination, the UN adopted the **Convention on the Elimination of All Forms of Discrimination Against Women** (CEDAW), which became effective in 1981. CEDAW is credited with inaugurating a transformative era in international human rights law with a specific focus on women. As mentioned earlier, international discussions predominantly revolved around discrimination against women (Article 1), and the CEDAW Convention played a central role in broadening this concept to encompass acts in both public and private spheres, committed by any person, organization or enterprise (Article 2, e).

1981: The **Committee on the Elimination of Discrimination Against Women** (CEDAW Committee) was established, drawing authority from Article 17 of CEDAW. The Committee is entrusted with three primary mandates: (i) receiving cases on individual or group violations; (ii) generating reports on systematic or grave violations of women's rights; and (iii) formulating general recommendations. In fulfilling the third responsibility, the Committee has issued two General Recommendations, numbers 12 and 19, specifically addressing violence against women – an aspect conspicuously absent from the original treaty.

1985: During the Third World Conference on Women, the **Nairobi Forward-Looking Strategies for the Advancement of Women** were adopted as part of the "Decade for Women: Equality, Development and Peace." This extensive document outlines strategies to combat violence against women, and garnered unanimous support from all participating governments.

1989: The CEDAW Committee issued the **General Recommendation n. 12** (1989), underscoring the obligation of member states to incorporate in their periodic reports the following information: (i) legislation aimed at safeguarding women from various forms of violence in their daily life; (ii) initiatives and services implemented to eliminate violence against women; and (iii) statistical data pertaining to this issue.

1992: In **General Recommendation n. 19** (1992), the CEDAW Committee points out the oversight in reports submitted by state parties, where the interconnection between discrimination against women, gender-based violence, and violations of human rights went unrecognized. The term "gender-based violence" was then defined as "violence that is directed against a woman because she is a woman or that affects women disproportionately" (paragraph 6). In response, the CEDAW Committee recommended incorporating "gender-based violence" into the definition of discrimination against women. The recommendation also underscores "family violence" as one of the most insidious forms of violence against women, prevalent in all societies (paragraph 23).

Since 1992, the CEDAW Committee has asserted that, in cases of violation of women's rights, states may bear international responsibility for the acts of individuals "if they did not adopt measures with due diligence to prevent the violation of rights or to investigate and punish acts of violence and compensate the victims." This novel concept of "due diligence" has significantly influenced subsequent declarations and conventions, such as the United Nations Declaration on the Elimination of Violence Against Women (1993), the Belém do Pará Convention (1994), the Beijing Platform for Action (1995), and the Istanbul Convention (2011). Following the recommendations of CEDAW, violence is now recognized as an international legal issue, a position upheld by the UN in subsequent resolutions and reports on violence against women.

1993: Amid the World Conference of Human Rights and the Vienna Declaration and Programme of Action, the General Assembly proclaimed the **Declaration on the Elimination of Violence Against Women** (DEVAW). As the first declaration exclusively dedicated to addressing the issue of violence against women, DEVAW holds the legal status of soft law, implying that states cannot be held responsible for its violation. Nevertheless, the declaration attained international significance by defining violence against women as

> any act of gender-based violence that results in, or is likely to result in, physical, sexual or psychological harm or suffering to women, including threats of such acts, coercion or arbitrary deprivation of liberty, whether occurring in public or in private life.
>
> (Article 1)

1994: A year following the Declaration on the Elimination of Violence Against Women, the Inter-American Human Rights System (IAHRS) introduced the first international convention specifically addressing violence: the **Convention on the Prevention, Punishment and Eradication of Violence Against Women,** commonly referred to as the **Belém do Pará Convention.** Distinct from the prior nonbinding declarations and general recommendations within the UN system, the Belém do Pará Convention holds the status of a legally binding instrument, allowing member states to be internationally accountable for human rights violations.

2000: The category of "woman" inherently intersects with various identity classifications, including race, gender, sexuality, and class. Addressing the intersection of gender with race, the Committee on the Elimination of Racial Discrimination (CERD) provided insights in its **General Recommendation n. 25** (2000). The recommendation acknowledged that

> racial discrimination does not always affect women and men equally or in the same way. There are circumstances in which racial discrimination only or primarily affects women, or affects women in a different way, or to a different degree than men.

In a complementary approach, the CEDAW Committee highlighted, in its **General Recommendation n. 25** from 2004, the importance of addressing "multiple discrimination against women" by implementing temporary special measures. Moreover, the Convention on Indigenous and Tribal Peoples' Rights from 1989, also known as Convention 169, underscores that the established rights should be applied "without discrimination to male and female members of these peoples" (Art. 3.1). In recent years, reports have been issued focusing on human rights considerations for Indigenous and Black women (IACHR 2017; ECLAC 2018).

2001: International courts such as the European Court of Human Rights (ECHR) and the Inter-American Court on Human Rights (IACHR) possess a judicial mandate to officially declare the international responsibility of a member state in cases of human rights violations.[1] Hence, they carry a differential mandate than entities like the CEDAW Committee and the Inter-American Commission on Human Rights, which are entrusted with tasks such as monitoring, making comments, reports and deciding cases with a friendly agreement. The subsequent analysis focuses on two leading cases within the Inter-American Human Rights System (IAHRS): the Maria da Penha Case v. Brazil, case n° 12.051, decided by the Commission in 2001; and *González et al. v. Mexico* ("Cotton Field"), issued by the Court in 2009.

The landmark case ***Maria da Penha Case v. Brazil*** (2001) marked the first application of the Belém do Pará Convention in the realm of domestic violence. This legal proceeding centers on the enduring cycle of violence suffered by Maria da Penha from her husband over a 15-year span. Despite numerous reports to state officials, the country neglected to implement any effective measures to prevent, investigate, process, or penalize this gender-based violence. Maria da Penha survived two murder attempts committed by her husband, which resulted in irreversible paraplegia and severe health injuries. Despite 15 years passing since the crimes occurred, the Brazilian national courts have not reached a final decision. The IACHR recognized the international responsibility of Brazil for negligence and omission concerning gender-based violence (IACHR 2001, para. 60), constituting a violation of the rights and obligations established at the Article 7 of Belém do Pará Convention, in conjunction with the Articles 1.1, 8, and 25 of the ACHR.

2006: Concerning the intersection of sexual orientation and gender identity, a group of experts from various countries independently formulated the **Yogyakarta Principles on the Application of Human Rights Law in Relation to Sexual Orientation and Gender Identity** (2006). This document holds particular significance as the first major international stance on the subject, notable for not being produced by an official human rights institution. This emphasizes the hesitancy within international law to address the LGBTQIA+ agenda. In 2017, these principles were further expanded to include state obligations related to the application of international human rights law, now including sexual orientation, gender identity, gender expression, and sex characteristics principles.

1 For more information, see the Statute of the Inter-American Court of Human Rights (1979); American Convention on Human Rights (1969) at Article 64; Statute of the Inter-American Commission on Human Rights (1979); European Convention on Human Rights (1950) at Section II; CEDAW (1989) at Part V, Article 17.

2008: The Inter-American Commission of Women issued the **Declaration on Femicide.** In this declaration, "femicide" is defined as the most severe form of discrimination and violence against women. The states are urged to establish and strengthen legislation to empower women, safeguard their rights and freedom, improve the criminal investigation system and the overall protection given to women affected by violence.

2009: The second landmark case is the ***González et al. v. México***, famously known as the **Campo Algodonero (Cotton Field)**, which was decided by the Inter-American Court of Human Rights. This case addressed the recurring and systematic practices of the disappearance and extermination of women in the border town of Juárez, Mexico. The families of three disappeared women – Claudia Ivette González, Laura Berenice Ramos Monárrez, and Esmeralda Herrera Monreal – initiated the case with local authorities. Subsequently, human rights organizations represented them before the Inter-American Commission and Court.

The context of violence in Juárez is characterized by two pivotal elements: gender stereotypes and the integration of women into the workforce. The preference for hiring women in the maquila industries enabled them to attain financial independence, thereby challenging the traditional roles imposed by patriarchal society. This transformative shift, where women assumed the role of the primary family providers, contested the established model of male control over property and female bodies (IACtHR 2009, paras. 129, 34). Numerous reports identify recurring patterns in the series of murders against women in the region: "the women were abducted and kept in captivity, their next of kin reported their disappearance and, after days or months, their bodies were found on empty lots with signs of violence, including rape and other types of sexual abuse, torture and mutilation" (IACtHR 2009, para. 125).

The mothers of the three women testified to the authorities' insinuation that each of their daughters was "out with her boyfriend" and that "if anything happened to her, it was because she was looking for it, because a good girl, a good woman, stays at home" (IACtHR 2009, para. 154). This rationale, once again, reinforced the structures of violence against women by attributing the blame to women for the violence inflicted upon them.

In this case, the Court established a significant precedent regarding the responsibility to prevent violence against women. Two moments warrant analysis concerning this obligation, one before the woman's disappearance and another before the discovery of her body. Regarding the first moment, the failure to prevent violence does not automatically result in the state's international responsibility. In this moment, instead of relying on a general context of systematic violence, the Court considered the specific demonstration of the state's acknowledgment of a real and imminent risk to a particular woman as crucial for declaring its international responsibility. In the second moment, when families report the disappearances to the authorities, the state necessarily becomes aware of the real and imminent risk in these specific cases. In this scenario, the state is responsible for the obligation to act with "strict due diligence," requiring rigorous and exhaustive search operations during the initial hours and days after the disappearance. The Court highlighted the importance that "police authorities, prosecutors and judicial officials take prompt immediate action" (IACtHR 2009, paras. 281–283).

Moreover, the Court not only consolidated its jurisdiction to interpret but also to recognize the international state's responsibility for violating the provisions of the Belém do Pará Convention.[2] The decision marked a milestone in addressing violence against women. Nevertheless, it still presented constraints in the use of the terms "feminicidio" or "femicide." Despite Marcela Lagarde's expert commentary presented in this case, the request made by the victim's representatives, and the use of the term even by the State of Mexico, the Court decided to employ the terminology "gender-based murders of women" (IACtHR 2009, para. 138).[3]

2011: The Council of Europe adopted the **Convention on Preventing and Combating Violence Against Women and Domestic Violence,** commonly known as the **Istanbul Convention.** Its scope encompasses all forms of violence against women, "including domestic violence, which affects women disproportionately."

The Convention provides the following definitions:

(i) violence against women is "a violation of human rights and a form of discrimination against women and shall mean all acts of gender-based violence that result in, or are likely to result in, physical, sexual, psychological or economic harm or suffering to women, including threats of such acts, coercion or arbitrary deprivation of liberty, whether occurring in public or in private life";

(ii) domestic violence is "all acts of physical, sexual, psychological or economic violence that occur within the family or domestic unit or

2 Even though the IACtHR had already considered its jurisdiction over the Belém do Pará Convention on a previous case – *Miguel Castro Castro Prison v. Peru* (2006) – the Campo Algodonero's sentence presented a large and crucial discussion on the issue, since the Article 12 of the Convention only mentioned the competence of the IACHR to analyze the violation of the international obligations prescribed at the Article 7. Through a teleological interpretation of the procedures established by the IAHRS in which the Court can only analyze cases submitted by the Commission, the Court consolidated its competence *rationae materiae* over the Convention. In this respect, the IACtHR considered that the State violated the mentioned Convention, Article 7 (b and c), in relation to the rights to life, personal integrity, and personal liberty of the American Convention (Articles 4(1), 5(1), 5(2), and 7(1) combined with 1.1).

3 In contrast, the Inter-American Commission has been adopting the term since the report "Acceso a la Justicia e Inclusión Social: El Camino Hacia el Fortalecimiento de la Democracia en Bolivia" from 2007.

between former or current spouses or partners, whether or not the perpetrator shares or has shared the same residence with the victim";
(iii) gender-based violence against women is "violence that is directed against a woman because she is a woman or that affects women disproportionately" (Article 3).

2011: Following a prolonged period of hesitation, the International Labor Organization (ILO) established the **Domestic Workers Convention,** No. 189. With this move, the ILO finally highlighted the significant impact that domestic work has on women and girls, emphasizing the ongoing undervaluation and invisibility of such labor within society.

2011: The UN issued the inaugural resolution on LGBT rights, accompanied by the first comprehensive study documenting violations of human rights against LGBT people globally. Subsequently, in 2015 and 2018, the Inter-American Human Rights System released regional reports addressing violence and the challenges associated with recognizing the rights of LGBTQIA+ persons in the Americas (IACHR 2015, 2018).

2013: Within the African System of Human Rights, the **Special Protocol on the Rights of Women in Africa,** also known as the **Maputo Protocol (2016),** was established as a complement to the general prohibition on sexist discrimination set by the African Charter on Human and Peoples' Rights of 1981. Drawing inspiration from existing international human rights standards, the Maputo Protocol specifically tackled the challenges experienced by women and girls in the African context.

Bibliography

CERD. 2000. "General Recommendation n. 25 on Gender-Related Dimensions of Racial Discrimination." Committee on the Elimination of Racial Discrimination (CERD), United Nations.

Committee CEDAW. 1989. "General Recommendation n. 12: Violence against Women." United Nations, Committee on the Elimination of Discrimination Against Women.

Committee CEDAW. 1992. "General Recommendation n. 19: Violence against Women." United Nations, Committee on the Elimination of Discrimination Against Women.

EC. 2011. "Convention on Preventing and Combating Violence against Women and Domestic Violence." Istanbul.

ECLAC. 2018. "Afrodescendent Women in Latin America and the Caribbean." ECLAC, UN.

Group of International Human Rights Experts. 2006. "Yogyakarta Principles on the Application of Human Rights Law in Relation to Sexual Orientation and Gender Identity." Yogyakarta.

IACHR. 2015. "Violence against Lesbian, Gay, Bisexual, Trans and Intersex Persons in the Americas." Washington, DC: OAS.

IACHR. 2017. "Indigenous Women and Their Human Rights in the Americas." OAS, IACHR.

IACHR. 2018. "Advances and Challenges Towards the Recognition of the Rights of LGBTI Persons in the Americas." Washington, DC: OAS.
ILO. 2011. "Convention 189 on Domestic Workers." Geneva.
Inter-American Commission on Human Rights – IACHR. 2001. "Maria da Penha Maia Fernandes v. Brasil." Caso 12.051. OAS, Inter-American Commission on Human Rights.
Inter-American Court of Human Rights – IACtHR. 2009. "Case of González et al. ('Cotton Field') v. Mexico." Costa Rica: OAS, Inter-American Court of Human Rights.
OAS. 1994. "Inter-American Convention on the Prevention, Punishment, and Eradication of Violence against Women (Convention of Belém do Pará)." Belém do Pará, Brazil: OAS.
UN. 1993. "Declaration on the Elimination of Violence against Women." United Nations.
UN Women, CSW. 1995. "Beijing Declaration and Platform for Action." Adopted at the 16th Plenary Meeting, on 15 September 1995. Beijing: The Fourth World Conference on Women.
WGDD. 2016. "Maputo Protocol on Women's Rights: A Living Document for Women's Human Rights in Africa." The report was given as part of a presentation on the "State of Ratification of the Maputo Protocol" during the AU Ministerial Consultation. Meeting held on 18 March 2016, on the margins of the 60th Session of the United Nations Commission on the Status of Women (CSW), in New York: The Women, Gender and Development Directorate (WGDD) of the African Union Commission.

Index

abolition 75, 163; of slavery 47, 51, 54n14, 71, 77–79, 78n5, 84, 86–87; of slave trade 46n13
abolitionist 54n14, 132, 135, 147–148; justice 132, 135
Abya Yala 29, 30
accountability 10, 85, 95n1, 114, 125–126, 130–132, 134
accumulation 2, 32, 37, 52, 122, 127; negative 44, 50; primitive 44, 44n8, 46n13
acolhimento 124–127, 134–135
acts of translation 120–121
adultery 57–58
advocacy 9, 11, 54n14, 88, 113, 117, 123n9; feminist grassroots 127; transnational 12
agency 40, 52, 53–54, 79, 169
alternation of power 145
amnesia 70–71
ancestral 3, 20, 107, 143; heritage 67; knowledges 143; lands 118–119; legacies 147; mobilizations 89
Anderson, Benedict 66, 68–69
Anghie, Antony 81
Aparelha Luzia 143
aquilombar 143–145, 148
architecture 7, 66; colonial 21, 40–41, 108, 112, 138, 165; of colonial slavery 50; of colonial violence 133; of femicide 19, 65, 114, 128; juridico-political 163; of modern juridical and ethical norms 31; of modern legal and ethical norms 127; of power 89, 138; state 79; of violence 3, 17, 19, 21, 40, 94, 162
archive 1, 15, 72, 75, 147; archival 15; archival silence 36; colonial 36–37, 144, 147; living 77; national 147; official 17, 71; racial economy of 17
authority 52–53, 58, 66, 77, 79, 86, 89, 99, 105n4, 136, 170; colonial 82, 147; epistemic 105; intellectual 102; judicial 55; legal 52; national 75; patriarchal 55; political 85; scholarly 99; sovereign 82; state 113, 122; transcendent 84
autonomy 12, 53, 79, 84n9, 122, 125
axé 110

Balibar, Étienne 70
Bantu 73n3, 95n1, 97, 110, 143
Barthes, Roland 66
being-with 57n17, 110–111
belonging 19, 65, 67–68, 86, 112, 119
Berlant, Lauren 66, 74, 82, 89
bigamy 58
biointeraction 149
biopolitics 108
Bispo dos Santos, Antônio 2, 149
Black Radical Tradition 2, 44
Black trans paranauê counter-coup 147
blame-shifting 33, 34, 37, 116
body-machine 112
bureaucratic: apparatus 69; and ideological systems 70; machinery of colonialism 55

Campt, Tina 129
capitalism 19, 44n8, 45–46; colonial 45; modern 44–45; racial 31, 45, 112, 146; Western 43
capitalist: discipline 55; dispossession 148; dynamics 50; imperialism 119n7; mode of production 44;

pre-capitalist stage 44; production 42; systems 46n13
capitão do mato 43
captive 28, 38; body 39–40, 54; subjects 43, 128
captivity 39, 40, 133, 144, 173
care 48, 50, 97, 104, 108, 112, 115, 124–127, 135, 147
Castillo, Susana Chávez 3
censos 70, 75, 78–79
Césaire, Aimé 32n4, 33, 44n9, 100
choreographies of survival 3, 5–7, 20–22, 90, 96, 98, 107–108, 144, 165
cisgender 5, 15, 15n7, 35, 55, 97, 132
cisheteronormative 15, 40, 56, 57, 58, 84, 89, 127, 145
citizen 22, 65, 72, 74, 76, 79, 82, 85, 87–88, 146, 163; infantile 74; infantilized 85
citizenship 65, 71, 82, 84–85, 87–89, 136, 169; effective 88; infantile 74; infantilized 78
civilized 31, 34, 74, 83
civilization 44, 73, 83, 86
civil rights 87–88, 127
class 45, 46, 51, 53, 58, 70, 98, 132, 146, 171; working- 51
coalition 3, 148–149; -building 146, 148
collaboration 13, 16, 99–101, 125, 132
colonial imaginary 30, 162
colonialism 1, 29, 31–33, 35, 44n8, 45, 48, 69, 73n3, 81, 127, 162; afterlives of 162; bureaucratic machinery of 55; counter-histories of 28; enactments of 162; European 29; exploitative 41, 49; first circle of 21; foundations of 19; fractures of 71; grounds of 87; institutionalization of 81; juridical 142; legacies of 84, 162; logic of 2n1; modern 72; Portuguese 38; role of 81; settler 32, 41, 48–49, 105, 121; trauma of 109
colonial justice 32, 55, 107
colonial racial-patriarchal order 1, 21–22, 65–66, 72, 74, 84, 87, 89–90, 98, 111, 116–117, 127, 137–138, 140, 148
color-line 32
Combahee River Collective 146
concubinage 40
Constitution 51, 58, 82, 84n9, 85, 88, 128, 144
constitutional 22, 51, 81–82, 128; code 81–82, 84–85, 89n3; democracy 133, 136, 148, 163; discourse 84; law 78n5, 81–82, 139; pact 83; preambles 84; representation 136; rhetoric 86
contract: racial 83; sexual 83; social 22, 45, 82–83, 85, 87
conversation 73, 105, 112, 116, 118, 123n11, 125, 142
co-optation 138
cosmologies 31, 97, 108, 120, 134–135
countercolonial 1–2, 19, 32, 43n7, 46, 49, 75, 98, 100, 112, 121, 143–144, 147–149, 162
countercolonial feminist 124; critiques 138; ecologies 107; kinships 112; mobilizations 112; praxis 1, 21, 89, 98, 132, 135, 143, 145; trajectory 135
court 54, 88, 118, 130, 141, 172–174; courtroom 54n14, 98, 107, 123, 130
crime 3, 9–11, 16, 36, 40–41, 56, 58–59, 98, 114, 130, 133, 136, 149, 172; of passion 14
criminal 11, 21, 40–41, 58, 85, 113, 126–128, 130–132, 136, 144, 173; justice 127, 132
Criminal Code of the Empire 35
critical fabulation 147

daily plebiscite 68
data 15–18, 20–21, 78–79, 103, 131n14, 141–142; collection 14, 99; empirical 101; qualitative 99, 163; statistical 132, 141, 170
death 3–5, 36, 57, 94–95, 111, 131n14, 133, 141, 144; politics of 58
decolonial 2, 32, 75, 98–99, 137, 163; justice 22, 133
decolonization 81, 145, 148
deep listening 6, 22, 98–99, 107, 121, 127–128
defiance 43n7, 47, 49, 128, 147
dehumanization 2, 39, 44, 54, 102, 110, 127–128, 163; dehumanized 3, 33, 42; dehumanizing 17, 38–39, 44n9, 95n1, 108–109, 128
demarcation 29, 123, 147

democracy 41, 74, 87–88, 108, 113, 136–137, 146; constitutional 133, 136, 163; liberal 1, 66, 85–87; racial 37, 75, 79, 87; representative 16, 59, 84, 133, 137, 140, 145, 148
democratic 84, 86, 136; ideals 22, 87; progress 65; representation 15, 22, 137; state 85
democratization 13n6; re-democratization 89, 113, 137
denegation 74
desire 39, 50, 68, 76, 120, 130
detour 75, 65
dialogue 99, 100, 102, 104, 105–106, 108, 110, 112, 120, 132–134
disorder 108
dissent body 36, 86, 101n3
domestic 13, 18, 46–47, 50–51, 86, 88, 132–133, 140, 146; labor 47–48, 51, 125; violence 13, 125–126, 172, 174; worker 47, 50–51, 125, 175
Du Bois, W.E.B. 32
dysphoria 145
dysselection 4, 4n4

ecosystem 4, 111, 149
education 12, 50, 76, 106, 116, 123; access 87, 106; rights 88; system 104
election 15–16, 86, 96, 122, 137–139, 141–143
emancipation 1, 54n15, 79–80, 89, 163
Empire 32, 33n5, 35, 37, 55, 71–73, 76–77, 81–82, 96n2, 100
encruzilhada 97, 161–162
Engels, Friedrich 46
enunciation 73–74, 98, 117
epistemic 2, 38, 75–76, 97, 100, 102, 106, 123, 136; authority 105; extractivism 101; violence 75, 100
epistemology 136, 146; colonial 37, 81
equality 65–66, 68, 86–87, 89, 114, 163, 169–170; gender 9, 13, 79
ethnography 99, 101–102, 107; legal 6, 22, 98
Eurocentric 20, 31, 42n6, 67–68, 83
exhaustion 1, 46, 109–110, 112, 162
exploitation 18, 32–33, 37–38, 44n9, 45n11, 47–51, 69, 81, 89, 101, 125
extraction 2, 20, 100, 102, 137; extractive 19, 37, 48, 101

family 21, 32, 52, 55, 57, 59, 65–66, 70, 77, 174; Black 49; colonial 51–53, 65; monogamous, cisheteronormative 57–58; nuclear 22, 55–57, 57n17, 67; Portuguese royal 80n6, 82, 92n2; providers 173; violence 170
Fanon, Frantz 19, 30, 44n9, 75, 80, 141, 148
fatherland 52, 66
fear 58, 70, 83n8
femicidal: *juridico-political order* 163; systems 28; violence 65
femicide 1, 4–5, 4n3, 7–21, 34, 58, 65–66, 107, 110–111, 115, 130–133, 136, 142, 169, 174; architecture of 65, 114, 128; criminalization 14, 127, 137; Declaration on 173; legal classification of 131
feminicidio 10–11, 174
feminism 9, 92n2, 97, 126; liberal 89
femocrat 138
femo-geno-cídio 11
Ferdinand, Malcom 45n12
Ferreira da Silva, Denise 4, 28, 39–40, 44, 133, 135, 135n17
fiction 17, 76, 133; legal 87
fieldwork 72, 99, 117
first wave 13, 87, 127
flesh 28, 37, 40, 45
forensic 15, 17
forgetting 65–66, 71, 89
fracture 28, 127, 162; colonial 30–32
Franco, Marielle 22, 94–95, 107–108, 118, 129–132, 140–142
Free Womb Law 49, 54–55
Freyre, Gilberto 37–38
front door 7, 18–19, 105, 145; violence 18–21, 28, 148

Gama, Luiz 54n14
gaze 30, 47; colonial 30–31, 38, 44, 76; dehumanizing 128; ethnographic 104; White 77
Gellner, Ernest 66, 68–70
gender-based: violence 1, 5, 7–8, 11, 13–21, 34, 41, 50, 58, 113–116, 124–126, 138, 169–172, 174–175
gender binary 15n7, 29, 35, 132
Gendered ontology of difference 35, 37, 40, 46n13, 67, 71, 85, 128, 133
gender nonconforming 131

gender norms 13n6, 15n7, 36; normativity 35; nonnormative 35
gender parity 137, 139
gender politics 138
gender-sensitive training 115
generation 4, 36, 77, 107, 109, 135, 162
geology 1, 19–21, 129, 133, 135–136, 148
Glissant, Édouard 66, 75, 122n8
Gonzalez, Lélia 38, 49, 75–76, 94, 103, 107
grassroots 11, 110; actions 95; activism 104, 110; activists 2, 14; advocacy 127; feminisms 96n2; feminist praxis 22; forms 124; kinship 111–112; mobilizations 14, 112, 114; movements 14, 20, 22, 89, 96–97, 105, 110, 112, 114–115, 127, 132, 135–136, 140, 148, 165; networks 112; politics 111; responses 135
grief 108, 130; grievable 132; grievance 130, 133; grieve 96; grieving 95

Haraway, Donna 45n11, 103
Hartman, Saidiya 3, 7, 28, 40, 114, 127, 147
heal 117, 126, 135; healing 106, 112, 126–127, 147
hearing 36, 74, 99, 117, 119, 123; legal 117; public 126
heritage 4, 67–68, 96n2
Herrschaft 69
heterosexuality 34, 55; heteronormative 15n7, 52, 55; heteronormativity 55; heterosexual 15, 97, 146
homogenization 31, 37, 50; homogeneity 68; homogeneous 161; homogenize 30
homosexuality 55–56
household 39, 47–48, 50–52, 79
housewifery 47; housewives 50
Human 12, 22, 31, 40, 48, 54, 65, 73, 127–129, 146, 149, 163; being 42, 44n9, 46, 112, 128; less-than-human 42; more-than-human 31, 108, 148–149; nonhuman 79, 163; not-human 136; script 30
humanism 12; monohumanism 31; monohumanist 31, 42n6
humanity 12, 31, 33–34, 40, 42, 49, 95n1, 108, 122n8, 128–129
human rights 3, 10, 131n14; agenda 13; discourse 12; law 169–175; reports 18, 113; system 12, 169, 171–175; theory 13; violation 13, 118n6, 170–175

ialodê 107
identity politics 145–146
imperial 30, 81; intentions 72; metropole 48, 70; monarch 84; palace 77; structures 81
imperialism 69, 105n4, 119n7
improvisation 97, 99
inclusion 15, 88–89, 128, 138, 140–141, 145, 163
Indigenous rights 119, 121, 123n9
infantilization 22, 73–74, 100, 103; infantilizing 75, 102; legal 53
infidelity 57–58
inheritance 52, 54
in/human 31, 42, 127
in/justice 116, 119–120, 127–128, 135
Inquisition 56
Institute of History and Geography 57n17, 75
institutional politics 94, 137–138, 141–148
international law 12, 14, 80–81, 172
interview 95, 98–99, 101, 103, 106–107, 119, 141, 143

James, C.L.R. 44
joy 112, 148
judicial: assistance 124; authority 55; decisions 12, 141; mandate 172; officials 174; power 55; system 113, 119, 122
judiciary 88, 113
juridical colonialism 142
jurisprudence 14–15, 98, 113
justice 3, 8, 11, 13, 20–22, 54–55, 90, 107, 112–114, 118–119, 121, 123, 127, 129–136, 145, 149, 163, 165; barriers 54; conceptions 20; concepts 33; critiques 134; demands 95n1; emblem 18; fight 54n14; ideas 32; modern 130; notions 121; principles 95n1; struggles 52, 120; theory 133
just war 33, 42

Kellogg, Susan 30, 47
Kilomba, Grada 7, 74, 99, 108

kinship 49, 56–57, 66, 97, 108, 110–112, 124, 127, 142; bloodline-based 52, 57n17; multispecies 149
knowledge production 7, 38, 100–101, 103, 105, 121

labor: coerced 33n5, 47; division of 32, 45–47, 50; domestic 47, 51, 125; emotional 106; enslaved 133n15; epistemic 102; exhausting 109; forced 45n11, 48; male 30n3; power 44; productive 46; reproductive 46–48, 51; rights 51, 125; waged 85
Labor Law (Consolidação das Leis do Trabalho) 51
Lagarde, Marcela 7, 10
land 1, 12, 18–19, 29n2, 34, 44, 45n11, 48, 57n17, 78n5, 95n1, 100, 110–111, 119–120, 123, 130, 162
language 4, 7–8, 11, 29n2, 57n17, 67, 72–75, 84, 105n4, 120, 126, 129, 162–163, 165; colonial 49, 75, 121; of the courts 120; of the law 10; legal 7, 12, 40, 81; legitimate 99; mastery of 99; monopoly of 73; national 125; official 73, 106, 125; of rights 12, 87; unified 73; universal 12, 65; White 106, 120
Latin: etymology 79; noun 67; prefix 73; semantics 52
legitimacy 68–70, 75, 85, 113; political 68, 84; scientific 38
Le Guin, Ursula 6
Lepecki, André 6
lesbianism 56
lethal 140; force 58, 121
listening effect 99
listen to 2, 96–97, 103, 106, 116–117, 119
literacy 87
livability 5, 17, 20, 119, 148
love 14, 38, 70, 74
Loveman, Mara 78
Lugones, María 29
Lusotropicalism 37, 49; Lusotropicalist 37, 41, 85

Malunguinho, Erica 143–148
Manicongo, Xica 36
map 16; political 94–95, 108, 129, 140, 148; politics 84, 112, 114, 135; rates 124, 131–132; structures 32
Maria da Penha: Law 124; Case 172
marriage 40, 53, 55, 58
Marx, Karl 44n8
masculinity 16, 40, 47; ultra-masculinity 15
mastery 99, 102, 121
mathematics of violence 7, 15–17, 79, 105, 132, 162
McKittrick, Katherine 15, 17, 102
Memmi, Albert 30, 32
memory 1, 4–5, 8, 19, 65–66, 104, 113; collective 3, 5; national 70, 77; selective 89
mestiçagem 22, 76
metaphor 7, 18, 28n1, 105, 108, 111
methodology 15, 22, 81, 98–99, 103, 116, 136, 162
Middle Passage 39, 42–43, 48, 143
migration 42, 70, 137
military 13, 42, 69–70, 86, 89n13, 95, 118, 130, 146
minus one 1, 4
miscegenation 38, 41, 76–77, 79
mocambo 43, 144
Mombaça, Jota 107, 127, 133
monarchy 80, 84, 86, 96n2
monoculture 47, 56, 83, 120, 149, 162
monogamy 32, 56–58
monolingual 73, 162
monologue 72, 75, 83, 162
monopoly 40; of the conditions of enunciation 74; of the Human 73; of institutional politics 145; of language 73; of legitimate physical violence 69; of violence 68–69, 113
multispecies 45n11, 111, 148–149; justice 149
myth 66; colonial 37; common origin 77; harmonious slavery 37, 85; harmony 75–76; independence 79; liberal 120; mythology 22, 79, 84; racial democracy 79; superwoman 108–109

Nascimento, Beatriz 17, 104, 107, 110, 144–145, 147–148
nation 35, 57n17, 66–71, 74, 76–81, 163; -state 1, 22, 59, 65–66, 68–76, 80–89, 123, 133, 139, 148

nationalism 59, 66, 68–71
neurosis 76; cultural 39
ni una menos 4
ntu 110–111, 147
nudity 33–35
Núñez, Geni 31, 56

object 102; objecthood 17; objectification 17, 34, 38–39, 44n9, 50, 100, 103, 136; objectified 33, 38; objectifying 100
objectivity 99, 113
occupy 86, 141–142, 144
Oliveros, Pauline 99
opacity 18–19, 122n8
Ordenações Afonsinas 56
Ordenações Filipinas 53, 57
Ordenações Manuelinas 36
otherness 39, 44n9
Oyewumi, Oyèrónké 29, 73n3

pact 22, 81, 83–84
Pahuja, Sundhya 80–81
parental right 48
paternalistic 41, 79, 86, 101
patriarchy 52, 140
patrimony 52
patriotism 66
the people 72, 77–78, 82, 136
perpetrator 16, 113, 115, 175
Pindorama 29
Pires, Thula 131
plantation 19, 44, 45nn10, 11, 85, 87, 107; politics 43
Plantationocene 45, 53
pleasure 38–39
police 9, 114–118, 124, 126, 132, 136, 174; force 113, 115; officers 41, 130; records 131n14, 147; reports 35; station 115–116, 126–127; violence 95, 118–119, 132
political economy of knowledge 20
political party 88, 104, 130, 139–143
politics of citation 102
politics of silencing/speakability 8, 71–72, 74, 77, 87, 100, 136
polyphonic 99, 103–104
positionality 21, 97–98, 103–104, 146
pretuguês 49, 75, 146
property 32, 36, 38–40, 44, 52–54, 58–59, 76, 79, 86–87, 140, 146, 163, 173; concentration of 52; private 52, 146, 163; propertylessness 53; rights 53
psychoanalysis 106; psychoanalytic 38, 73, 136; psychoanalytical 106
public paramnesia 66, 74, 89
punitive justice 113

quilombo 19, 43n7, 49, 143–144, 146–148; Mandata 143, 145–146, 148; urban 143
quilombola 1–2, 120; peace 147
quotas 137–139; gender 137–140; legislative 139; party 139; racial 106

racialization 4n4, 44, 56
Racial ontology of difference 32–33, 35, 44, 77; Racial and Gendered ontologies of difference 21, 28, 30, 38, 45–46, 49–50, 53, 56, 58, 89, 127
racial schema 44
racism 17, 41, 44, 66, 70–74, 95, 103, 141
radical legal praxis 22, 98, 112, 135
Ramos, Guerreiro 100
recognition 4, 13, 21, 48, 50, 54–55, 68, 95n1, 97, 100, 121–123, 127, 131, 139, 145; legal 11, 51, 53, 87; politics 121, 136
re/de/composition 90, 128, 134–135, 137, 147–149
redress 90, 99, 114, 117, 121, 127, 129–132, 134–136, 143, 146, 149, 163; architectures of 129; generative 1, 3, 98, 124, 136
redressive: actions 114; extra-legal claim 146; forms of resistance 144; justice 119, 125, 143, 148; mechanisms 112; pathways 22; praxis 137; responses 133
refuge 110, 124, 126–127
refusal 1–2, 7, 15n7, 17, 19–20, 43n7, 49, 105, 108, 118, 121–126, 129, 134, 136, 144, 148, 162–163
reintegration of possession 145–146
re-membering 65, 114, 135, 144, 146
Renan, Ernest 66–67, 76
repair 3, 114, 129, 134–135, 163
reparar 129, 133–134
reparation 10, 81, 129, 131, 147, 149, 163

reparative: claim 146; framework 132; justice 22, 85, 113, 119; practices 133; responses 133
representation 15, 17, 22, 54, 78, 83–86, 98, 104, 118, 123n9, 136–140, 146, 163; paternalistic 41; political 136, 138, 140–141; vicious circle 145
repression 39, 70, 74, 82
reproduction 39, 48, 146; social 46, 49
republic 77, 86; republican 71, 77, 84, 88
rest 111; right to 112
restoration 95n1, 114, 134–135
Rich, Adrienne 8, 55
right to kill 56, 58
Russell, Diana 9

sacrifice 53, 67
Saffioti, Heleieth 50
Schwartz, Stuart 55
seed 22, 98, 107–108, 110–111, 114, 135, 163
Segato, Rita 7, 11
sexism 71, 73–74, 88, 103, 140
sexuality 37–39, 56, 74, 171
shelter 124
Simpson, Audra 105, 121–122
Simpson, Leanne B. 21, 105n4, 134
slavery 28, 40, 42–45, 47, 54n14, 96n2; afterlives of 38, 51, 89, 107, 114; archives 17, 77; Black Atlantic 72; chattel 48; colonial 4n4, 12, 28, 31–33, 39, 41–44, 48, 50, 70–71, 76–77, 81, 109, 114, 121, 129, 135, 144, 146; conditions of 39; economic structures of 53; economy of 53; hierarchies of 48; historiography of 50; institutionalized 49; institution of 39, 43; legacies of 49; legal 83; plantation 85
Slavery1 42, 44
Slavery2 42–45
slave trade 46n13, 55, 83; African 42; Black Atlantic 42; transatlantic 19, 43
social Darwinism 72
sodomy 36, 55–56; improper 56
sovereign 36, 108; authority 82; intellectual territory 102; people 85; will 122
sovereignty 67, 81, 83n8, 86–87, 105, 113; absolute 49; food 12, 123; Indigenous 123; popular 86; Portuguese 29; state 123
speak: about 100; on behalf 78; for 77; nearby 21
speech 74; absence of 73; capable of 73
Spiller, Hortense 28, 39, 48, 135n17
spiral 1, 149; temporality 20
standpoint theory 103
state of nature 83
statistics 14–15, 17, 78–79, 132
stereotypes 14, 145; gender 141, 173
succession rights 53
superwoman 108–109
survivor 41
Syndicate of Domestic Workers 51

thingification 41, 44, 100
Third World 13, 81, 170
tibira 56
tombar 4, 162; tombamento 4
total violence 13, 40, 43, 49, 58, 133n15
traditional politics 145
transformative: justice 22, 95n1, 98, 125, 133, 135; law-making 147; legal efforts 11; potential of radical legal praxis 112, 117, 121; potential of the seed 111; process 75; representation 140; soil 163; transitional justice 113–114
translator 88, 106, 123n11
trauma 66, 109, 116–117, 134; traumatic 66, 116–117, 143
travesti 15n7, 36, 98, 107, 131n14
Treaty of Tordesillas 29
Trouillot, Michel-Rolph 65, 71, 165
Tupinambá, Glicéria 47, 119–123

Ubuntu 95
un/gendered 50, 76, 128
unpreparedness 85–86, 88
unspeakable 7–8, 40, 77
un-worlding 148

vergonha 33–34
victim 16, 41, 113; -blaming 10, 41; ideal 41; stereotypical 41
victimhood 41, 47, 127
virility 34
vital force 110, 135

vitality 49, 107; politics of 6, 22, 98, 108, 110–112, 134, 136, 147, 149, 165; principle of 147; spaces of 126
voice 18, 40–41, 99–100, 104, 106, 140
vote 53, 86–88; right 88

war 6, 12, 33, 42, 83n8, 95–96, 147
Weber, Max 69
White: supremacy 41, 83, 112, 144; supremacist 31, 72, 76, 78, 127, 162; guilt 41
White conquest-driven masculinity 21, 28, 30–34, 37–38, 47, 52, 58–59, 69, 71, 86, 126, 137–138, 163; White masculinity 76
Whiteness 38, 41, 52, 77, 99, 140
Whitening 31, 77, 78n5, 79
Williams, Eric 43–44
womanhood 15n7, 40, 48, 53, 89
world-making 90, 105, 123, 135, 148; otherwise 120; project 20; strategies 7
writing 3n2, 6–7, 101, 105n4, 162–163; history 28, 76; polyphonic mode 103
Wynter, Sylvia 4n4, 19, 42–44

Yusoff, Kathryn 19

zero degree 28

FSC
www.fsc.org
MIX
Papier | Fördert
gute Waldnutzung
FSC® C083411

Kolibri 360 GmbH
Ferdinand-Jühlke-Straße 7
99095 Erfurt, Deutschland
produktsicherheit@kolibri360.de